WAR IN THE NEXT DECADE

WAR IN THE NEXT DECADE

edited by

Roger A. Beaumont
and
Martin Edmonds

The University Press of Kentucky

*A University Press of Kentucky
Military Study, Robin Higham, Editor*

ISBN: 0-8131-1291-5

Library of Congress Catalog Card Number: 73-77251

Copyright © 1974 by The University Press of Kentucky

A statewide cooperative scholarly publishing agency serving Berea College, Center College of Kentucky, Eastern Kentucky University, Georgetown College, Kentucky Historical Society, Kentucky State University, Morehead State University, Murray State University, Northern Kentucky State College, Transylvania University, University of Kentucky, University of Louisville, and Western Kentucky University.

Editorial and Sales Offices: Lexington, Kentucky 40506

Published jointly in Great Britain by The Macmillan Press

To

Mary Ann Beaumont

Eve Edmonds

Contents

	Preface	ix
1	The Horizons of War: Problems of Projection *Martin Edmonds*	1
2	The Emergent Military *Morris Janowitz*	21
3	Reserve Forces: Mobilization Demand in Modern War *Martin Edmonds*	35
4	The Future of the Reserve Officer Training Corps *Laurence I. Radway*	55
5	Youthful Officer Retirement: Matrix for Political Action *Alden Williams*	69
6	Strategic Ideas and Defense Policy: the Organizational Nexus *Colin Gray*	89
7	Militia in the Seventies: a Conflict Paradigm *Philip S. Kronenberg*	110
8	The Burgeoning Arsenal: Developments and Projections *Robert Snowden Ficks*	135
9	Science, Technology, and the Future of Warfare *Roger Williams*	157
10	The Military Bureaucracy: a Case Study of a Civilian Contribution *Peter Nailor*	180
11	Polemology: Promises and a Problem *Roger A. Beaumont*	203
12	Summing Up *Roger A. Beaumont*	211
	Notes on the Contributors	215

Preface

The next quarter-century is perhaps the most crucial of the twentieth century in the realm of military affairs. For military affairs have become human affairs to such an extent in the nuclear age that no matter what one's political, ideological or intellectual position, it is getting harder and harder to find steady ground from which to remain objective. This volume, therefore, has attempted to gather informed opinion from military analysts and if it has erred in any direction it is in that of creativity. Since the essence of creativity is individual effort and the scanning function is also vital, the editors have attempted to gather together as many varying positions as possible. It may be noted by those who read the volume closely that the editors themselves do not agree on certain basic presumptions. We feel that this is a strength rather than a weakness and that if anything has clouded the effectiveness of military analysis in the century to date, it has been the tendency to assume a fixed position without really considering alternatives.

No one in the volume, then, speaks for anyone else, but taken *in toto* the volume is more hopeful than may be justified by the flow of events. Indeed, someone looking back at this work from a perspective of twenty-five years may view its contributors and editors as latter-day prototypes of Norman Angell. Nevertheless, whatever the statistics of conflict analysts may show, the sense of the imminence of violence and war is greater at this point in history to a larger number of mankind than in any other point in time. As Marshall McLuhan noted in *War and Peace in the Global Village*, it is this immediacy that is rapidly changing the impressions and the basic assumptions on which national states have hitherto been founded. Certainly the quantum dimensions of change, the last major colonial war and the end of the *Pax Britannica* in the first quarter-century, the end of European hegemony and the Hitlerian malaise in the second quarter, and the wars of expanding literacy, technology, ideology and population which began to burgeon in the third quarter leave one apprehensive to say the least.

We hope, nevertheless, that the thoughts and ideas provoked by this eclectic collection will contribute in some measure to the last twenty-five years of the twentieth century being known as its most tranquil and uneventful period.

ROGER A. BEAUMONT AND MARTIN EDMONDS

1 The Horizons of War: Problems of Projection

MARTIN EDMONDS

Projecting future forms of war is an uncertain preoccupation. It is in essence no different, however, from the problems of defense planning and management, which are likewise characterized by the notion of uncertainty. Decision-makers, be they politicians or servicemen, are not only concerned with internal uncertainties, which originate largely in the technological character of weapons development, but also with external uncertainties, which stem mainly from the so-called international strategic environment. Both categories of uncertainty, which are not mutually exclusive, are exacerbated on the one hand by the lengthy lead times, costs and complexities of modern weapons systems, and on the other by the speed and intensity with which international crises can flare up anywhere in the world. The situation is in some measure epitomized by the recognition that a future war will likely have to be fought with forces in being and by the elaborate intellectual activity in the area of conflict management. These two considerations themselves are in effect the outcome of planning and policy decisions; the former are decisions of a decade or more previously, and the latter in the present time frame, perhaps in recognition of the inadequacy of previous policies and decisions as well as of the desire to avoid war.

The challenge of defense planning, like the challenge of prophesying future forms of war, is to minimize uncertainties and limit risks.

2 War in the Next Decade

It is to balance and equate defense policy, in contradistinction with the strategic environment, with the fulfillment of that policy. But, at the same time, the requirement is to keep the means by which the challenge has to be met within stringent financial ceilings, and in a manner politically compatible with the values and ideology of society.

To meet the challenge, defense planners have developed and experimented with sophisticated management techniques. Most of these new methods have had an economic bias. The tendency has therefore been to attempt to equate capability with cost, and thereby achieve a measure of economic efficiency. Despite these techniques, there remains a gap between the external and internal environments of defense planning. Within this gap lies the essence of the strategic dialectic and the dialectic of war. Can any state be assured that its defense plans, once formulated, are relevant to a future war projected fifteen years or more ahead?

The 'rationalists' have developed politico-military scenarios depicting future possible war situations. From them, projections based on the results of stochastic processes, probability distributions and forecasting methods have been produced; and yet there is little evidence that such projections have been successful. Alternatively, those who have projected future war and have based their arguments on experience, intuition or historical precedent, have an equally unconvincing record. The ratio of failure to success in these ventures has been high.

Why, then, attempt a study of the horizons of war through the 1970s? First, there is the argument that it adds to the debate. Second, it only attempts a projection in the medium term, accommodating the probabilistic constraints in military technological forecasting. And third, and most important, the emphasis is changed. The contention here is that attention should not, as has been the tendency in the past, be given only to the technological and strategic considerations of war; the focus should be on the dynamics of military institutions and their impact on society. But civil-military relations are a two-way affair; it is for this reason that the 'resource base' upon which this study is made is widened further to incorporate significant trends in society as they impinge upon the military sphere. That 'state policy is the womb in which war develops' is a statement which is as valid today as it was when Clausewitz first coined it. It is regrettable that this fundamental point is so often overlooked by those studying the causes and conduct of war.

It has now come to be accepted that strategic studies and defense analysis as fields of intellectual activity have become more widespread and sophisticated since the Second World War. Explanations for this growth in interest focus upon the importance and implications of nuclear weapons, and upon the wide and multifarious impact of technical and scientific developments in military hardware. Both of these developments are customarily linked within the general term 'the Military Technical Revolution'. Military strategy, strategic theory and defense studies have consequently centred upon the problems of military capability and on broad questions of what a state can do, under what set of assumed circumstances, with what military weapon systems and organization at its disposal and with what likely, or range of possible, outcomes. The many techniques of operations research, mathematical model-building and economic analysis have been applied to these problems with giddy and sometimes unquestioning enthusiasm.

For many people, however, it is anathema to have asked questions of military strategy and to have devoted time and energy to these types of problems; the morality and integrity of those engaged in this activity have been heavily criticized from a number of standpoints, ideological, religious, psychological and ethical. No matter how laudable, thoughtful and sincere these objections may be, the reality of the situation cannot be ignored merely because it is conceived to be repugnant or unfashionable. The issues of defense, security and strategy are real issues. They relate to the practical problems faced by those responsible for state policy in providing for security both at the present time and in the future.

These essentially military problems are unquestionably important; much value can be derived from the results of intellectual energy devoted to facing these problems and endeavouring fully to understand them. But the whole process has in the past tended to be limited to the point of distortion. Whilst within its limitations the quality of analysis and scholarship is unquestioned, the breadth of the whole problem has left too much uninvestigated; the parameters of the study of security problems have been too narrowly drawn. The explanation is simple: the study of strategic and military problems has tended in the past to operate from the assumption that 'security' is synonymous with 'defense'. Within this assumption it is subsumed that 'defense' means military defense, interpreted in both the 'active' and 'passive' senses of the term. If, then, 'security' as a concept is taken to incorporate more factors than specifically military ones, not only are the operational parameters for a projection of war in the 1970s widened, but also the whole issues of preparation for war, and the cause of war, are reinstated where they properly belong, in the political spectrum. And, in parenthesis, many of the criticisms of the more 'traditional' studies of strategy and defense may be accommodated.

The concept of security may indeed be ambiguous; what one man perceives to be adequate security, another may well not. There are wide differences of opinion as to what normatively constitutes security, and what represents a threat. At least, however, there can be some degree of consensus in the general proposition that security does not of necessity have to be a military consideration, nor that a threat to a 'feeling' of security can only come from a military source. In terms of feelings of security and perceptions of threats, war, defense and the military must be placed in context and, preferably, in rank order. Consideration should also be given to the argument that either too much security or the absence of a threat can also constitute a danger to society.

Security as a concept is popularly interpreted as the absence of a threat; like insurance, it is seen as an essentially negative concept. But it also has positive connotations. It must imply that a given situation can be improved, or at least maintained in a situation of equilibrium in contradistinction with the environment. It becomes compatible with the broadened parameters of security and with this positive interpretation of the concept to argue that the possession of a formidable military capability, especially one that is large, complex and technologically advanced, may represent a dual security threat. The first is that such a capability would be likely to attract an opposite, if not necessarily an equal, force. This is based on an assumption of the action-reaction phenomenon in arms races, especially between militarily powerful states. The second is that such a military establishment would represent an opportunity or investment cost, the size, depth and breadth of which could compromise many of the other features of security. A society under these circumstances would, for example, be unable to contend with major, or even minor, internal political, economic and social problems that threatened its stability owing to an overcommitment to the provision for security against an external military threat. The problem becomes particularly sensitive when an essentially hostile external power employs the policy of encouraging political or social disorder within a society, thereby dividing attention and forcing a potentially wasteful reallocation of scarce resources to meet these new security threats.

The second and perhaps the most important effect of widening the parameters of security as a base for projections of war, is to reintroduce into the equation the problem of war ends as distinct from the means of war. War ends in this context refers to the political objectives for which war is being fought; it is not the narrower interpretation of the traditional military war objectives of defeat of the opposing forces, military surrender, or the attainment of a military strategic objective. Again, the tendency in the past has been to divorce the political and the military objectives in war. The problem of the German surrender during the Second World War illustrates this point. Further, the tradition has been to see and to perceive the military as an organization which is set apart from politics. Political issues are not matters of concern for the military; like the civil service, the military establishment is generally considered to act as an executive agency for policies laid down by government. To a considerable degree, advanced industrial societies in the West have been convinced by the myths and liberal democratic traditions surrounding the military as an institution, with the result that it has come to be accepted that there is a qualitative distinction between military means and political ends.

But military means and political ends are not separate, no matter how politically expedient it is to believe it or how important the routinization of military subservience to civilian control is to the overall image of the governmental and political system. Two examples may serve to illustrate this point. They are taken from movements which were generated from within society and which were directed against the military. They were not directed against the military as an organization or as a social group, but against the military as the physical manifestation of political aims and objectives. The military were, in other words, the tangible, physical evidence of goals, objectives and policies with which the objectors fundamentlly disagreed. One is the Campaign for Nuclear Disarmament (C.N.D.) in Britain during the middle and late 1950s. It was directed primarily against the policy of the British government to develop, procure and deploy fusion weapons. The Campaign organizers hoped that by their example they could bring home the issues to the British public and by their force of argument persuade the government to alter its policy and unilaterally abandon nuclear weapons. A secondary objective was to stimulate similar disarmament agreements among the nuclear powers, following what was assumed to be the British example. It was the contention of the C.N.D. movement that the use of nuclear weapons served neither the political objective for which they were intended, nor the guarantee of security for the country in the face of the nuclear retaliatory capability of the Soviet Union. The leaders of the movement attacked the premise behind deterrence theory as vehemently as they did its logic; they argued that the penalties incurred in proving that deterrence did not work, or that accidents could happen, were far from being commensurate with the apparent benefits of possessing the nuclear deterrent. 'Passive' defense policies could, alternatively, assume other forms. Security through nuclear means was seen, for the C.N.D. movement, to be as big a threat as it was a guarantee.

The other example is that of the Vietnam War. It is an important event in understanding the unity of military means and political ends for, being a limited war situation, the goals for which either party to the conflict fought had to be reasonably clearly defined. Opponents in the United States to the war objected both to the system of selective service currently operating, by which manpower was made available for active service in the war, and to the political objectives which the United States hoped to achieve in Vietnam by military means. Doubts about the merits of the objectives and their justification were expressed time and time again by people in all sections of American society. Even to those for whom the ostensible political objectives were acceptable, namely the containment of communism in South-East Asia and the maintenance of democratic systems of government in the area, the appropriateness of the means employed did not engender sympathy. The most perplexing feature of the war for most observers was the realization by those in authority that the war was fundamentally a political issue and that it could only be resolved by a political solution. Yet when the time came, there was always a last attempt to force a military defeat. Time and time again the United States reverted to traditional form in that it put its confidence in the military establishment to bring about the final capitulation of the enemy.

The impact of the opposition to United States' involvement in Vietnam was heightened by the effect that the war had had upon American society as a whole. The economy had been both dislocated and made vulnerable, generations had been divided to the point that tolerance had almost ceased to exist, political parties had been discredited by their inability to find, or agree on, a solution, and individuals and groups had experienced loss and personal tragedy. With the possible exception of industry, particularly the technologically advanced and military-orientated corporations, hardly anyone had benefited from the war. In the long run, the war may be seen as having forced the United States to take a closer and more critical look at itself, with consequences that may possibly be eventually desirable; in the short run, however, the consequences of the war were menacing. And in all this turbulence, the section of the community whose image had been most tarnished by the war was the military; but they were not entirely alone.

Arising immediately from this Vietnam War experience, many developments in American society have been set in train that might be considered as serving a poor foundation for military security planning into the late 1970s and early 1980s. The implications of such phenomena as 'the military-industrial complex', the 'military-academic complex', the 'Vietnam moratorium', the Chicago 'conspiracy' trials, and 'Pinkville' and 'My-Lai' are hard to evaluate.

Their impact upon American society may take a long time to be absorbed. But at least in the short run, Vietnam has raised in the minds of many young Americans the fundamental question of their obligations and duties to society on the one hand and their individual conscience on the other. In an open society such questions are basic; and upon the answers to such questions, which relate to the tenets of American society and the values that it has historically held important, the future commitment to defense and security rests. 'The legitimacy of the draft is in a sense a subtraction from the legitimacy of the state. It represents the threat system of the state turned in on its own citizens however much the threat may be disguised by a fine language about service.' The double standards of Nuremburg have suddenly become, a mere generation later, a central issue for many young Americans.

The dichotomy of legal obligation and individual conscience, whether expressed in the context of the United States' involvement in Vietnam or of the United Kingdom's decision to procure and deploy nuclear weapons, is synonymous with the dichotomy of the means and ends of war. Assuming that defense planning is directed towards the eventuality that a state might have to go to war, this means–ends dichotomy is only relatively straightforward if it is confined within military parameters. Military means, seen as weapons systems, men and doctrines, and military ends, seen in terms of the attainment of military tactical or strategic targets, are entirely compatible if it is assumed that the repercussions of military planning on the economic, political and social life of the society are ignored, and if it is assumed that the act of employing military force in itself does not alter the nature or degree of the political goals that are hoped to be gained as a result of military success. The large proportion of military defense planning makes these assumptions; it is placed upon a two-dimensional plane, and consequently the only constraints upon military and defense planning for security are the quality of military intelligence information, the morale and preparedness of the armed forces, and the availability of resources with which to translate what are perceived military needs into practical reality.

When the parameters are widened, and when the concept of

security embraces military and non-military considerations, the problem of the relationship between means and ends of war becomes disproportionately more problematical. When, for example, the constraints upon the military include a voluntary system of manpower recruitment in place of a system of conscription, or when military objectives subsume political ends, planning for defense and security has to take into consideration the whole range of political, social and economic implications of such a policy. As the contribution of economists to military defense planning in the 1960s was to introduce the notion of 'efficiency' into defense decision-making by applying, for example, techniques of marginal incrementalism to specifically military problems, so, given the widened parameters of security, additions to the military capability of the state must be seen in relation to the whole spectrum of opportunity costs and marginal reductions in overall security incurred by such a policy. The costs that could be incurred might include such considerations as the 'quality of life', economic stability, the political acceptability of the ends for which the increased military capability was intended, or diminished standards in welfare, education, leisure, and technical and scientific potential. It is entirely compatible with these widened parameters that disregard for any of these fields might well represent a security risk, inasmuch as the stability of society is threatened and the whole social and political structure is thrown into disequilibrium.

In projecting the horizons of war in the 1970s, therefore, it becomes as important to give attention and weight to those threats to society which are self-inflicted as to those that are perceived to be posed from outside. It is assumed here that it is the professional responsibility of the political scientist to examine policy content and to make judgment upon the future political implications of those policies currently being formulated or put into effect. A value judgment of this sort would not be incompatible with the role of the political scientist as analyst Unless the concept of security is broadened, and unless defense is seen within a total societal context, the possibility, if not the likelihood, is that the greatest political threat to society, in terms of the quality of life and the values that that society represents, is the system of military security itself. At present, the demarcation between security defined in military terms and security defined in broad societal terms remains clearly marked along traditional lines. The danger becomes evident when a society, confronted with a changing internal and external environment, can only respond in military terms, or is constrained from making alternative reaction because of the neglect of these alternatives through an overcommitment to the military. It is as though inputs into the system are always interpreted in military terms as either external war threats or internal threats to 'law and order'. And in these circumstances, feedback becomes positive in that the response to these inputs exacerbates the situation which gave rise to the perception of a threat in the first place.

The situation in Northern Ireland since 1969 might serve to illustrate this last point. The sources of internal opposition to the Northern Ireland government stem from the past inability of the political system to resolve long-standing differences between religiously motivated communities. Having abandoned any confidence in the Stormont government to respond to their respective interests, the two communities have resorted to sporadic outbursts of violent action. This was immediately perceived as a threat to 'law and order', and the Northern Irish and British governments responded by sending troops to the troubled areas. By their presence, it can be argued that violence has been mitigated and law and order have been in evidence; but the apparent consensus is very artificial. Perhaps it is the belief of the British government that time will cool, if not heal; and while this cannot be considered out of the question it should be remembered that the problem has existed in Northern Ireland for nearly three hundred years. The fundamental difficulty is that the solution to the problem is system change, rather than system maintenance. By seeing the problem as something that requires a military response, the opportunity for a system change, transformation or adaptation becomes more and more remote.

How, then, can projections of the horizons of war be made, based upon a broadened conceptualization of 'security'? Two requirements have of necessity to be fulfilled. The first is to identify those areas where there already exists a degree of overlap between security planning on a purely military basis and security planning on a broader front. Two problems complicate this exercise: firstly, advanced industrial societies are highly complex both in their structure and in their dynamics. Events, decisions, processes and responses happen in complicated and unexpected ways. Secondly, the overlap is hard to establish because of the disparity between interpretation and reality. Traditions, images and interpretations of civil-military relations in most societies tend to cloud the extent to which any overlap already exists. Traditional images of the military as being essentially a group apart from the broader issues are reinforced by such security devices as the Official Secrets Act which limit both knowledge and understanding of the nature and dimension of civil-military relations. Somewhat paradoxically, because the military are seen, and like to be seen, as being extra-political, outside politics, there tend to be outbursts of horror and consternation when it is known that the military have taken an interest in political, social or economic problems.

Nonetheless, there is an increasing number of studies of the military and their relations with the rest of society which reveal that the overlap is considerable. The findings of these studies suggest not only that military and defense policies have a considerable impact upon society, of which the military and defense planners are well aware, but also that such decisions are often taken on grounds that make more political, economic or social than specifically military sense. Studies of elites in society, both in the United States and in Britain, and of the dual function of the party and the army in the Soviet Union, suggest that the separation of the civil and the military at decision-making levels is not as wide as traditional interpretations would immediately suggest.

The second requirement is to make clear the methodological basis upon which projecting the horizons of war is based. Exploratory forecasting, based on an ontological process of extrapolating from identifiable current trends, meets this requirement. Such techniques of forecasting are usually applied to possible future developments in technology, and there is no methodological reason why a similar technique should not apply to sociological phenomena. By systematically examining trends in civil–military relations, devoting particular attention to areas where purely military considerations overlap broader political, economic and social forces, it becomes possible, within tolerable degrees of error, to isolate and categorize the extent to which war, and war preparation, have changed direction and emphasis. This does not, it should be noted, conflict with the supposition that intuition has served to be the most accurate projector of war; intuition suggests that war is moving from the military to a multi-dimensional plane, and the 'rationalist' approach of exploratory forecasting taken here is not focused on questions of how wars will be fought but upon questions related to what wars are likely to be fought about, equating means with ends.

There are several identifiable areas of overlap between purely military considerations and economic, political and social forces. In the general context of decision-making in defense, for example, the civilian has been assuming a more and more influential role. This is not only due to a greater continuity in office than his military counterpart, but also because of the increasing administrative and essentially bureaucratic function of central defense departments. The impact and influences of Mr Macnamara in the United States and Mr Healey in Britain should not be underestimated in this context. Through them, many civilian analysts and advisers on defense problems were incorporated into the defense decision-making process, on the premise that many military problems and issues could be interpreted as essentially organizational, economic, sociological or mathematical problems. This assumption in recent times has come under criticism; the record of decisions made upon purely economic, sociological or mathematical theoretical interpretations has been singularly poor, the TFX/F111 decision emerging as the most notorious. This is not, however, to assume that decisions taken on primarily military criteria would have fared any better. But the pendulum is swinging back and the military appear to be reasserting their primacy in defense planning, even though civilian participation will continue to play a significant role.

In defense economics, broad questions have been raised both about the structure of the defense industries and their productive capacity and flexibility. These questions in their turn have been seen in relation to questions about the structure of the economy as a whole and the impact of defense expenditure upon it. As a supplementary, some concern has been expressed over the relationship between defense industries and the government, and the poorly defined interdependence of the one upon the other with neither being wholly accountable. Defense spending has been a major field of concern. As the delicate balance between growth and inflation becomes more precarious, fanned by recurrent balance of payments difficulties and international currency crises, so attention has been turned to ways and means by which some sort of stability can be restored to, or maintained within, an economy. Defense spending has been seen as one expedient method of budgetary control. though in adopting this essentially non-military line of policy, not only does defense spending on the economy tend to become more pervasive in its secondary and tertiary effects, but it also raises one of the political anomalies of Keynesian economics, recognized by Keynes himself. This is that a commitment to full employment and the control of inflation might necessitate a society having to absorb much of its own surplus production without in turn generating more income. Expenditure on defense might well provide that function, leading to the supposition that the economies of advanced industrial societies may have to come to rely on there being a permanent, and large, area of defense expenditure.

Recent studies of military organizations suggest that changed political as well as military technical environments have had their impact. Traditional concepts of morale, discipline and order have come under scrutiny. Many of the accepted tenets of military life have been threatened, amended or ridiculed, and many more have been abandoned. Recruitment, for example, has suffered; the manpower requirement of the military has changed, whilst the image they portray in the mind of the public does not encourage appropriately qualified or motivated men to volunteer for service in sufficient numbers. The career problems and status of the regular soldier have been exacerbated by a widening diversity of roles, functions and responsibilities, many of which he is now expected to master. The problems of being able to propagate the military life as a worthwhile career, and to project the military establishment as a whole as an organization of prestige, status and opportunity, are becoming increasingly difficult.

The popular image of the military has not been enhanced by such events as Vietnam, Czechoslovakia, Algeria, Suez, Dominica, etc. The whole concept of recruitment by conscription has come under fire to the point that, in the United States at least, the system is almost totally discredited. It is open to question whether the introduction of an all-volunteer system represent an expedient or are demonstrative of a change of heart. The situation was indicative of a deep-rooted malaise when a substantial proportion of a generation of young men, eligible for national service, appeared to hold their opponents in higher esteem than they did their own political leaders. Military discipline has not avoided criticism. There are mounting pressures, again in the United States, for a more democratic army. Whether this is a function of a better-trained and educated technocratic military organization, rather than a feature of undercurrents of opposition to the military and political ends for which the military establishment is maintained, is again open to question. But in either case it would suggest that within the armed forces, as indeed within society, there are discernible indicators that there exists a strong feeling of antagonism, based on skepticism, even cynicism, to what the military represents, however false this image may appear to be. This antagonism, whilst far from being universal, is nonetheless fairly widespread, especially among the young. The feeling perhaps is closely akin both to the conceptual phenomenon of alienation, central to Marx, and to the idea of anomie, formulated by Durkheim.

These concepts help to clarify what is an important contemporary development within advanced industrial societies. They assist especially in interpreting attitudes towards security as defined in purely military terms. There are many contributory reasons other than military ones, for instance, for the development and growth of a feeling of alienation; of necessity, they relate to the fundamental contradiction between 'real life', seen narrowly in this context as the reality of military power capability and organization, and 'reflections', taken loosely to be concerned with conceptions of man's purpose, aspirations and destiny. The contradictions and paradoxes inherent between the two, as they apply in the military-security context, are most strikingly brought out over the question of nuclear weapons. If the early discussion of whether to develop the hydrogen bomb raised, in the minds of the scientists responsible, the incompatible but simultaneous questions of ethics on the one hand and perceived military requirements on the other, it is doubtful whether the ordinary citizen can be expected, with partial knowledge and with a culturally determined value system, to make sense of, or make rational decisions about, these seemingly irreconcilable issues. That a sense of anomie should be seen alongside that of alienation is hardly surprising: the conflict of moral standards between the tenets of Western civilization and the act and conduct of war, and especially nuclear or 'insensate' war, must raise in the minds of many citizens, irrespective of class, a sense of double standard and of moral decay. On the issue of war, the Churches are ambivalent, natural scientists vacillate between ethical doubts and continued research in the interest of the pursuit of knowledge, and politicians – on the whole a group about whom populations are increasingly becoming cynical – tend towards the expedient and have so far failed to take a moral stand. And in the meanwhile, the doubtful partnership of the bomb, chemical and biological warfare and genocide, and the 'Christian way of life' continues to exist.

It is sometimes forgotten that young men and women under the age of thirty-five have never known the non-nuclear world. Those under twenty-five have never lived in one. Young people of these generations are generally speaking better educated, even though they have been exposed to the pressures, challenges and comprehensive coverage of the mass media. Little seems to escape the camera or the tape-recorder. Wars, riots, famine, disaster, crime, violence and decadence are the hosts upon which News depends. It is tempting to over-exaggerate the effects of the mass media; but man has, nonetheless, to relate what he sees and hears as matters of common report to the values and ideology of his society. How, for example, are modern weapons, the products of massive scientific and technological research effort, to be made reconcilable with the realization that mankind can be eliminated at will? Or how meaningful is it to talk of devoting more resources to military security when the threat to life and the quality of life through pollution, or an inadequate welfare service, is more immediate and pressing? And how can action in Vietnam, Czechoslovakia, Biafra or Northern

Ireland – all of which are covered in graphic detail by the mass media – be made compatible with the principles and values that the states which were partially responsible for these events are meant to epitomize?

The contradictions seem to be becoming more apparent year by year. The continued presence of the United States in S.E. Asia, and the continued Soviet 'occupation' of Czechoslovakia serve to keep these contradictions in focus. Over Vietnam, for as long as the United States retained an armed, active force there, two discrete but related consequences were likely to result. The first was that the great expense and loss in human, material, financial and psychological terms not only began to take its toll, but also made the healing period longer to complete. The second was that the gap already existing in American society widened still further. The gap widened, as much because of the impact of the war upon American society as because of the astounding capacity of the Vietnamese people to withstand the formidable military might of the United States armed forces and to continue the battle. The lack of success of the United States, and of their conventional faith in naked military power, raised questions about many of the assumptions that had long been accepted by all Americans. The Viet Cong and the Viet Minh successes served to vindicate the Maoist thesis, at least in the eyes of the younger generation, of the unity of military and political means and ends. It is more than possible that the practice of this Maoist philosophy as exemplified in Vietnam, Algeria, Cuba and Laos may serve as a blueprint not only for internal active opposition to traditional types of society, but also for defense planners and governments alike.

Alienation, arising out of the contradictions apparent in the reality of war and the reflections of society, has manifested itself in many ways. Sometimes it has been active and positive, at other times passive and negative. Examples of the former would include the anti-war, anti-NATO and anti-arms sales demonstrations and lobbies, the draft card burning rituals of American conscripts, Vietnam teach-ins and the ever-increasing output of exhortative (and frequently inaccurate) literature and information on military affairs. Among the better-organized anti-war movements would be C.N.D.

Among the latter might be considered the problems of recruitment with which many Western states are confronted. Principal among these is perhaps Germany, where it has been sugested that there is a widespread and strong political awareness that a war in Europe would be purposeless, for, no matter what the outcome was in terms of victory, defeat or stalemate, Germany, as the battleground, would inevitably suffer most. Another feature would be the ever-increasing body of analysis of such subjects as the 'military-industrial complex', the 'Permanent arms economy' and the 'Pentagon Warlords'; and the trend in the cinema, theater and art might be considered in this context as well. As much attention is also being given to international *détente* and the thaw in the Cold War as to military strategy; but whether this new interest is motivated by optimism about reduced tension or is part of the reaction to past 'cold warrior' discussions of strategy remains an open question. It is likely a combination of both. The general picture that emerges, however, is that defense policy and military capability, as problems of permanent concern, are some of the major contributions towards discernible indicators of alienation developing in advanced industrial societies. And this trend is not confined to the West, either. Though the perspectives of the post Second World War era may have been accurate at the time of their inception, they, and the language in which they have been conceived, have persisted as the basis for security; this anachronism has developed as a source of opposition from within. 'Conventional wisdom' on war and security no longer seems to provide answers to the questions that are currently being asked.

There is evidence in military decision-making circles that there is an awareness of potential intra-societal threats; there is evidence also that the military are in the process of developing and analyzing the appropriate military response. What has not been in evidence is any move to analyze and examine the sources and causes of these potential internal threats, or to work out an appropriate political remedy. Falling back on the knowledge that nuclear weapons are a reality, and that their existence must be taken into account in security planning, defense planners appear to have arrived at the conclusion that, over the whole spectrum of war, the emphasis will move from the nuclear threshold and the entire deterrence/defence debate to unconventional war and insurgency on a small scale. The future threat is disruption of society by selective use of violence and terrorism. Recent military studies in Britain, for example, have suggested that there is a pressing need for a whole new inventory of 'sub-lethal' weapons. The United States already has a lead in this field through counter-insurgency experience in Vietnam, and much of the experience has been reinvested in the sale of counter-insurgency weapons to Latin America for use against guerrilla operations.

The future outlook on the likelihood of internal wars appears to be a gloomy one. Not only does it appear that for political, sectional, racial, economic and social reasons internal conflicts are likely to increase, and in consequence will represent a threat to the 'security' of society, but also the reaction by those in authority seems to continue to be a dependence on a purely military solution. The conclusions of Lasswell's hypothesis of the 'Garrison State' appear to be coming true, even if it is for quite different reasons. It is as though the feedback process of external and internal threats to society remains positive. The circle is closed when the source of an internal threat to the stability of society is a consequence of alienation arising from the impact of essentially military and military-related phenomena on society; the threat then becomes all the more menacing because it is a military response to the problem which has been decided upon. Suggestions have been put forward, for example, as to how to effect control of internal opposition and how to maintain 'law and order' and the status quo. One is that weapons should be developed that can single out an individual from within a crowd without harming those around him. On the assumption that crowds always have to be led, which is tenuous indeed, this might be a fair suggestion. Another is for the development of chemical and biological weapons that help to subdue, or incapacitate, a potentially hostile group. But however humane these suggestions may be at first sight, the possible political or social consequences of these weapons should they fall into the 'wrong' hands hardly bears contemplation. The crude techniques used by the Nazis might serve to illustrate the ghastly possibilities such developments could bring about.

The logic behind this projection of the horizons of war is not complicated. On the simple premise that security is a broad concept, and that it is not exclusively a military domain, it becomes possible to argue that the responsibility of decision-makers is as much to balance military requirements and military ends as it is to equate the requirements and political aspirations of society as a whole. The internal threats to mankind, many of his own making, are as immediate and lethal as those that are perceived to exist exclusively from outside military forces. External threats in the past have been manufactured by leaders of states to justify a course of action, the ultimate intention of which was to strengthen their control within the state. The future may well see the reverse of this phenomenon. Internal threats may well necessitate leaders who have the political and moral strength to diminish the perception of an external threat so as to enable society to adapt to, contend with, or overcome the problems that have to be faced from within. If commitment to external threats either compromises the capacity of society to meet its internal problems, especially where that society is generally accepted as being an 'open' one, or raises fundamental contradictions between the means and ends of war, then a thorough and major reassessment has to take place.

By examining areas of overlap between the conflicting needs of the military and of society with regard to internal and external threats to security, some progress in exploratory forecasting of the horizons of war can be made. From the selected studies in this volume, concerned with specific areas of overlap in the contexts of decision-making, military organization and defense planning, and preparation for war, the general pattern that emerges is that premises behind security and the perceptions of war have moved to a different footing. Both the ideological camps are having similar problems. But what will emerge at the end of the 1970s is still hard to determine. The military-technical revolution at the top end of the spectrum seems to have reached a political, technological and financial plateau; if the focus turns to the lower end, society as a whole, as well as the military, immediately becomes involved. But it means that the military ends of violence and the political ends cannot be conveniently divorced. Whether governments are in their turn likely to pursue the political solution as opposed to the military one, whether they have a mandate to do it or not, is the crux of the problem. As Albert Einstein has observed, 'Intelligence recognizes that man's security and happiness depend upon a well-functioning society; that a well-functioning society depends on the existence and observance of laws; and that men must submit to these laws in order to have peace'. It rests on man's intelligence to learn from experience and to plan ahead with laws compatible with his 'reflections'.

2 The Emergent Military

MORRIS JANOWITZ

How can one speak about the military profession in the post 1970s when one can not readily anticipate the outcome of immediate and crucial events? It has become popular to skip over current uncertainties and make bold projections into the longer-range future. Often such forecasting is not only highly inaccurate but it may be self-defeating. It can be self-defeating if predictions become self-fulfilling prophecies because they inhibit creative thinking and limit options.

To speak of the military profession of the post 1970s is to identify those institutional policies and practices that require change. Rather than becoming enamored with predicting the future, I prefer to focus on the changes that men must accomplish in order to manage by rational means the human environment. Prediction based on extrapolations of current trends are particularly dangerous in international relations since change does not evolve gradually and at a uniform rate. Both in the deployment and use of conventional weapons by the major powers, and in the evolution of nuclear weapons systems, the last years of the decade of the 1960s may well be one of the basic transformation comparable to the period of 1945. The phase of American foreign policy from 1945 to 1970, a phase of a quarter of a century, can be thought of as a distinct period.

The Changing Politico-Military Context

First, during this last twenty-five year phase, the prospects of nuclear war were very remote indeed. It has been argued that during this period nuclear technology developed a delicate balance of terror, which was perhaps not so delicate as relatively stable, because its dimensions could be calculated. Political leadership and political arrangements accounted for the absence of major war, or rather accounted for the ability of the Soviets and the Western bloc to work out an arrangement to exist under the threat of accidental and premeditated nuclear war. The essential political formula was that the Soviet bloc believed that the United States' political leaders firmly controlled their military establishment and that the United States had ruled out a preemptive nuclear attack on the Soviet Union. In short, the political initiative and political posture of the United States was crucial during this period as the Soviet Union expanded its nuclear weapons system.

As 1970 came to an end, this political formula was being fundamentally strained by the uncertainties that MIRV-type weapons introduce. Political communications must become more mutual and two-way; but currently neither side was able to extend to the other the essential political guarantees, although it was abundantly clear to each that any nuclear initiative remains self–defeating. In addition, the nuclear balance was gravely complicated because the United States and the Soviet Union independently or in concert cannot extend the political formula of the last twenty-five years to include relations with China as she develops her nuclear weapons.

Second, during the last twenty-five years conventional military forces were employed by the United States to implement two increasingly divergent foreign policies: one in Western Europe and one in the Far East. In Western Europe, the stationing of American troops and the system of defense alliances were reasonably compatible with European national political aspirations. In the Far East the stationing of troops and their direct involvement were relatively compatible with local national aspirations until the end of the Korean War. Progressively the tasks of American forces have become more and more difficult because of opposition they encountered from local nationalist political forces; especially the nationalist sentiments of the developing nations. Vietnam represented the epitome of the stalemate of military force and nationalist political elements.

In exploring the tasks of institution-building for the military profession during the next two decades, it is possible to make very grim or merely grim assumptions about international relations. In the nuclear arms race, it might well be assumed that the Strategic Arms Limitation Talks (SALT) will fail and MIRV weapons will become standard equipment. In South-East Asia, it could be assumed not only that peace objectives will fail but that in the aftermath of disengagement of American forces the result will be to incorporate into the National Liberation Front, significant portions of the present South Vietnamese military potentials (less manpower and more weapons). In short, the domino theory could be made to work if American efforts contributed to the development of a Vietnamese military potential which would threaten neighboring states.

My observations about the future of the military profession are not based on any particular assumptions about the outcome of specific international negotiations. They are based on a more general assumption. Namely the crucial issue facing the military profession rests on whether it has the ability to recognize the paradox which nuclear weapons and contemporary nationalist movements raise; that the growth in the destructive capacity of both conventional and unconventional weapons has been paralleled by an extension in the limitation of the political effectiveness of force. The use of force has traditionally operated within circumscribed limits and contemporary political considerations have served only to narrow the limits. This is what is emphasized in the 'constabulary concept', a notion of military force as defined in *The Professional Soldier*. 'The military establishment becomes a constabulary force when it is continuously prepared to act, committed to the minimum use of force, and seeks viable international relations, rather than victory, because it has incorporated a protective military posture' (p. 148). In other words, the outbreak of general war is no longer inevitable in the calculus of political leaders.

The military profession believes that it has unique characteristics because of its responsibility for the management of the instruments of violence. Rationality in the the military profession means that it must, in the contemporary scene, accept the notion that a successful officer can be one who does not fight, but contributes to deterrence and the resolution of international conflict. It is truly unique to be trained to perform tasks that one hopes never to perform. Therefore, the basic question is whether I am justified in making the radical assumption that in decades ahead the military profession will increase its capacity to understand the limitations on military force and will be able to incorporate such an understanding into its doctrine, training and organization.

Of course, such an assumption must be seen in the light of the lessons to be drawn from the Vietnam War. These lessons deal not only with a host of tactical and organizational issues, but involve the questioning of fundamental strategic concepts. For example, in 1961 and 1962 ground force planners concluded that the limitations on military force in Vietnam were such that one million to one million two hundred thousand men would be required for a land engagement. How was that reality denied first by U.S. political leaders and then by the military professionals themselves?

The Emerging Military Format

But the impact of Vietnam on the future of the military profession has already been felt. First, the political definition of the national interest has come to include the public demand that future engagements similar in scope and strategy to the Vietnam conflict be avoided. Second, the frustration of Vietnam, plus the inequalities and rigidities of selective service, have created a crisis in the legitimacy of the conscript system of manpower. The result is that maintaining a volunteer armed force will be a persistent and increasing theme in the years ahead. In the near future United States military posture will be conditioned, and limited, by this changing manpower system. The professional military is likely to emerge as (1) a smaller establishment, (2) recruited permanently on an all-volunteer basis, and (3) organized predominantly on a force 'in being' basis with a de-emphasis of the older tradition of a cadre for mobilization.

All of these three elements articulate with one another. The pressure for and the need for a smaller force does not guarantee proportionate reductions in manpower costs. Economists have committed themselves to estimates and there is good reason to anticipate that like most military budgeting they are understatements of actual expenditures.

But the move toward a fully volunteer force is not merely a matter of cost and efficiency. It has emerged as an ideological goal for a variety of groups in the United States. For some, it is a desirable objective because it is an expression of individual freedom. Those who speak of the need for individual initiative in business enterprise system are the same ones who urged the end of selective service and who are opposed to all forms of national service. At the same time, many of the sharpest critics of the current economic system also agree that the military service should be organized without a draft. For these, despite practical and moral objections, the 'volunteer army' is offered as a basis for producing greater consensus in a society divided by a range of social and political issues.

An armed force 'in being' which is highly transportable has a strong appeal to the military profession seeking a solution to competing pressures. While professional officers prefered to build such a force on a modified selective service system, they have, of course, accepted the move toward an all-volunteer service.

The initial implication of these policy directions are abundantly clear; the result will be to reverse the pattern of civilian-military relations of the last two decades. To reduce reliance on or to eliminate the draft, to recruit a fully volunteer force with longer tours of duty for officers and enlisted personnel and to shift from a mobilization to a force 'in being' format will make the military much more of a self-contained establishment. Clearly, the military will not revert to the professional isolation of the period between the First and the Second World Wars. The resources and skills which the military require, and the central importance of military operations in current affairs, will prevent such a gross transformation. But much civilian pressure on the military profession will have the effect of emphasizing the organizational autonomy and the separate character of the armed forces. However, the task of effective institution–

building will have to be the opposite. The task will be to develop a military profession which is closely articulated with civilian society. The underlying issue is not merely the danger of military opposition to civilian political leadership, but rather the question of professional vitality and legitimacy as well as sensitivity to the need for change.

The great danger will be if the military profession comes to be seen as a distinct and separate establishment by civilian society and in turn if the military profession begins to see itself as alienated from civilian society. To prevent such developments, and to increase the military's understanding of the limitations on the use of violence in international relations, institution-building in a wide range of areas is required, as for example recruitment, education and career development.

My focus will be on officer personnel although the issues of enlisted manpower are real. It is essential to keep in mind the format under which the military profession operated during the post-Second World War period. The professional officer corps is characterized by (1) a very broad base of recruitment, that is, in terms of social class, educational background, geographical region and even in terms of more intangible social personality. There is no specific social type which tends to make up the bulk of the recruitment; (2) a significant, but declining, number of the officers served as enlisted personnel (in the early 1960s over one-quarter of the ground officers had some enlisted experience, including the National Guard; (3) the bulk of the officer corps is composed of personnel with relative short-term career commitments. This includes not only the bulk of the junior officers with two to four years of obligated tours of duty, but many middle-level officers whose careers end after five to ten years of duty. Although the senior posts are dominated by academy trained officers with long-term career commitments, the personnel mix of the armed service currently operates with a constant inflow and outflow of civilian-oriented officers; (4) a significant portion of the officers, but again a declining portion, are men who held civilian posts before they entered the armed forces or were mobilized as reservists and then chose to remain in the armed forces. Although this system might contribute to higher training costs it also has economic and social relevance for the officer's civilian employment after retirement. But the issue at hand is not only the economic cost but the character of civilian-military relations and the type of armed force that such emerging manpower systems will produce. The trend toward a smaller, fully volunteer standby force will alter this personnel mix and change the pattern of recruitment.

Recruitment. Movement toward an all-volunteer force is certain to narrow the base of recruitment into the officer corps. First, the number and range of R.O.T.C. units from which the bulk of the officers corps is drawn is certain to contract. This is not mainly a matter of agitation at selected college campuses against R.O.T.C. units. The pressure on R.O.T.C. units will be to produce a supply of officers and an emphasis will be placed on a smaller number of successful units. These will tend to be located in rural areas and in the south and west where the tradition of entrance into the military profession is the strongest. Often these R.O.T.C. units will be at universities with more modest academic standards.

Second, the armed forces will seek a higher component of officers who are trained in the service academies, a step which has already been taken by increasing the size of the student body at these institutions. While such a step may be necessary, it is an additional trend toward social separation, if more officers are trained at the academies in contrast to R.O.T.C. and O.C.S. units. While the system of selection into the service academies is broadly based, increased use of academic graduates will also in the future narrow recruitment because military family background is likely to become even more important in academy selection. It is important to note that the pool of such military families and the number of their offspring are increasing because of the expansion of the armed services during the last twenty years. Some such increase is acceptable because the percentage of officers whose fathers were in the military profession is still below the amount of occupational inheritance of other professions, for example the medical profession. But excessive recruitment from military families – officers and enlisted – would not only serve to narrow the basis of social recruitment, but would also contribute to a separation of the officer corps from civilian society. Any increased reliance on government sponsored military preparatory schools or even privately sponsored preparatory schools would also specialize social and geographical background.

Third, there is a danger that recruitment from the ranks into the officers corps may decline. As the military places greater and greater emphasis on a college degree, the trend will be to recruit from college graduates rather than train and promote from the ranks. Of course, the services have shown considerable ability to offer a college education to highly motivated enlisted personnel.

The issue at stake is not only a broadly based military officer corps, but its academic, creative and leadership potential. To focus on academic test scores which have come to characterize American university life is to miss basic elements. How can we account for the extraordinary leadership and statesmanlike cadres of higher officers who rose to prominence during the Second World War? They were not selected by means of psychological or academic tests; self-selection was crucial. The pool of outstanding officers was in part the result of the attraction of an academy education for the sons of respectable families without financial resources. This was the strength of the academies in the 1920s and 1930s, especially during the depression. The rise of the state universities and the opening up of the talent search by the prestige universities has weakened the relative position of the service academies for recruiting outstanding leadership potential.

Institution-building for the professional officers corps will in the future require extensive lateral entry if recruitment is to remain representative and vigorous. The professional military since the end of the Civil War, and especially since the turn of the century, has opposed lateral entry with great vigor. But it seems impossible to cope with a fully volunteer service and its emerging skill requirements without opportunities for lateral entry. Lateral entry can involve limited tours of duty, and in this respect is close to reserve status. The difference would be that an active duty assignment would be a routine event and not only in an emergency. Lateral entry includes the opportunity to take up an extended career in the professional military, two, five, and even ten years after graduation from a civilian university. Such lateral entry would be crucial both for a variety of technical assignments, and also for specialists in area and language work.

Education and Career Development. In the emerging armed forces, the education of the professional military man is designed not only to supply him with essential skills but to provide him with the necessary linkages with civilian society. Education emerges as one of the main mechanisms for articulating the military with civilian social structure. The tasks of the constabulary force require increased awareness of the larger society. However, the training and operational realities of much of the emerging military force along with its recruitment process will tend to separate the military from larger society. The education of the officer, which, of course, cannot be thought of independently from his career development, will have to carry the main burden of meaningful relations with the larger society.

In the past, the ground forces have had the major responsibilities for politico-military affairs and have supplied the cadre of officers for these tasks. Not only the mission of the ground forces but their style of life have predisposed them in this direction. But in the future the ground force 'in being' with its heavy emphasis on air transportability will become more like the current air force. Its organizational life will be contained mainly within the confines of a military base. Given the limited supply of uniformed personnel, the pressure will be to remove military personnel from logistical roles and thereby opportunities for civilian experiences will be diminished. Higher headquarters will be removed from metropolitan centres and placed on military bases or in remote areas. The trend will be toward garrison life in which each military professional will strive for the high-prestige assignment of an operational role. Even residence and social contacts will be more and more garrison-based since fewer personnel will be living off base. Preparation for military duties will separate the armed force both in residence and daily existence from the larger society.

A more detailed examination of career lines is required. As the military establishment moves toward a constabulary format with an overriding emphasis on deterrence, the range of tasks to be performed increases. The traditional ideas of a standard or prescribed career comes to have less and less meaning. The effectiveness of the military profession will depend on its ability to reward and integrate a wide range of careers. But this is not an easy task. First, the military are certain to continue to define the unit commander of manned conventional forces as the central role, and to think of such assignments as being at the heart of the professional prestige system. However, the dilemma of the commander at each level in the military hierarchy is that training, experience and concern with the internal management of the system does not necessarily increase his understanding of the politico-military context of higher command and of the consequences and limitations of force. Moreover, he must learn to live with the idea that if he is really successful, national objectives can be achieved by his sheer existence and not by his involvement in actual operations.

Second, the tasks of manning the automated system of mass destruction and their counter-defenses will consume a large portion of the personnel of the future military profession. The need to prevent nuclear accidents and the responsibility for managing the disposal of nuclear garbage and dangerous or obsolete weapons prevents these tasks from becoming routine. They are essential tasks but ones which do not necessarily develop military statesmen.

Third, the military see a broad range of specialized tasks as falling under the rubric of politico-military affairs, for example the management of military alliances, military assistance programs and involvement in arms control. The importance of these tasks are clear and increasing. However, it is a fundamental error to think of these assignments as constituting a set of specialized staff assignments. Every task and responsibility of the armed force – no matter how tactical, 'military' or routine – has its politico-military implication. The ineffective and disruptive disposal of obsolete chemical weapons, the uncalled for use of bayonets for local security around an overseas base, indicate the fusion of tasks and career lines in the military profession. It has not been and will not be the case in the future, that only high-ranking officers are involved in politico-military affairs. It is no longer the case that an officer first learns his purely military skill and then in mid-career requires exposure to the consequences of force in international relations. These tasks are now diffused throughout the entire structure. Even the command of tactical military units – both at home and abroad – needs to be seen as the symbolic presence of American goals rather than concrete and specific force levels.

Institution-building for the future will involve both educational and career changes. Like professional development in a wide area of contemporary civilian society the officer will require both higher degrees of expertise in his particular area of competence and at the same time heightened consciousness of the responsibility of the military establishment as a whole. The all-volunteer force may well, despite its disadvantages, supply a unique opportunity for restructuring the military profession.

It will be necessary to eliminate the worldwide personnel system which periodically distributes, rotates, and redistributes military personnel. Instead a modern equivalent – and I say equivalent – of the old-fashioned regimental system could well be developed both for the army and air force. The navy could strengthen and make realistic the notion of a home base. The experience with gyroscope units is a step in this direction. Such a system would permit each officer to have a basic affiliation with an operational, planning, logistical or educational unit, and would represent his primary affiliation. It could make possible a higher degree of cohesion and solidarity and the conservation of the best element of military tradition, which has been weakened by constant rotation. It would help to reduce family disruption and to increase career satisfaction.

Such a system would also permit and in fact enhance rotation of assignments required for professional development. It would make possible a greater degree of geographical specialization, essential both for operational units and for personnel with area and language skills. It would increase effectiveness in those functions which require long-term contacts with foreign governments and alliance organizations which today suffer from endless rotation of personnel.

A greater degree of career and geographical specialization in a personnel system of increased stability could articulate with an educational system designed to strengthen both civil-military relations and increase the awareness of the military about the limits of force in international relations. First, there should be no objection to starting professional officer education at an earlier age. It is well recognized that youngsters mature earlier, that a good part of high school is a waste of time, and that much of current unrest is the result of the prolonged dependence that youngsters must endure in high school and college. It should be possible for the academies to permit entrance after three years of high school. (In addition, one element in handling R.O.T.C. recruitment would be to make it possible for R.O.T.C. cadres to serve on active duty as enlisted personnel for a period of one or two years when they find college too boring and too confining. For this time, they would receive constructive service credit if they elected a long-term professional career.)

Academy instruction should include the junior year of instruction at a civilian university. This would be the equivalent to the junior year abroad and would supply an important educational experience. The military profession is already moving toward a larger and larger number of officers with higher degrees, and there should be a coresponding emphasis of obtaining these degrees at civilian universities in order to maintain effective civilian linkages.

But the basic transformation of professional education must focus on increased sensitivity to the consequences of the use of force. It is the case especially that junior officers need to be introduced to the broad professional educational objectives that are supposed to be the responsibilities of the advanced level schools (command and general staff colleges and service war colleges). But it must also be recognized that both the curriculum and the approach of such instruction at all levels require a recasting. Much of current instruction involves generalized discussion of current issues. The study in depth of politico-military affairs with concern for concrete details is required.

At the academy level, basic instruction in the social sciences is not enough. The social science analysis of tactical and strategic issues needs to be developed with a concern for political and economic and social aspects of military operations. For example, at West Point such an approach would involve joint endeavor by the social science faculty, the office of Military Psychology and Leadership and the tactical department to present realistic and simulated problems. The same type of instruction would be appropriate at the command and staff level. Yet it should be kept in mind that there are limits to the role of classroom instruction in developing a statesmanlike approach to the management of military affairs. Actual apprenticeship is an essential ingredient. It could well be that the war college level of instruction could be curtailed or even eliminated. During this time period, officer instruction could include a host of new experiences such as assignment to a civilian government agency, in community work or as participant observer with an outstanding military officer.

Basically, the evolution of military education is designed not only to prepare the officer for higher commands but to assist him in the transition to civilian life. The emerging military career line will involve a second career in civilian life. The advocates of a volunteer army speak of the reduction of personnel turnover but the military profession, despite the hope of the economists, will continue to be a young man's game. The future armed forces, because of strains and tension, will have to make possible the exercise of authority in the prime of life. The vitality of the armed forces depends on its age grading system, and this point is well recognized by the Israeli army. Even if the armed forces permit a significant number of officers to remain on duty outside of the promotion system, early retirement and the second career is and will remain crucial.

Military Authority. Finally, institution-building for the emergent military requires continual attention to the issues of military authority and discipline, particularly as it relates to internal management. Because of the equalitarianism of American society and the emphasis on informal personal relations, civilian society views with suspicion the practices of military authority. The military profession had engaged in considerable self-scrutiny about its authority relations, and has slowly adapted itself to the requirements of technical and team management. But there can be no doubt that the gap between garrison life and the realities both of operations and of combat is very great. Under conditions of operational duty and especially under the requirement of stress combat, there emerges the close fraternal authority required for group solidarity.

The military profession must recognize that many civilians view with suspicion a fully volunteer armed force because they fear a retrograde in authority, with harsh and unfunctional discipline, unrelated to the realities of modern military life. There is a belief that with the removal of the reluctant draftee, and the pressure he places on the system, the style of life dramatized in *From Here to Eternity* would return. These fears may be unfounded but they exist for many American civilians who recall or exaggerate the excessive formalism and arbitrary discipline which they have experienced in garrison life. There can be no doubt that a cultural factor is here at work; the professional military seems to assume that informality weakens leadership and limits response to direct commands.

It will not suffice to claim that civilian fears are unfounded; the military profession will have to confront this issue and expose its practices to full public scrutiny. Any misunderstangings as to how the armed forces operate would greatly weaken civil – military relations. The professional military will, in the future, be concerned with strategic concepts, and realistic military doctrine, and it will hope to be judged on these issues. However, it will be judged by civilian society in part on the patterns of discipline and authority it uses in its daily and operational life. The military profession of the future must also be prepared to participate in discussions of fundamental questions of human goals and to explore hypothetical issues including the military format of a world without war. There is no reason why the military profession should not avoid such an analysis since a world without war would not be without its equivalent peace officers.

3 Reserve Forces: Mobilization Demands in Modern War

MARTIN EDMONDS

In discussion and analysis of the defense policy and military strategy of a given state, the usual tendency is to either ignore entirely, or to regard as of marginal significance, the role of reserve forces. Yet the subject of reserve forces is important in its own right, if for no other reason than that they are an integral part of a state's overall defense posture and can provide some indication, within specified time scales, of its potential military strength and capability. Less importantly, though significant within a different context, is the impassioned and emotional response that discussion about the place of reserve forces customarily evokes among soldier, reservist and civilian alike.

In a few states where the principles and objectives of defense policy and structure differ from those generally found in the West, reserve forces can be found to provide the most important contribution to the over-all defense posture. Israel, Sweden and Switzerland, whose defense systems are loosely categorized as being that of a 'Nation-in-Arms' are familiar examples.[1] In the event of an emergency, the defense departments of these three states have the capacity to mobilize a high proportion of the adult population within a short period of time. In China, where the defense capability might still be crudely described as 'labor intensive', reserve forces in the form of the People's Militia are a highly significant factor, numerically speaking.[2]

The reserve force of a state is where the military and the civilian societies overlap. This is fundamental to an understanding of any military reserve system. It is where the self-image of the soldier and the civilian, and their respective attitudes to one another, are brought into sharpest focus. And it is from the juxtaposition of the civilian and the soldier within the same organizational framework that important concepts about the structure of society, the rights and duties of citizens and the ethos of society are highlighted. For example, within a study of the reserve forces of Britain and the continent of Europe, basic differences between the two societies are brought into stark relief. In the former, voluntarism continues to be the principle behind recruitment into the armed forces, whether regular or reservist; no legal obligation is made upon any individual to contribute actively to the defense of the state. The point has been made that it is the Englishman's right not to bear arms.[3] On the continent, the situation is reversed. Although each European state differs in practice, all operate from the assumption that able-bodied adult males have an obligation before the law to serve in the defense forces, unless legally exempt, and subsequent to that service, to be available to be recalled should the need arise. The obligation covers not only the limited period among the regular forces but continues with periods of training up to a specified age limit.

Discussion of the status, size and efficacy of reserve forces has in the past few years become more complex and intense, especially in the West. This does not mean, however, that the problem has not been one of concern among the Eastern bloc states. In the West, the question of reserve forces has focused on two broad planes: the first is the role of reserves within the North Atlantic Alliance, and stems from a reappraisal of European defense following the period characterized by the adoption of a strategy of 'flexibility in response' and by the move towards *détente* in Europe. This reappraisal, as it related to reserve forces, covered the question of how reserve forces should be evaluated as part of the combined military strength of the European members of NATO in the assessment of NATO forces relative to those of the Warsaw Pact; this on-going activity assumed an air of urgency following the invasion of Czechoslovakia in July 1968. The attention given to European reserve strength was further concentrated following the suggestion that there was the possibility of the United States withdrawing a substantial proportion of its ground troops stationed in Germany in response to internal public and Congressional pressure.[4] In the event that the balance of military forces between NATO and the Warsaw Pact becomes too much in favor of the latter, and if the United States withdraws forces from Central Europe in the wake of France and Canada, there is likely to be mounting pressure for the European powers to fill the gap. No state appears to have a great deal of faith in the United States airlift capability to be an adequate substitute in the event of a sudden Central European conflagration.[5] The capacity of the European powers to meet these probable deficiencies would depend on their willingness to bring their regular forces up to establishment, as well as to bring the NATO contributions up to agreed levels, and provide for adequate reserve strength. At present neither action, with the exception of Britain which enlarged its contributions to NATO ground forces by one brigade in 1969,[6] has been undertaken by any European state; if anything, the reverse has been the case.

The second plan relates to the discussion of reserve forces within each state. Depending upon the state and the policy issue, such debate as there has been has been intermittent. In no other state in Europe, however, has the question of reserve forces been more hotly argued than in Britain in the past few years. There are several contributory reasons for this: paramount is the radical alteration in British defense policy in 1967 from an 'East of Suez' role to one which was primarily towards Europe.[7] This change raised questions about the use of tactical nuclear weapons in Europe, force structures and the demands that a European role would make on ground forces especially. Related to this change of policy was the controversial decision to restructure and reorganize the whole system of military reserves which was taken in 1965 and brought into effect in 1967. Combined with the reorganization was the virtual disbandment of the civil defense forces.

In 1962, France also effected radical changes in defense policy; in the ensuing reorganization, a system of Operational Defense of the Territory (D.O.T.) was established. It was to have important and far-reaching effects upon the structure and role of the French reserve forces. The general effect has been to reduce the commitment of reserves to conventional mobile war in support of the regular forces, and to redefine them almost exclusively in a regionally based home defense role.[8] In Germany, the question of reserves has assumed an urgency, for within Central Europe it is the Germans who must face the initial force of invasion. Further, it is the Germans who are most affected by possible United States troop withdrawals and by understrength NATO contingents. The basic issue for Germany is the cost of building up an efficient reserve system, well manned, well equipped and efficiently run. Internal political, social and economic pressures mitigate against this being achieved, at least in the short term.[9]

It is never clear from commentaries, reports and analyses of reserve forces what precisely is meant by the term. Only a brief survey of the reserve systems operating in the various states of Europe demonstrates that there is no uniformity regarding what reserve forces are or the roles that such forces are intended to fulfill. Generally speaking, this is because reserve forces are defined by what they do, not what they are. However, the distinction that is usually implied when the category 'reserve forces' is used, is that between the regular and active forces, and those that are on a part-time basis. Arising out of this implied distinction is the professionalism of the former with full-time military service experience, and the semi-professionalism of the latter, based upon a limited period of military service brought up to par with intermittent periods of training. Basically the distinction is a qualitative one, though it can be found that in some roles or functions the reserve might well be qualitatively superior to his regular counterpart.[10]

The regular/part-time distinction is only a general one, and does not operate in all instances. Within the armed forces of several states certain regular forces are designated 'reserve', inasmuch as they are trained for, and allotted a flexible role designed to provide additional support and reinforcement to other regular forces when and wherever it is needed. The British Third and Fifth Divisions of Army Strategic Command would fall within this category.[11] Nor does the distinction cover the situation where role, rather than status, would appear to be the determining factor, and which is the basis upon which most commentators discuss reserves. Some roles are called 'reserve' though undertaken by regular forces. In Norway, for example, the regular forces are divided between those who, in the event of attack, fight a forward action to stall the enemy for as long as possible, while the remainder, operating within the network of military administrative units, mobilize the total defense effort, comprising mainly reserves. Parts of the regular forces are thus serving as an integral part of both the reserve system and the professional standing army.[12] The same situation applies in Britain where regular officers command T.A.V.R.* units

Another instance where the distinction would fail to apply is that of the role and function of para-military groups. These have an indeterminate status, and assume a wide range of civil and military roles. In some instances they absorb large numbers of trained and skilled personnel; in Italy, for example, the Carabinieri number, with 'other security forces', almost 100,000 men compared with the army's 313,000.[13] The gendarmerie in France – though roughly parallel systems operate in Turkey, the Netherlands, Luxembourg, Belgium and Greece – is a good example of a para-military organization. It is responsible to the minister for the armed forces, and its principal role is internal security. Among its military responsibilities are to keep a census on military reservists, to serve as agents for national service selection, and to act as one of the main channels for D.O.T. mobilization.[14] It is probable, however, that in the event of war most para-military organizations, with the exception of frontier guards, will perform their usual peacetime function.

The question of what is and what is not a reserve force has to be asked; this invites in turn a parameter to be established before further analysis can be undertaken. The first assumption must be that reserves are not defined according to the role or function they perform. For this reason, when reference is made to reserve forces, it must be with regard to a specific category of military manpower, organization and equipment. Of these three variables, manpower is the most important. A reservist is an individual who is in civilian employment first and foremost, but who has, or assumed, an obligation whether voluntarily or compulsorily determined, to take up

* Territorial Army Volunteer Reserve.

arms in defense of the state when called upon to do so. The obligation does not presuppose any specific military role or task.

On the basis of this parameter the issues of whether reserves serve the purpose of support, supplementation or substitution of the regular forces can be incorporated without encountering contradictions. Paradoxes could arise, for example, when reserves undertake roles or tasks for which there is no regular armed force counterpart. Under these circumstances, it is difficult to decide whether the reserve is a reserve unit in support of the regular forces, because it is acting as a substitute for the regular forces, or whether the reserve unit by nature of the unique role that it performs within the total defense posture, is comparable with a regular unit.

In the light of the above parameter, three broad, fundamental issues must now be raised. The order in which these issues are examined is crucial, for, being interdependent, the danger is that one will serve as the premise for the remaining two. Cardinally, the first is the question of what reserves are for. The supposition here is that the role and purpose of reserves is specified within the defense policy objectives of the state. Defense policy, therefore, prescribes the ends to which reserve forces will make a supposedly meaningful contribution. Clearly, *a priori*, there is a broad area for interpretation as to what form that contribution should adopt, and it is around this question that most argument and loose terminology is centred. The second is the question of what reserve forces can do, *a posteriori*. Ideally there should be a high degree of compatibility between policy, corresponding with ends, and what reserves are capable of doing, being synonymous with means. This compatibility, either in theory or practice, is seldom evident at either the state or the international level. The third problem is where reserve forces come from. This is essentially a civil-military problem involving the legal and moral obligations of the citizen to offer himself for the defense of his society or state; but it also concerns the quantitative and qualitative problems of available manpower resources, and as such represents a constraint upon what reserves can do.

As with the interrelationship of means and ends, so the availability of manpower can be a determinant of, or at least a constraint upon, the ends that defense policy is intended to achieve. Moreover, whether the manpower is available or not may be a function of what the specified ends of defense policy are. Similarly, the means problem of what reserve forces can do in terms of their skill and expertise, organizational commitment and ability to integrate within a military as opposed to a civilian structure, is a function of the numbers and quality of manpower and equipment. The interrelationship is a close and sensitive one between the means and ends and locus of reserve forces; for this reason, whichever is considered to be the priority issue will determine and prejudice the other two.[15] Most authors who have discussed reserve forces have taken ends to be paramount. In so doing they have interpreted ends as requiring a specific form or reserve force capability, and to back this contention up have made extravagant claims for the skills and availability of civil manpower to meet their demands. Indeed, many elaborate and ingenious schemes for finding reserve manpower have been devised to justify individual interpretations of defense policy ends.[16] In Britain, one author accused the government of looking at the means problem of what reserve forces can do before examining the ends of defense policy, and concluded that it was for this reason that the British reserve forces were drastically cut in 1967.[17]

In recognition of the dangers inherent in producing an axiomatic argument when looking consecutively at the means, ends and locus of reserve forces, the method here is to examine each in a vacuum separately. The object is not to prescribe what reserve forces should do to achieve what ends and by what means. It is to explore what are the factors that have to be taken into consideration, based on the experience of Western powers since 1945. Only coincidentally will any form of comparative study emerge.

What, then, are the ends of reserve forces? What purpose do they serve? In practice, it appears that reserve forces usually serve one or a combination of four purposes. The rationale behind each of these purposes differs between states. The first, which relates to what are generally classified as first-line reserves, is to have reserves as an expedient method of maintaining a balance between the manpower needs of the regular standing armed forces on the one hand and budgetary constraints on the other. Here the distinction between wartime and peacetime military establishments is important. Those men who are called up specifically to bring regular forces up to wartime establishment might conveniently be distinguished from all the others by referring to them as 'reservists' as opposed to reserves or reserve forces.[18] The 'reservists' are customarily those men who have recently left the armed services but who carry with them in their return to civilian life an obligation to be available for recall; in Britian this applies to those who have served as regulars in the armed forces, and on the continent it generally applies also to recently retired conscripts. In a few instances, these reservists, such as doctors, are called to the colors because of their individual skills rather than for their military experience.

The rationale behind this purpose for reserves, in addition to balancing the requirement to keep as large a force as possible in preparation for a crisis, with the costs involved in doing so with a full complement of men, is the effect upon men and morale if the professional armed forces were to be held continually on a war footing. Many roles and functions, highly necessary in war, would not be necessary in time of peace; consequently there is no need to have men serving these functions becoming bored and impatient and wasting their time and the service's money. Doctors, again, are a case in point. This device, however, is not without drawbacks; over and above the obvious point that in the event of a sudden crisis the forces immediately involved would be understrength, their possible success would rest on the speed with which 'reservists' could be mobilized.[19] A less obvious, but real disadvantage, is that a peacetime regular unit has to use its manpower for perhaps two, three or more tasks in addition to their specialized military ones. For example, artillerymen may have to do paperwork, maintain trucks, and engage in public relations work as well as be good gunners. It is not uncommon that 'reservist' troops, who train, albeit intermittently, on one task only, prove to be more efficient than their immediate regular counterparts.

The second purpose for reserves is as a means of adding to the regular armed forces' capability. The intention here is to enable the state to bring greater military force to bear on the enemy at a particular point in time than that existing within the wartime establishment regular forces alone, or to enable the regular forces to wage war over a longer period of time by replacing losses in men and equipment as they occur. Neither of these purposes requires the short mobilization time as is necessary for the 'reservist's' function. The classification of reserve soldier for these functions is second-, and sometimes third-, line reserve forces, and it is here that the area of greatest uncertainty is centered. The uncertainty relates to a number of factors, of which the likelihood of medium to long-term conventional war is foremost, given the existence and possession by NATO and the Warsaw Pact, of nuclear, atomic, chemical and biological weapons. Other problems relate to the availability and training of manpower, to equipment and to costs.[20] A further purpose, related to the above two, is the need to give the regular forces flexibility. With substantial reserves, so the argument goes, the armed forces can delegate certain functions and be redeployed more effectively where they are needed more. In a state that has a defense policy covering a number of alternative ends, but which cannot be handled concurrently with regular forces, additional flexibility through increased reserves might be considered to be essential.[21]

The third purpose for reserve forces is that of home defense. The tasks that are generally subsumed under this category are to minimize the after-effects of a nuclear attack, to combat internal insurgency situations, and to provide organized resistance in the event of invasion or occupation. It is this over-all home defense function alone that is assigned to the forces in states that operate on the basis of a system of 'Nation in Arms'. Many European states, particularly the smaller ones, are giving greater attention to this third purpose of reserves, but it is France, with the Operational Defense of the Territory system, that is leading the way. With the exception of France, the reserve forces assigned to this purpose are usually the oldest in age, and the most poorly equipped. They generally work, however, in conjunction with civil defense units on a local basis. Exceptions to this rule would include nationally based functions, such as manning communications networks designed to operate in the event of a nuclear attack so that no area is cut off.

The final purpose of reserves is nebulous, but one to which the regular forces place considerable importance. This relates back to the civil-military basis of reserve forces. Reserves are a method of getting regular recruits, and a way of projecting an image to the public through contact and experience. Tradition may play an important part in this role also, especially where participation in reserves is on a regional or local basis. Reserves, indeed, can and have played an important social function. Finally, on a negative point, there is to be considered the institutional reluctance and apprehension in getting rid of something that has always been there, on the premise that because it is there it must be doing some good, even if it is hard to discover.[22]

When the question is asked what can reserves do, the answer is not dependent upon what they are required to do, but upon what constraints act upon them. These limit what can be entertained. In addition, the distinction between what they can do and what is expected of them must continually be borne in mind. The assumption behind this section is that military forces, both regular and reserve, have now come face to face with what has been categorized as the equipment 'sophistication barrier'.[23] The significance of this phenomenon for reserve forces can best be seen in relation to its implications for the professional regular forces. Where regular forces are involved, concern has been expressed in recent years in many advanced industrial societies not only about the cost of modern military equipment, but also the cost of training military personnel to use it, to keep them abreast of the state of the art and to meet the costs of depreciation, use and replacement. Training has become so costly and so complicated that doubt has been cast on the two-year contract in place of the minimum three-year one, as a way of attracting more recruits into the armed services, because of the limited time it would allow to train them adequately and to integrate them in the military establishment as a whole. The cost of training is so high that it pays to give generous bonuses to trained military personnel to remain in the armed forces rather than to recruit new replacements. The qualifications demanded not only of officers but also of other ranks have risen considerably, not only in military and technical skills but also in the techniques of management and decision-making. This applies to all the armed services but more especially to the more technical branches of the air force and navy.

The disparity between the regular serviceman and the reserve is, consequently, increasing despite individual instances where the reserve may prove able to keep up. But 'most serious is the fact that, on the continent, conscripts who form the basis not only of manpower but also trained military men for reserve roles are now face to face with the sophistication problem.'[24] In Germany especially it is feared that on the basis of present experience, future generations of equipment will be too complex for short-term conscripts to master.[25] It may well be that the two-tier armed forces is on the cards, at least in Europe. Such a structure would involve short service local defense militia, simply armed, and highly trained professional forces equipped with advanced weapons. It would eliminate all but possibly the first line category of reserve forces and establish home defense as a part of the total standing defense posture of the state.

Working from the assumption inherent in the concept of the 'sophistication barrier', a number of limitations on what reserve forces can do immediately become apparent. These are supported with empirical evidence from current Western reserve systems. The first relates to the skills that are expected of reserves within the context of the roles that they might be expected to perform. It cannot be expected that reserves can match the technical and military skills combined, or the readiness of the professionals; this disparity becomes even more apparent between the different branches of the armed services. Enthusiasm, a characteristic particularly of voluntary reserve services, is hardly a satisfactory substitute. There may be close parallels between civilian trades and those in the armed services but to suggest that a direct transfer of personnel from one context to the other is either possible or satisfactory within the time scales allowed for in mobilization for war, would be to make too many demands on the compliance of the individuals concerned.[26] Though the labels given to military and civilian skills may be the same, the exercise of them differs enormously; this is especially true where military management is concerned. Those optimists who believe that industrial or military training schemes can duplicate each other, grossly underestimate the organizational and sociological problems involved.

The skills required by the military in conventional war are closely related to the type, intensity and duration of training, and the aptitude of the trainee. Reserves, however, 'have a primary occupational commitment ... to their normal civilian careers'.[27] Either voluntarily, or by legal obligation, they devote some of their time to training sessions ranging from short-term active duty training exercises to in-service conferences and correspondence courses. The amount of time spent on training depends not only upon a stipulated minimum appearance but also upon counter-claims from family and employer alike.[28] In theory, the amount of time is short and, except in the cases of senior officers, rarely in excess of three weeks in any year. In practice, the situation is much worse. The rule is that training is not given, or is of a fairly rudimentary kind with exceptions found where voluntary reserve systems operate and where first-line essential 'reservists' are concerned. In France, for example, reserve officer training is restricted to three weeks in eight years, and correspondence courses have been abandoned;[29] in Germany, the estimate is that only 5 to 6 per cent of reserves receive training after their period of compulsory service is finished, and even then it is only within small units and at approximately three-year intervals.[30] Most of military reserve training in Germany is undertaken by the Werband, a private voluntary military organization.[31] In the Netherlands, where only officers are considered reserves, the probability is that the reserve soldier will never receive training, and certainly not after he is twenty-eight years old.[32] It should be noted also that under training must come the quality of training that European reserves receive whilst they are doing their compulsory national service. No European state has a conscript's tour of duty extending beyond two years, except in a few cases – particularly in the air force; assuming a period of time acclimatizing the conscripts to military routines and bearing in mind that the average age is around eighteen years, the period left for effective training, and to acquire combat 'experience', is limited indeed.

In training reserves, disparities also occur throughout Europe regarding methods as well as equipment. Some states train according to the skill of the particular reservists; reserve units are therefore based according to whether they are infantry, artillery, signals, etc.

Others train regionally, and reserves turn up at the nearest reserve unit no matter what their previous training might have been. On very rare occasions is there evidence that reserve units have trained in other than small isolated units. As mobilization demands in modern warfare would require large-scale unit movement and coordination, the degree of previous experience and readiness is open to question. The exceptions to the rule are those states with militia or total defense systems.

A third limitation on the effectiveness of reserves arises out of their organizational structure and their place within the integrated defense system. The limitations of the structure of reserve forces are apparent from the system of training. The fundamental problem, however, is that reserves are part-time men, who live all over the country. The location of reserve personnel bears no relation to the location of specialized military units nor to the system of reserve force mobilization according to age and function. Some reserve systems, as for example in France, accept the regional distribution of reserves, and within their D.O.T. system mobilize mainly on a regional basis.[33] Others – for example, Italy – shift their reserves around for training according to the skill of each soldier and the strategic or tactical location of his unit. The only exception is with the Italian Alpine reserve units.[34] Some operate a dual system, as in Britain. The organizational problem, however, is simplified when reserves are not trained for conventional external roles, but for home defense tasks. The Norwegian 'total defense' system,[35] the Danish Home Guard,[36] and now the French D.O.T. home defense systems, would lend weight to this argument.

The major organizational problem, however, is not within the reserve system itself; it is the problem of integrating reserves with regular units. Some reserve units may have the advantage of having regular officers in command who have been responsible for training, and some may have close ties and liaison with regular units. But this appears to be the exception, especially among second- and third-line reserve forces. The basic problem is a combination of the disparity in skill and training between the two, and the perceptions they have of each other. Further, much depends on the organizational flexibility of the professional force to absorb incoming reserve units. There is considerable weight to the argument that these organizational problems may be so complex and huge that the most effective function for the regular forces to perform in the event of mobilization beyond the wartime establishment level, i.e. with second-line reserve forces, would be to assume purely administrative, organizational and training roles, and leave the fighting to the reserves.

A repeated complaint among reserve units, especially those in the first line, is that their effectiveness is limited by inadequate provision of equipment with which they can train. Even in Britain, where the reserve forces have been contracted and where the first-line reserves, the T.A.V.R. 1 and 2 categories, are held at a relatively high degree of readiness, equipment is restricted to small quantities for basic training purposes only.[37] In Germany the inadequacy in the supply of modern equipment is even more marked.[38] The issue is basically one of available finance, not only for advanced equipment ready to be used in the event of crisis, but also to meet the costs of maintenance, depreciation, stockpiling and use. The financial problems jump drastically the more complex and sophisticated military equipment becomes. These financial problems are doubly difficult for 'capital intensive' branches of the armed forces. It is a reasonable enough observation to make that few, if any, states can afford to equip their reserve forces either with front-line equipment or in substantial numbers. And, even if they could, the manpower problem would still have to be overcome.

These limitations must be seen in relation to the operational context within which reserves might be expected to operate. Broadly speaking, the spectrum of war in which reserves might be likely to be involved is from conventional war in support of regular forces, either as replacement or as supplement, to home defense civil action. Throughout the spectrum, a limitation on the use of reserves is the time required to mobilize them, relative to the speed with which a crisis could occur. With European and NATO thinking revolving around rapid Soviet moves, as demonstrated over Czechoslovakia, aimed at taking out small areas of, say, Norway, West Germany, or Denmark, and thereby confronting the West with a *fait accompli*, reserve reaction time would appear to be crucial. The suggestion here is that were the Soviet Union to venture to invade Europe it would either be a rapid and decisive *fait accompli* snatch of a small area, in which the European reserve reaction time would be too long, or it would be a massive full-scale frontal attack, in which the European reserves would be totally inadequate. There does not seem any merit in entertaining building up reserves for the half-way house situation and incur little more than high opportunity costs in the process.

As a result of the constraints acting upon the capability of reserve forces, the temptation is to suggest that if European reserve forces are to be employed at all, their most realistic function would be in home defense. To suggest that they could meaningfully operate to increase a state's wartime establishment would merely expose the limitations inherent in the system. In this respect, Britain's use of reserve forces, or, more accurately, her 'reservists', beyond that for which they are already earmarked, is highly suspect. What may be suspect, alternatively, is the breadth over which the Defense Policy White Paper has been cast and the resources that have been allotted to these tasks. None of the continental powers plans to operate their reserve forces outside their borders in large numbers; many use them exclusively for home defense. It would seem a bizarre argument for Britain to increase her reserves to meet the demands of a conventional war in Europe when her European partners show little intention to do likewise. Essentially the difference between Britain and Europe is that the former uses trained reserves to bring regular forces up to establishment, i.e. 'reservists', whereas the latter tends to use conscripts for the same purpose. Neither method would suggest professionalism in depth, nor would it appear to envisage a war in Europe lasting a long time on a conventional footing. Britain tends to see resorting to nuclear weapons when the NATO forces can no longer control the situation,[39] whilst the European states, on the basis of their reserve policies and because it is their homeland which would receive tactical nuclear weapons, tend to envisage longer-term guerrilla-type action against occupation or invading forces.

The final question is where reserve forces come from. This is basically an ecological problem and one which should not be dismissed. It involves not only the availability of manpower and skills but also the prevailing public attitude to military service and the ends of defense policy. Traditional means of acquiring reserve manpower are by voluntary entry, compulsion, or by a variety of ways of selective service. The obligations imposed on a reserve soldier depend on his skills, rank, age and, sometimes, his residence. The pattern tends to be the same in all states that the youngest, and those with the most recent military experience, will first be called to the colors. Exemption from reserve obligation in those states where it is compulsory is based on medical grounds or the relative importance of the individual's civilian job to the war effort. Munitions workers, for example, are more valuable in that job than doing reserve training. The qualifications and exemptions are endless. Again, only in the militia-type, citizen armies, do these many complications seem less important.

Many Western states are currently facing recruitment problems in their regular forces, and many are substantially understrength. Voluntary recruits do not appear to be coming forward, and in some states military conscription – especially of a selective service, discriminatory kind – is coming under fire. The regular armed forces are currently unable to combat the demands made on the citizen in civil life to attract him to a military career. The situation is worse for the reserve forces, for many of the reasons for poor recruitment into the regular forces also apply to them. The obligation to train with the reserves appears to be becoming a sensitive problem for the National Guard in the United States,[40] for example, and opposition to having R.O.T.C. units on university campuses is commonplace.[41] Since the United States has opted for a voluntary system of armed forces recruitment, in the face of opposition to the draft, a regular source of National Guard recruits has been cut off.[42]

Whatever the solution to the manpower problem, the attendant problems of organization, training, costs and skills should not be overlooked. It could very well be that the method of meeting the manpower shortage only exacerbates the problem that caused the manpower shortage in the first place. On the assumption that a man will enter an organization voluntarily if that organization is seen by him to be relevant, both personally and to the society of which he is a part, the task for defense planners, whether civilian or military, is to seek to relate national security policy and the structure of the armed forces to the interests of the individual. Failure is likely to sustain feelings of alienation, both within and outside the armed forces.

It is, for example, a paradoxical state of affairs to put within one defense policy statement the objective of deterrence and an implied belief that such a policy will prevent war, alongside a policy of the early use of nuclear weapons in Europe in the event that conventional means should fail, and the elimination of any meaningful means for home defense.[43] To make national security considerations relevant to the individual requires a substantial change in attitude within the population and a careful reappraisal by governments and the military alike of the place of the armed forces, and the reserves, within the society. Within this appraisal, which must probe the core of civil–military relationships, there must be an examination of the fundamental issues of the recruitment, career patterns, structure, political influence, legal basis, function and status of the armed forces as a whole. It might well be that the 'sophistication' of the armed forces and the awesomeness of the power that is entrusted to them, with little accountability, together with the mass media coverage of the events of recent wars, has driven a wedge between the soldier and the civilian.

The problems that beset the role of reserves on a national scale are compounded on an international one. With the prospect of further troop withdrawals from Central Europe, and further manpower shortages among NATO assigned forces, Europe may well be faced with an acute military manpower crisis in the 1970s.[44] At the same time, NATO is committed to a strategy of flexibility in response which subsumes a reluctance to use nuclear weapons but a conviction that they will be used if the military situation leaves no military alternative. The theory behind the strategy is to have conventional forces capable of withholding a Soviet attack to allow the various mechanisms of hot-line diplomacy and crisis management to avert the first nuclear exchange. It is generally agreed that NATO does not possess that conventional capability, either in terms of regular, reservists or reserve equipment and manpower. SACEUR warnings and requests for reinforcements continue to be thwarted. The solution to the problem does not rest with reserve forces, irrespective of historical precedents,[45] nor in the belief that effective reserves can be built up quantitatively and qualitatively and mobilized in time. The separate reserve systems of Europe are ill-equipped, under-trained, badly organized and unintegrated for a conventional war in Europe. It is doubtful if they could be mobilized in time. The West may well have to look for security elsewhere; it might be in Mutual Balanced Force Reductions, or other associated arms control agreements. Alternatively, there may be a future for security along the lines of the French model, by retaining the basis of alliance either through the North Atlantic Alliance or through the Western European Union. Home defense manned by reserves, coupled with a highly professional military establishment for specialized tasks, offers itself as an attractive alternative. It may also provide a solution to the widening gulf that exists between those who honorably and responsibly defend society and those who are members of it.

NOTES TO CHAPTER 3

1. D. Rapport, 'A Comparative Theory of Military and Political Types' in S. Huntington, *Military Politics* (New York: Free Press, 1962) pp. 88–98. Also M. Foot, *Men in Uniform* (London: Chatto and Windus, 1962).

2. F. Hoffman, 'The Red Chinese Militia', *National Guardsman* (Washington: Aug 1965) pp. 2–6. Also E. Joffe, *Party and the Army* (Cambridge: Harvard University Press, 1965).

3. C. Barnett, 'Armed Forces in transition', *Royal United Services Institution Journal* (London: June 1970) p. 14.

4. See, for example, Senator Mansfield's repeated attempts to cut US troops in Europe between August 1966 and November 1971.

5. J. Newhouse et al., *US Troops in Europe* (Washington: Brookings Institution, 1971).

6. *Statement on the Defence Estimates*, 1969 (London: H.M.S.O. Cmnd 3927).

7. First announced in the *Defence White Paper*, 1967 (London: H.M.S.O. Cmnd 3357).

8. 'France and her Army' Service de Presse Information No B/30/10/6, Ambassade de France (London, 1966) pp. 14–16. Also Col R. Y. L. Gallais, 'The French Reserve', *National Guardsman* (Washington: July 1966) pp 11–14.

9. R. Frykland, 'West Germany builds a National Guard', *National Guardsman* (Washington: Sep 1964) p. 9. Also E. Waldman, 'German Reserves and Replacements, *Military Review* vol. 47 (April, 1967) p. 22; *German Security White Paper 1970*, German Government Information Office (1970) pp. 85, 115–37.

10. This is particularly the case when peacetime regular forces are severely understrength and troops have to dilute their expertise by undertaking a wide range of other tasks. See below, p. 42.

11. Lt-Gen. Sir J. Mogg, 'Army Strategic Command. Role and Capability', *Royal United Services Institution Journal* (June 1969) p. 16.

12. W. Lanouette, 'The Norwegian Reserve Forces', *National Guardsman* (Washington: Feb 1967) pp. 11–12.

13. *International Defense Review* vol. IV, 1969, pp. 335–6, cit. *The Military Balance*, 1969 (London: ISS. 1969).

14. Col L. H. Landon, 'Military Service, Reserve Forces and their Training in the French Army', *Army Quarterly* (Oct 1967) p. 99.

15. The means-ends calculus is entertainingly outlined in the Chinese T'i-Yung problem. L. W. Pye, 'Description, Sensitivity and Analysis' in A. Ranney (ed.) *Political Science and Public Policy* (Markham, Chicago: 1969) p. 225.

16. C. Barnett, op. cit. p. 18.

17. C. Douglas-Home, *Britain's Reserve Forces*, Royal United Services Institution (London: 1969) p. 55.

18. I am grateful to Brig. W. Thompson for suggesting this terminological distinction to me.

19. No information is available for mobilization times of 'Reservists'. The 48 hour TAVR 1 standby may be taken as a rough guide. See 'The Territorial and Army Volunteer Reserve' *Army Quarterly* (Apr 1967) p. 34.

20. See below, pp. 44–50.

21. Lt-Gen. Sir W. Pike, 'Some defence aspects of the reorganisation of the reserve Army', *Army Quarterly* (Apr 1967) p. 37. Also C. Douglas-Home, op. cit. pp. 5–6; *The Times*, 21 Jan 1968.

22. Institutional inertia. For a discussion see P. Blau, *Dynamics of Bureaucracy* (Chiagco; Chicago University Press, 1955) pp. 202–14.

23. D. Watt, 'Balanced Force Reductions', *Royal United Services Institution Journal* (June 1970) p. 43.

24. Ibid. p. 43.

25. Ibid.

26. 'Compliance' is used here in Amitai Etzioni's terms. *Comparative Analysis of Complex Organisations* (New York Free Press. 1961) pp. 3–21.

27. C. Coates and R. Pelegrin, *Military Sociology*, Social Science Press (Maryland, 1965) p. 230.

28. *The National Guard 1636–1970. A fact sheet*, National Guard Association. (Washington, 1970) pp. 6–7.

29. Lt-Col H. Landon, op. cit. p. 100.

30. E. Waldman, op. cit. p. 25.

31. Ibid. p. 26.

32. W. Lanouette, 'The Netherlands Reserve Forces', *National Guardsman* (Washington: Nov 1969) pp. 28–9.

33. Gen. A. Beaufre, 'French Defence Policy', *Royal United Services Institution Journal* (Oct 1969) p. 6.

34. 'The Italian Reserve System', *National Guardsman* (Washington: 1965).

35. W. Lanouette, 'The Norwegian Reserve System', op. cit. p. 38.

36. Lt-Col. I. Vase, 'The Danish Home Guard', *National Guardsman.* (Washington: Feb 1968) pp. 11–12.
37. Lt-Gen. Sir W. Pike, op. cit. p. 36.
38. R. Frykland, op. cit. p. 10.
39. *Statement on the Defence Estimates*, 1969 (London: H.M.S.O. Cmnd 3927).
40. 'The National Guard 1636–1970', op. cit. pp. 6–8.
41. L. Radway, The future of ROTC in this volume. See also Lt-Cdr J. W. Corey, 'A wetter better NROTC', *United States Naval Institution Proceedings* (June 1970) p. 68.
42. S. Tax (ed.), *The Draft* (Chicago University Press: 1967) esp. W. Oi. 'Costs and Implications of an All-volunteer Force' p. 224.
43. e.g. The British and German Defence White Papers, 1970.
44. D. Watt, op. cit. p. 43.
45. C. Barnett, op. cit. pp. 14–15.

4 The Future of the Reserve Officer Training Corps

LAURENCE I. RADWAY*

The Educational Issues

R.O.T.C. has been part of the educational landscape for more than fifty years.¹ Units exist at over three hundred and fifty American colleges and universities. Yet some members of the academic community have long been critical of the program, for reasons largely unrelated to current controversy over the Vietnam War. Campus skeptics are inclined to describe R.O.T.C. courses as 'guts' or to dismiss them as 'Mickey Mouse', devoid of theoretical interest, laden with trivia, and unworthy of academic credit. If pressed, liberal arts purists will concede that instruction in navigation or military courtesy is no more inappropriate than instruction in welding or photo-journalism, and that viewed solely as an intellectual operation, stripping a Browning automatic rifle is not fundamentally unlike dissecting a cadaver. But to the critics such parallels do not redeem R.O.T.C. For they contend that vocational training has no place in a liberal education and that professional education is best deferred to the post-baccalaureate period.

Campus critics are also restless about the quality of R.O.T.C. instructors and the nature of their teaching methods. Material is said to be drilled into the hapless student in a fashion derived from age-old efforts to provide routine skills to masses of poorly educated enlisted personnel. The instructors themselves are felt to possess

* An earlier version of this article was prepared under the auspices of the Inter-University Seminar on Armed Forces and Society.

less intellectual distinction than their civilian counterparts. Less often, but perhaps more tellingly, they are compared unfavorably with more promising *military* officers. Why, it is asked, are so many incoming heads of R.O.T.C. units starting their last tour of duty before retirement?

More recently, concern has been expressed that R.O.T.C. may jeopardize the autonomy of its host institutions. Under federal law, it is noted, no unit may be retained at a university unless the latter adopts, as part of its curriculum, a course of instruction 'which the secretary of the military department concerned prescribes and conducts'.[2] In most cases the services determine the subjects, syllabi, and teaching materials used in R.O.T.C. courses. The navy reserves the right to deny its R.O.T.C. students permission to major in certain fields not deemed useful to a naval officer. Host institutions are also required by statute to award the rank of professor to the senior officer of each R.O.T.C. unit. He thereby acquires faculty status although he is not paid, evaluated, reappointed, or promoted like other faculty members, and in practice he is not recruited like them either. The conclusion has been drawn that R.O.T.C. units resemble 'foreign embassies within otherwise sovereign territory'.[3] This analogy acquires more bite when it is observed that the staffs of these particular 'embassies' operate not only on the technical skills of the 'natives' but on their belief systems, and that they aim to develop attitudes, e.g. with respect to nationalism, discipline, and obedience, which leading figures within the host 'country' do not necessarily share.

It would be nice to report that campus complaints were ordinarily accompanied by constructive suggestions for improvement. Such, unhappily, has not been the case. Nevertheless, in the past few years R.O.T.C. has been modified in ways which seem to take into account some points made by critics. One or another service has introduced two-year programs, accepted cuts in academic credit, invited civilians to teach designated courses, reduced drill requirements, or settled for less than full faculty status for junior instructors. If they have not responded immediately to every considered criticism,[4] the armed forces have given more ground than is commonly supposed; and with ingenuity, imagination, and good will on all sides, it is conceivable that they could meet many of the objections to R.O.T.C. raised on educational grounds.

The Political Context

The intensity of recent anti-R.O.T.C. sentiment, however, leaves little doubt that it is inspired by campus opposition to the war in Vietnam. A few institutions have taken steps to terminate the program. Others seek to eliminate all credit for R.O.T.C. courses, deny academic status to all military instructors, or convert required programs into voluntary ones.[5] Beginning on a few prestigious campuses in 1969, the protest movement subsequently spread from Puerto Rico in the east to Hawaii in the west. More than thirty R.O.T.C. headquarters buildings were firebombed in the spring of 1970. Ohio state, long a prolific source of reserve officers, was the scene of repeated R.O.T.C. riots. As army Chief of Staff Westmoreland admitted. 'Today it takes a man of determination and maturity to wear a uniform on many of our campuses.'[6]

Unrest at the universities hurt enrollment not merely by discouraging potential individual applicants but more importantly by inducing some schools with compulsory R.O.T.C. programs to convert them into voluntary ones.[7] By 1971–2 only twenty-five institutions maintained a compulsory program, and twelve of these were at military colleges. Enrollment also suffered from a decline in draft quotas, for this relieved the pressure which had driven many undergraduates into campus units.[8] Between 1966–7 and 1969–70, the total number of students in R.O.T.C. fell from 260,000 to 156,000.[9] By 1971–2 the total was only 88,000. Paradoxically, this coincided with an *increase* in officer production. One reason was that the decline in freshmen enrollment was not immediately reflected in a decrease in the number of graduating seniors; another was that the drop-out rate fell significantly. The latter phenomenon could be explained by the shift to voluntary programs, the introduction of a new option limited to the last two years of college, an increase in the number of students awarded tuition scholarships,[10] and a widespread fear that resignation from R.O.T.C. might be followed by a draft notice and enlisted service in Vietnam.

The decline in the drop-out rate did not, however, allay the Pentagon's concern. Individual services took special steps to strengthen their programs. The army, for example, raised subsistence allowances for advanced students, liberalized course offerings, and mounted an energetic public relations campaign.[11] Its chief of staff stated bluntly that the army needed and wanted R.O.T.C.[12] Such measures were supplemented at the Defense Department level in June 1969 by the appointment of an *ad hoc* committee (hereinafter called the Benson Committee) to review the entire range of relationships between R.O.T.C. and host institutions.[13]

It is easier to state that the creation of the Benson Committee was part of a larger defensive strategy than to be certain of what was being defended against whom; for if the Pentagon was confronted on one side by an increasingly militant academic world, it was confronted on the other by some highly conservative members of Congress. The House Armed Services Committee, led by J. Mendell Rivers (D., South Carolina) had begun its own study of R.O.T.C. immediately after the campus outbreaks in the spring of 1969. Its report, apparently completed by 7 August 1969,[14] concluded that if R.O.T.C. were attacked at any university, the government should not only cancel the program at once but also withdraw all defense contracts from the institution. A week later the army announced that it would terminate R.O.T.C. at Harvard and Dartmouth, whose faculties had voted to phase out the programs as currently enrolled students completed them.[15] Army officials were later to observe pointedly that several dozen other schools were eager to move in if the Ivy League moved out.[16]

It was exceedingly unlikely that the newly elected Nixon Administration would wish to fly in the face of these signals. Its defense secretary, Melvin R. Laird, had won his spurs as an influential member of the House of Representatives, one, moreover, usually sympathetic to the defense establishment. At the same time, members of the Benson Committee could not ignore the specific educational issues which had long been debated at host institutions. The result was a report which one anonymous member of the Committee described as 'quite a bland document'.[17] And while he ventured the opinion that conservative Congressmen were likely to think it conceded too much ground to campus critics, the official statement accompanying release of the report stressed the Committee's disagreement with campus militants over such matters as course credit, faculty status, the wearing of uniforms, and drill. At the same time Dr Benson advised newsmen that R.O.T.C.'s true strength was in the state universities, and that some Ivy League schools had been advised to leave it.[18]

The Benson Report

Against this political background it is now appropriate to analyze the Benson Report in more detail.

With respect to curriculum, the Committee concluded that at 'the great majority' of institutions R.O.T.C. courses were comparable in quality to the rest of undergraduate education. True, some of the strictly military textual material was 'insufficiently challenging'. But materials designed for 1969–70 'show more promise' and the services were exhorted to prepare better materials in the future. Host institutions were taken to task for failing to exercise initiative. They were urged to propose curricular improvements and to offer to teach some courses themselves. But while the report recommended 'the use of civilian faculty where possible', it also noted that 'the armed services desire continuing contact for a four-year period' between R.O.T.C. student and military instructors.

On the touchy issue of academic credit, the report concluded not very resoundingly that R.O.T.C. instruction 'merits serious consideration for undergraduate credit'. The Committee conceded that credit should not be given for drill, and that each institution must evaluate for itself the credit to be assigned each course. But failure to award credit, it observed, would discourage students from entering the program.

In endorsing the report, the Defense Department's Advisory Panel on R.O.T.C. Affairs added a few words of its own on curricular content.[19] It proposed that the purpose of R.O.T.C. be restated to emphasize that the object was 'education' rather than 'training'; the very title (Reserve Officers Training Program) was said to be unfortunate. In particular, the Panel suggested that the navy should review its goal of producing an 'immediately employable ensign' with a view to deferring until after graduation some of the practical instruction in its present curriculum.

On the issue of institutional autonomy, the Benson Committee proposed that universities safeguard their prerogatives by rejecting or discharging unqualified R.O.T.C. instructors. Moreover, it observed that schools which were reluctant to give the title of professor to the senior officer of a military detachment could call them visiting professor, adjunct professor, affiliate professor, or visiting lecturer with the rank of professor. Finally, the Committee acknowledged candidly that the statutory authority of military departments over R.O.T.C. curricula was inconsistent with traditional prerogatives of the university. It recommended that the legislation be revised 'to indicate a cooperative effort between the service and the university'. But it did not indicate which of the two should have the last word if cooperation failed.

The message of the Benson Committee to the academic world was essentially this: 'You have the power if you are willing to use it. Create an effective campus committee and go to work.' Host institutions were reminded that they were free to make R.O.T.C. less conspicuous by organizing it as a 'program' or a 'center' instead of a department, by increasing the proportion of civilian instructors, and by transferring more drill to summer, although 'there is an irreducible minimum of drill which it would be wise not to do away with'.

The question remains whether these conclusions were realistic. On how many campuses, and to what extent, will civilians in fact challenge military judgments concerning R.O.T.C. course content? How far is it possible to treat military instructors like their civilian counterparts? Is it enough to observe that universities possess the authority to reject unsuitable instructors and that the University of Michigan, to cite one case, has actually refused to accept 25–30 per cent of all service nominees?[20] Will civilian institutions search aggressively for talented officer instructors by placing confidential calls to former superiors, raiding the staffs of other military installations, or dangling the prospect of research funds and other professional opportunities before prime prospects? Or is it more likely, as charged in a *New York Times* editorial sharply critical of the Benson Report, that host institutions will not be able to exercise 'ultimate jurisdiction' over either program or personnel.[21]

There is some evidence that the Committee was uncertain about its own message. The report stressed that its recommendations were for the present only. If the armed forces became smaller, or if an all-volunteer army were adopted, said the report, R.O.T.C.'s 'very existence' might be called into doubt. And in any event, as study of future manpower systems progresses, 'the R.O.T.C. question must be considered further in a very fundamental manner'. These remarks placed the Committee safely if not firmly on both sides of the question.

The Larger Issue of Civil-Military Relations

Thoughtful analysis of the desirability of R.O.T.C. must at some point come to grips with the issue of civil-military relations. Two themes run through the Benson Report on this question. One defends the utility of a 'blend' of civilian and military values. The report finds it good that R.O.T.C. students are exposed to both 'highly motivated' officers and 'critical thinking' civilian teachers; the interaction of the two is 'an important educational experience' for students and a broadening experience for R.O.T.C. instructors. The other theme defends the idea of civilian 'influence' *per se*. Other systems of officer procurement 'yield more to domination by the military organization acting on its own'. Moreover, if R.O.T.C. were removed from campuses, 'there would be grave danger of isolating the services from the intellectual centres of the public which they serve and defend'.

Several observations must be made about these important contentions. First, it is true that civilian university programs produce a large part of the officer corps. In the fiscal year 1964–5, just before the Vietnam build-up, R.O.T.C. produced 26 per cent of all new officers while other college-based programs produced an additional 15 per cent.[22] In the next five years R.O.T.C. produced 65 per cent of all new army officers. In 1970, more than 25 per cent of army generals on active duty were R.O.T.C. graduates. It is also true, however, that the retention rate for R.O.T.C. graduates, even for those who have held full tuition scholarships, is far below that of service academy graduates.[23] In part for this reason the latter still predominate at the higher levels of all services, especially in the navy. Second, removal of R.O.T.C. from campuses will not of itself 'isolate' the services from educational centers. The service academies regularly recruit young instructors who have studied at civilian universities. During their careers most regular officers will be assigned to civilian universities for graduate work. Third, while campus interaction may have been an important educational experience for some R.O.T.C. students, it has been a disillusioning one for others, namely those who have found R.O.T.C. courses and instructors less satisfactory than civilian ones. Invidious comparisons are probably more common when military and civilian programs coexist on campus than when they are conducted in separate locales. Fourth, the need for this particular method of checking and balancing the power of an officer corps is probably less acute in a country like the United States, where officers are divided among four highly competitive services, and where they lack the power and prestige which many of their foreign counterparts derive from membership of a privileged social class. European cadet schools often became citadels of an established elite; America has long delegated to a representative legislature control over most appointments to its service academies.

Off-Campus Options

Nevertheless, most Americans would probably agree that it is wise to recruit from a variety of sources and, in particular, to avoid undue reliance on the service academies. It is another question, however, whether R.O.T.C., with its educational and political complications, is the only or the best way to do so. To raise this issue is to invite attention to off-campus alternatives.

The Benson Committee itself explored some of these. For example, it examined the prospect of relying more heavily on O.C.S. But the services, it found, thought 'their long-range chances of securing quality officers are better with R.O.T.C'. What was probably meant, but unsaid here, is that O.C.S., at least for the army, does not attract enough college graduates, and that the retention rate of such graduates is lower than the rate for their R.O.T.C. counterparts.[24]

The Committee also examined recruitment systems confined largely to the summer, notably the Marine Corps Platoon Leaders plan for undergraduates. But after observing that the marine corps was having trouble filling its quota of students, the Committee concluded that its approach would be impracticable for other services. In contrast to this judgment is the subsequent conclusion of the President's Commission on an All-Volunteer Armed Force that 'serious consideration' should be given to increased use of Platoon Leader Corps-type programs.[25] At any rate, one wishes to know why the marine corps plan is insufficiently productive. Are students discouraged by the requirement of two months of summer training when other programs require only one? Suppose all services required two months? Does the marine corps, with its special mission and traditions, appeal to fewer students? Have marine corps officers suffered from lack of 'extended contact' with military instructors during the school year? How?

A variation of the marine corps' approach, analyzed by the Committee under the heading of 'new methods', would keep the academic year unencumbered by drill and by all R.O.T.C. courses except those taught by the civilian faculty. A senior officer would remain on campus merely to recruit students, keep an eye on them, advise about course selections, and possibly organize an evening program of extra-curricular lectures. The disadvantages, according to the Committee, are that this does not 'blend' civilian and military studies during the year; that students might not wish to devote a long summer to military training; that they might require more post-commissioning instruction; and that the on-campus contact might be insufficient to develop an interest in a military career.

A second variation envisages instruction in routine military skills at off-campus centers or 'extra-curricular units', while host institutions assume responsibility for 'an educational concentration embracing their own concept of the ideal officer'. The Committee concluded that an immediate shift to such a plan would paralyze the existing system because 'in the present anti-Vietnam War mood few institutions would submit programs, and many students would not stay with the programs'. Nevertheless, it concluded, not very decisively, 'This proposal apparently has some merit and could at some time be put to partial use.'

With the model of a French training program in mind, the report also considered whether undergraduates might supplement daily civilian courses with training at military installations during weekends. The hitch here, it concluded, is that American colleges are widely scattered, often 'miles away' from a significant military installation, so that such a plan would be feasible only in a few metropolitan areas.

One emerges from all this with an impression that the Committee did not think the time ripe for major changes. Its report did not deal with one rather obvious possibility, namely that students might devote one or two semesters to *full-time* training at a military installation. This would be congruent not only with existing programs for National Guard and reserve enlistees but with the growing tendency of educators to encourage restless students to take leave of absence at least once during their undergraduate years. Nor did the Committee do full justice to the prospect of evening or weekend training away from campus. It is possible, for example, to envisage a network of Regional Officer Training Centers (to preserve the traditional R.O.T.C. initials) located at public facilities, including but not limited to military installations. Local armories or public schools are potential sites. Certainly, in the automotive age the geographical problem should not be so difficult as the Committee implied.

Introduction of an off-campus plan would dissolve the somewhat unstable compound of training and education which characterizes existing R.O.T.C. curricula. It would do so not, however, as the Benson Committee proposes, i.e. by making R.O.T.C. courses more 'civilian', but by making them more 'military' and removing them from the university. It would also permit the services to substitue a contract with the individual for a contract with the institution. The university, presumably, would continue to call attention to this way of meeting one's military obligations. But its involvement would be so minimal that local critics would lose the leverage they now possess by virtue of the fact that R.O.T.C. is officially sponsored by the institution.

An evening or weekend off-campus plan, moreover, could make the civilian input into the officer corps more representative than it is under R.O.T.C. as now constituted. First, it could include younger college *graduates* interested in switching careers. Second, it could include educationally deprived young men who are not now attracted to R.O.T.C. in sufficient numbers[26] – members of minority groups, drop-outs, and recently discharged veterans with officer potential. Third, the undergraduate component would not have to consist so largely of men from the subset of colleges and universities which happen to have R.O.T.C. units and which choose to keep them in the face of anti-R.O.T.C. sentiment. The point here is of the utmost importance. R.O.T.C. may be expected to survive best at southern and western institutions where there is less dissatisfaction with the educational or political implications of the program. It is likely to be slashed first and most deeply at institutions which produce a disproportionate share of political executives, higher civil servants, legislators, editors, scientists, foundation officials, lawyers, bankers and educators concerned with foreign and military policy. The danger, clearly, is that a shrinking R.O.T.C. program may widen the gulf between our future military and civilian leaders.

Instead of narrowing the pool of potential participants, there seems to be reason to widen it. By the same token, instead of perpetuating autonomous training programs, there seems to be reason to coordinate them and to provide more administrative continuity. The latter goals, too, could be advanced by off-campus centers. By sharing facilities, equipment and personnel, pre-commissioning training operations could be integrated with the training of officers or enlisted men of National Guard and reserve components. In addition, it may be possible to create inter-service facilities. Less likely, but not inconceivable if only the cake of law and custom can be broken, are national defense officer training centers at which candidates for the army, navy, marine corps, and air force could undergo common courses of instruction before proceeding to study matters peculiar to the individual services.

Finally, there is the issue of cost, which is related to the possibility of economies of scale. It will be more expensive to maintain many small and relatively unproductive campus-based units than a few large off-campus centers. No one can foretell with certainty whether or to what extent present R.O.T.C. units will shrink. One factor will surely be the probable temper of the American academic community after Vietnam. Again, it is difficult to speak with assurance, but it is sobering to recall that anti-militarism has been as much the rule as the exception among intellectuals and college students,[27] and that this is the second, not the first, time that R.O.T.C. has been attacked. Between 1921 and 1936 it was the compulsory character of the program which drew most criticism and prompted the creation of organizations like the Committee on Militarism in Education.[28] Moreover, this earlier protest rested on a very broad base; it began not in the Ivy League but in such great state universities as Wisconsin and Minnesota. A pool of students taken in 1932 disclosed that nearly 40 per cent opposed all R.O.T.C., and 81 per cent opposed compulsory R.O.T.C.[29]

There is clearly economic as well as military risk in continuing to rely on a campus-based enterprise to produce so large a fraction of the total officer corps. The army has also conceded that declining draft pressures will become a greater factor in the future.[30] Finally if the draft is superseded by an all-volunteer armed force, the economic pressures for some pooling arrangements are likely to grow.[31]

The concept of off-campus centers is not, of course, free from difficulties, and one may be certain that these will be emphasized by practical men, who tend to prefer the present with all its inconveniences to the perils of a still unknown future. Some service officials fear that such centers would be expensive and unproductive, particularly if students found the commuting burdensome. Others assume that what is intended is wholesale and immediate abolition of all existing R.O.T.C. units, even flourishing ones. But a more sensible first step surely would be to create one or two pilot centers to serve as additional avenues or supplementary tracks to a commission. Even so modest an experiment may not be politically feasible while some members of Congress and some military officers are 'uptight' about student behavior. But sooner or later the logic of declining enrollments seems likely to force a major change.

NOTES TO CHAPTER 4

1. The Land Grant Act of 1862 required state universities to offer military instruction, but did not provide support, standards, and supervision of the kind the federal government now makes available to R.O.T.C. units. Army R.O.T.C. in its present form dates from the National Defense Act of 1916. Navy R.O.T.C. was introduced in 1926.
2. The R.O.T.C. Vitalization Act of 1964.
3. Gene M. Lyons and John W. Masland, *Education and Military Leadership* (Princeton: Princeton University Press, 1959) p. 175.
4. In 1953–4, for example, the army rejected a Harvard faculty committee recommendation that R.O.T.C. be cut to three years, that it include more academic-type courses taught by civilian faculty members, and that most of the technical training be confined to an expanded summer program. *Ibid.* pp. 220–1.
5. The extent to which state university students are required to take R.O.T.C. is a matter of state law and service custom. The navy has a compulsory program only at the Citadel. As recently as 1963–4, however, about one-half of all army and air force enrollees participated in required programs. By 1971–2 this had dropped to one-seventh.
6. Address by General W. C. Westmoreland to the 54th Annual Meeting of the Association of Military Colleges and Schools, Washington, D.C., 9 Mar. 1970.
7. Fifty-two army units became optional between 1966 and 1969, thirty-eight of them in 1968–9. Fifteen air force units became optional in the same period, ten of them in 1968–9.
8. Continental Army Command, *R.O.T.C. Newsletter*, IV 1, Fort Monroe, Virginia (Jan–Mar 1970).
9. Association of American Universities, *Survey Report: Status of R.O.T.C. Programs at AAU Member Institutions*, Feb 1970 (Washington, D.C.), Table 6-A.
10. The R.O.T.C. Vitalization Act of 1964 extended to army and air force students tuition scholarships previously available only to naval R.O.T.C. students.
11. A favorable article appeared in the *Reader's Digest*. Testimonials from the American Legion and other patriotic and miltary organizations were publicized. The army distributed a brochure complete with slides, press releases, and suggestions about how parent's day, homecoming, open house, band concerts, unit blood donations, photography contests, and communion breakfasts could be made occasions to boost R.O.T.C.
12. *New York Times* (8 July 1969).
13. The Chairman of the committee was Dr George Benson, political scientist and former president of Claremont Men's College. Other members were: E. Howard Brooks, Vice Provost, Stanford University; Claude E. Hawley, Dean of John Jay College of Criminal Justice, City University of New York; Brigadier General Clifford P. Hannum, Deputy Director of Individual Training for R.O.T.C. Affairs, Department of the Army; Rear Admiral Sheldon H. Kinney, Assistant Chief for Education and Training, Bureau of Naval Personnel; Herbert E. Longnecker, President, Tulane University; Donald R. Mallett, Vice President, Purdue University; Major General Lester Miller, Director of Personnel Training and Education, Department of the Air Force; and Dayton S. Pickett, Assistant Vice Chancellor for Academic Affairs, University of Illinois.

14. But not released until 4 Oct 1969. See *New York Times* (5 Oct 1969).
15. *New York Times* (12 Oct 1969).
16. Address by General W. C. Westmoreland to the 54th Annual Meeting of the Association of Military Colleges and Schools, Washington, D.C. (9 Mar 1970).
17. Report of the Special Committee on R.O.T.C. to the Secretary of Defense, Washington, D.C. (22 Sep 1969).
18. *New York Times* (21 Sep and 4 Oct 1969).
19. Members of the Advisory Panel were Herbert E. Longnecker, President, Tulane University; William C. Friday, President, University of North Carolina; Reuben A. Holden, Secretary, Yale University; Benjamin E. Lippincott, Professor of Political Science, University of Minnesota; John D. Millett, Chancellor, Ohio Board of Regents; Clarence R. Mall, President, PMC Colleges; Charles E. Odegaard, President, University of Washington; and Paul C. Reinert, President, St Louis University.
20. Association of American Universities, *Survey Report*, p. 13.
21. *New York Times* (5 Oct 1969).
22. *Report of the President's Commission on an All-Volunteer Armed Force* (Washington, D.C.: (1970) p. 72. The total of 41 per cent of all college-based programs conceals important service differences: army (63 per cent), air force (35 per cent), navy (17 per cent).
23. 'Between 80 and 90 per cent of service academy graduates can be expected to remain in the service upon completion of their obligated tour of active duty (now five years), as opposed to less than 50 per cent for R.O.T.C. scholarship graduates and under 25 per cent for O.C.S. graduates.' *Ibid.*, p. 77.
24. *Ibid.*
25. *Ibid.*, p. 75.
26. *Report of the Special Committee on R.O.T.C. to the Secretary of Defense*, p. 58.
27. Charles C. Moskos, Jr, *The American Enlisted Man* (New York: Russell Sage Foundation, 1970), p. 179.
28. Wisconsin abolished compulsory R.O.T.C. in 1923. Approximately two dozen other institutions either made it optional or dropped it entirely betwen 1921 and 1935. See Arthur A. Ekirch, Jr. *The Civilian and the Military* (New York: Oxford University Press, 1956), pp. 217–37. See also Lyons and Masland, *Education and Military Leadership*, pp. 47–52.
29. Ekirch, *The Civilian and the Military*.
30. Continental Army Command, R.O.T.C. Newsletter IV 1 (Jan–Mar 1970).
31. See *Report of the President's Commission on an All-Volunteer Armed Force*, pp. 75–6.

5 Youthful Officer Retirement: Matrix for Political Action[1]

ALDEN WILLIAMS

Considering the undemocratic histories of large active and retired military establishments, it is remarkable that the United States celebrates its bicentenary with little worry about its retired military force of a million careerists, more than one-third of them former career officers. United States retired officers alone outnumber all but five of the world's total active militaries. Most of these former officers are in their forties, served the military mission for at least twenty years, and confront 'retirement' with practical family obligations and at least twenty more years to fill before their civilian contemporaries retire. Four out of five of these modern retirees will be too young, too encumbered financially, and too restive mentally to do anything but seek second careers and be active civilians. Will they re-enter civilian society and politics as obediently as they departed it in the late 1940s and 1950s? Or will these 'old soldiers', neither about to die or fade away, give United States politics a reactionary turn?

As a stereotype group in American society, retired military officers have been blamed for many of the frustrations of America's crisis in military goals. They are tied to the industrial-military complex, vilified as a group for the puerile mischief of a few, and novelized as villains awaiting a signal to put one of their number in charge of rediscovering the Real Enemies of America. Most interesting is the way these stereotypes persist in spite of the absolute lack of evidence – in the form of organized political action by retired military personnel – to support it. As an organized group, retired officers have not acted out *Seven Days in May*, the Fletcher Knebel and Charles Bailey novel of a right-wing civilian-military conspiracy to seize United States executive power. No such post Second World War case exists in the public record, and it is doubtful that closed files would reveal any, or that the evidence could remain secret very long. To be sure, numbers of retirees have been guilty of questionable conduct as employees of defense-related industries. Individual retirees here and there have been indiscreet and probably, at times, criminally subversive. However, there is no convincing evidence that either retired military officers in defense industries, or isolated malcontents and the psychologically disturbed, can wield anything like the influence attributed to them. What, then, is the political problem of large-scale military officer retirement in the coming decades?

The problem has two sides. On the one hand, it is the drafting of practical, equitable, and humane retiree legislation that serves both national security and the individual. On the other hand, it is the development of maturer public understanding of the many similarities and fewer differences between military retirees and their civilian cohorts. This chapter summarizes findings on both sides of the problem, because the official policy environment and the demonstrated behavior of present retirees together are the real matrix of retired officers' political action and the proper starting point for public understanding.

Part of the polity's problem is that retired soldiers are reminders. Americans tend to be pragmatic, liberal, and idealistic. Hence, they are uncomfortable with reminders of old dreams that have not been fully realized and old programs that have not been completed. Americans' preoccupation with economics, technology and, more recently, broad social justice, has been punctuated by the demands of national and international security, created by wars, alliances, and massive military assistance ventures. Military retirees may be the most tangible link between the yesterday, today, and tomorrow of national security policy. Retired soldiers' numbers and annual

Youthful Officer Retirement: Matrix for Political Action 71

costs are living reminders of what security was once thought to be worth. But retirees set off highly selective memories. A people can simultaneously be proud of shrewd and successful expenditures – like those necessary to win the Second World War or contain Korean aggression – and alarmed about the delayed costs of those ventures, such as the costs of retirement pay for old soldiers who fought the wars but could not be scrapped like surplus airplanes on a Pacific island. However, the notion that retired career military officers represent some sort of reactionary residue in civil democracy might have remained an innocuous part of American political mythology had two parts of the problem not become too big to ignore: the size of the retiree community and, correspondingly, the costs of retirement pay.

Dilemmas of Rational Policy

These two elements – the number of retirees and their costs – are both large and relatively inflexible. The more than 750,000 retired officers and enlisted men on the rolls at the beginning of the 1970s will more than double by 1990 at an annual average rate of 37,500 net additions, equal to more than two infantry divisions a year. These totals do not depend on new Vietnams or Berlin crises. They are based on military careerists now in uniform who will definitely retire with pay. Three out of four officers will retire as middle- to upper-level managers in the army, air force, and marine ranks of colonel, lieutenant-colonel, and major, or their navy counterpart ranks of captain, commander, and lieutenant-commander.

Retirement pay of some $4.4 billion in fiscal 1973 is an enormous expense, even within the staggering dimensions of Cold War and Indochina defense budgets, and multibillion-dollar weapon systems. Shortly before the Second World War, 39,000 United States military retirees drew $55 million a year, some 6 per cent of the typical peacetime military budget in the 1930s. Total mobilization during the Second World War shrank retirement's share of the wartime budget to $49 million a year in 1943. By 1947, the first full fiscal year of peace, retired pay jumped to $140 million a year. It reached $500 million a year by 1957 and doubled that figure by 1963. With the events of the 1960s, it became clear that the anticipated 'hump' of personnel retiring about twenty to twenty-five years after the Second World War was not a hump but rather a steady increase sustained by Cold War force levels. Estimating future costs is an actuarial nightmare, always complicated by pending legislation to 'rationalize' military retirement, but projections of $10 billion to $15 billion a year for pay alone by 1990 are not outrageous. As will be discussed below, military retirement has been the only non-contributory government retirement system, that is, financed entirely by new appropriations every year. Retirees maintain with some justification that they contributed to retirement benefits by working for inferior wages during their active years. It is also idle to guess how large a proportion of the overall security budget by 1990 will go for retirement pay. Respectable estimates range from the present 5 per cent up to 25 per cent. The point is that retired pay costs in the next twenty years will not depend on what the United States decides now to do and spend for security. Decisions leading to retired pay costs in the 1980s and 1990s have already been made. One can reliably say that whatever happens to the national security dollar in the 1970s, military retired pay is a budget fixture that is rising more steeply than any other personnel expense, and more steeply than nearly any other material or functional item in the United States security budget.

So long as costs were low, that is, well under a billion dollars a year during the 1950s, Congress paid little real attention to military retirees and retirement. There was no political advantage in taking sides on the retired military issue so soon after the Second World War and Korea, at a time when notions like 'massive retaliation', 'more bang for the buck', 'missile gaps', and the 'new look' in defense doctrine framed the field for Congressional battles on security appropriations and service roles and missions. Only in the defense reorganization of 1958 did Congress and the Eisenhower Administration act on the retirement pay problem. In a move bitterly resented by many retirees, Congress separated pay for active forces from retirement pay so that retirees no longer received automatic raises, or 'recomputation', when the active forces got a raise.

At the end of the 1950s and in the early 1960s, when retirement pay costs climbed toward a billion dollars a year, Congress had to turn its attention to the mushrooming costs. The number of retirees affected the cost, of course, but Congress could not address the numerical aspect for several reasons. For one, retirement policy was and is considered inseparable from active force policy. Early retirement and retired pay are means of regulating the active forces, and almost any change in retirement policy would have to be related to short- and long-range needs, including the need for flexibility in the size and composition of the active forces. In the second place, the size was fixed for years to come and could not be drastically reduced during the 1960s without radical cuts in the active forces, which were deemed impossible in light of security needs. Moreover, radical changes would have undermined the implicit 'contract' which would-be careerists feel they have with the government, thereby weakening retirement policy as an inducement to enter and remain in military service.

Congress thus faced a dilemma: military retirement cost too much to be ignored, but it was too closely related to national security to be radically changed. Attention was therefore diverted from the central issue to two other issues that gave Congress an opportunity to talk about military retirement without really talking about cost and size. The first issue was retirees in defense-related industry. Congressional subcommittees between 1958 and 1970 reviewed evidence that hundreds of retired senior officers – generals, admirals, colonels, and navy captains – had found jobs with firms doing defense business with the government. As noted earlier, the questions of how much influence these officers really had on defense procurement, and of how their retirement activities could be realistically regulated by law, were not satisfactorily investigated.

The second issue, an outgrowth of Congressional attention to Cold War education and speech review policies in 1962, focussed on the 'pro-Blue' indiscretion of army Major-General Edwin Walker. Walker's vigorous right-of-center troop indoctrination programs for United States troops in the Federal Republic of Germany were the focus of 'muzzling' hearings in the Senate, where it appeared that Walker probably had more organizational and spiritual ties to retirees than to active duty officers. The extent of support for Walker among active careerists was not measured by Congress and could not be. However, it is generally accepted that most officers felt Walker had probably exceeded the bounds of permissible conduct, and had been indiscreet. General Walker was retired soon after the incident erupted, and his erratic behaviour and association with militant, far-right causes and organizations after retirement effectively isolated him from the rest of the retired community and from active duty officers.

In Walker's case, quite a few officers were ready to feel that his guilt was exaggerated, but their feelings stemmed from a general assumption among military careerists that whatever the evidence, verdicts are liable to go against military professionalism or the 'professional ethic' when the issue is fought in open Congressional hearing. No Congressman has more military constituents than civilian constituents, and when the issues are so framed, the typical Congressman must defend 'civilian supremacy', generally to the disadvantage of the military. Service supporters in Congress know this best of all, and for that reason Congressmen such as the late Mendel Rivers of the House Armed Services Committee, current chairman F. Edward Herbert, and John Stennis of the Senate Armed Services Committee took pains to keep the discussion of ballooning retired pay, an inherited cost, from becoming a weapon in the hands of opponents of present military costs. The issue was thus reframed as follows: (1) how to keep retired pay attractive for recruiting purposes without returning to the fiscal risks of 'recomputing' retired pay when active pay was raised; (2) how to equalize the treatment given regular retirees with the much larger number of reservists who completed full careers as 'extended active duty' officers; and (3) how to make military retirement a contributory system, like social security or a company pension fund, rather than an 'unfunded obligation', whose dollars had to be voted and paid out of current tax revenues every year.

The dilemmas which Congress created for itself, perhaps unavoidably, by trying to regulate retirement costs without disturbing security policy are interesting in themselves, but equally interesting is the relationship between Congressional prerogatives and political action by retired officers. The link is direct. If a given political action by retired officers were organized, conspiratorial, and potentially violent and unconstitutional, it would be dealt with by a combination of presidential and court action. But since the chances of that kind of retiree politics are low, the political regulation of retirees reverts to Congress, which, though slower and less responsive, jealously guards its prerogatives with respect to the laws governing retirees' conduct.

How, then, can a polity like the United States regulate its retired officers if its formal control mechanisms are not fully suited to the task? The executive and the courts are largely set up to deal only with spectacular – and unlikely – retiree misconduct. Congress is not constituted to deal with abstracted or root problems of retired officers politics. Furthermore, on what is the assumption of potential retiree misconduct based? The answer to both questions lies in a closer examination of the young retired officer as he really is in the 1970s, and not as he is pictured in novels and stereotypes of the martinet in mufti.

Private Lives and Public Understanding

The assumption of possible political misconduct depends first on corollary notions about the military establishment. The military is the largest internally non-democratic institution in the United States, and the only institution that has a monopoly of violence when it acts externally for the state as a whole. The values reinforced in individuals who spend a career as responsible leaders in this institution suggest some conflict between military and civilian norms when the careerist rejoins society. Second, the assumption of possible misconduct depends on a prior assumption that career officers are by no means a cross-section of American society. They are self-selected by a host of personality characteristics, and they are self-selected from a still relatively narrow section of society where change is resisted and organizational clarity is prized, including clear organization of values about national security. When the two prior assumptions are combined, what emerges is not so much a 'military mind' as a psychological type that finds fulfillment and identification in military institutions and procedures.

General assumptions about retired officers are one thing, and specific evidence is quite another. Research on the ballooning retiree population throughout the 1960s and early 1970s indicates that former career officers do indeed identify with both their own services and the military establishment as a whole. But it also indicates that retired officers by no means fit a single clear mold and do not express markedly different political opinions from other American males of comparable age or social and economic circumstances. If there are differences between retired officers and their civilian peers – differences with political implications, that is – they lie in the retiree's less flexible view of democratic politics and processes, and in his tendency to relate both his political and personal non-political frustrations to the fluid character of democratic policy-making.

To illustrate these assertions, we have to examine officers in middle-aged retirement at their point of greatest visibility – at the points where career identification and retirement behavior are most likely to be related. The three most visible points are the period of transition from military to civilian life, the period of reoccupation in the civilian labor market, and the period of assimilation in civilian social, community and political life. The modal profile of the young retired officer that follows, based on ten years of diverse researches, is an approximation of thousands of largely field-grade retirees in their forties. It fits no one officer precisely, and how useful it is for predicting retiree politics depends on the fast pace of change of attitudes of, and about, the United States military.

One clear finding has been the difference in retirement adjustment between officers whose careers included the Second World War and retired in the late 1950s and early 1960s, and so-called the 'Cold War' retirees who were recruited, commissioned, and socialized throughout their careers entirely in the Cold War crisis in American military goals. Wherever the data allow, those differences are brought out in the following discussion.

Patterns of Transition: Military to Civilian. In a narrow sense, the officer's transition from military careerist to civilian begins when he makes the first irrevocable move toward retirement – submitting final military paperwork, buying a house, accepting a civilian job – and ends when his second career stabilizes with a permanent job and residence. That period varies widely, but is rarely less than a year and is often much longer. In a broader sense, transition begins in subtle ways much earlier than an officer's first irrevocable steps, and ends, if it ends, when he no longer relies on a military institutional response to most of his problems. Respondents said transition may be 'like, I never left the army', or it may be the 'most aimless, terrible period of my life'. More typically for recent retirees it was 'just like changing your wardrobe; there was nothing special about it.'

We would expect the retiree to be politically less active during the transitional period than at any later time. His principal concerns are financial. He is probably temporarily disenfranchised, local political processes are neither familiar nor personally salient, and he is too new to the community to have become a source of reference on military aspects of domestic and international policy. The officer who systematically and realistically plans for retirement is still an exception. What more often passes for planning is wishful thinking, thinking which is unrealistic in at least three respects. In the first place, the about-to-be-retired officer is rarely aware of how much structure the military has given his life. He knows that he will have to set his own hours after he leaves active duty, but he does not realize how closely his active duty day-to-day schedule has been related to corporate military purpose, and how schedule cannot exist without purpose. In the second place, retirees tend to ignore, or have no basis for recognizing, the difference between changing careers and changing jobs at middle age. The civilian in his forties who changes jobs, even involuntarily, can usually convince himself that his life has more functional continuity than can the officer who stops serving the pervasive military mission of national physical security. In the third place, retirees frequently misjudge their own training, experience, and abilities for a civilian society they have not fully known, despite their having spent most of their off-duty hours 'in' that society. Unfortunately, society allows the middle-aged breadwinner less margin of errror in judging his abilities than it allows the young man just starting out.

Life does not begin at forty for the young retired officers; instead, one said, 'it doesn't do a damn thing at forty' other than roughly coincide with the self-reexamination psychologists have found most men undergo in their late thirties and forties. However, for the retired officer this normal self-reexamination blends in with attempts at objectively explaining his retirement from the military. Interviews revealed a convergence of psychological pressures on the retired officer during transition, some positive and some negative. On the plus side, there is the stimulation, even excitement of having 'resolved' an increasingly ambiguous personal military situation by retirement. The stimulation comes from having reduced ambivalence, not from how wise or unwise the retirement decision (if voluntary) objectively was. On the minus side, there is an undeniable ambivalence for many officers about retirement from the service, even when it is voluntary and deliberate. In short, the retiree cannot know, until he has actually done it, how he will react. The services can be remarkably inept about inducing highly desirable, would-be retirees to stay in the military. Even at field-grade level, the administrative machinery of retirement serves effectively to give the retiring officer the impression that he is, after all, dispensable. Even the highly desirable officer can entertain doubts about how much he was actually needed, in a system built upon the dispensability of the individual.

Most officers know at least a year ahead of time the approximate date of their retirement, whether it is involuntary due to force cuts or repeated failure to be promoted, or truly voluntary. Even with the services providing more planning assistance, however, it has been found that probably no more than one in three retirees has confirmed plans six months before he leaves active duty. The other two out of three begin planning some time in the final six months, and half of these wait until the final ten weeks or do no planning at all. Surprisingly, there is no strong evidence that the early planners are better satisfied with post-military life in their first ten years of it.

No amount of counseling cushions a bank account. An officer retiring after twenty creditable years loses most supplementary benefits and receives 50 per cent of his active duty base pay with periodic adjustments for increases in the cost of living during the rest of his life. Retirement pay can range up to 75 per cent of active pay for officers with thirty or more years' service. However, the fewer career years an officer has, the lower will be his retired pay during the top-expense years in which he has adolescent and college

BASIC MONTHLY RETIREMENT PAY FOR FIELD GRADE OFFICERS COMPLETING 20, 25, AND 30 YEAR CAREERS IN 1973[2]

Rank	20 years	Length of career 25 years	30 years
Colonel/Captain	$898.65	$1,188.75	$1,546.88
Lt-Col/Commander	$812.85	$1,051.88	$1,262.25
Major/Lt-Commander	$703.65	$ 879.56	$1,055.48

age children. It does not particularly comfort a forty-five year old lieutenant-colonel, the father of three children under eighteen, to learn that if he lives into his seventies, his retirement pay will amount to a 5 per cent return on a $100,000 trust fund. It is not a principal he can use for emergencies, and even the paper principal dies with him.

Retirees' relative lack of planning and government indecisiveness surrounding retirement policy are less important in themselves than in what retirees think about them. Are they sources of discontent? Do retirees blame their former services, or the military in general, for their resettlement difficulties? Characteristically, retired officers do not blame their own services or the military establishment, even for troubles that are within the services' power to relieve, such as more considerate treatment of retirees at military base hospitals. If such criticism is occasionally made, it carries none of the vehemence with which retirees attack civilian agencies such as Congress and the Office of the Secretary of Defense for what they regard as political expediency or 'breach of faith' when these agencies seem to violate old but unwritten contracts with retirees. Moreover, the average career officer has seen and doubtless participated in numerous cases in which service needs or benefits have been sacrificed, in his view, to political expediency. His service, and the military generally, were not the culprit. Here, interviews disclose a sharp difference between retired regular officers and retired reservists who served an equal number of years on 'extended active duty'.[3] Reservists, supposedly but not necessarily more 'civilian' in their outlook, have been found to be about five times as likely to accuse civilian agencies, including Congress, of political double-dealing and 'breach of faith'. Paradoxically, retired regular officers are more tightly constrained by rules on income and political activity than retired reservists, and are more likely to suffer the real inequities of the double standard.

However, both regular officers and career reservists draw equal pay for equal years and face the same retirement expenses. Hence jobs and finances, not politics, remain the overwhelming concern of most retirees in need and search of a second career.

Second Career Patterns. The image of retired military officers flocking into defense industry and security policy-making is a distorted picture of the youthful military retired community as a whole. Even using a liberal definition of 'defense-related' jobs, more than 95 per cent of middle-grade retirees who find stable, true second careers are located in lines of work far removed from any position of direct influence on national security policy, armed force management or Pentagon purchasing.

Retirees hold a striking variety of jobs. Compared with the civilian labor force, more retired officers tend to settle satisfactorily with large (more than 2,500 employees) businesses. However, many officers prefer to mix the bureaucratic attractiveness and paternalism of the large organization with the independence they have managing decentralized offices of such businesses. Among the appeals of large business is the fact that large corporations are less liable to take advantage of the retiree's government income by paying him less, although his is likely to have some difficulty in negotiating his late-entry share in the company's own pension program. It is hardly surprising that some 60 per cent of retired officers settle in sales, managerial and administrative jobs. Although on active duty they may have been responsible for technical operations as complicated as modern aircraft or communication systems, retired officers rarely have the current technical, scientific or engineering qualifications of a civilian project systems manager, for example. Moreover, retirees who hope to revive scientific or technical credentials dating back to pre-service or early service days find that old degrees, particularly in the hard sciences, are hopelessly out of date. Sales attract numerous retirees because sales jobs are always open to self-confident men, even without experience, who are willing to take a risk. Typically, retirees who sell most successfully – and they are a small fraction of those who try – are in institutional sales rather than hard commodities. If he has the aptitude to start with, the typical retiree can sell bonds, community services, or other intangibles more easily than cars, cookware or men's clothing. Among unsuccessful retiree-salesmen, the two reasons for failure most often cited are, the subservience that officers feel sales require, and the difficulties of adjusting to a cash-exchange relationship after a career where cash was not an important currency of exchange.

Transferability of skills has had a lot of attention, but the real explanatory factors in second-career success are difficult to pin down. Albert Biderman and Laure Sharp found, and the present research as well, that transferability of skills has meaning for field-grade officers only in cases of very specialized skills, e.g. directly transferable operations, research skills, or corporate-level accounting. Otherwise:

> In analyzing the considerations that entered into employer's and job counselor's evaluations of retirees' job qualifications, it was concluded that various civilian common-denominator criteria, such as education, articulateness, personality characteristics and status (for which rank achieved was an indicator), were given uppermost consideration. In both hiring and assigning men, the study found, employers usually did not attempt specific matching of jobs and specific military-acquired skills.[4]

The different skills and outlooks of so-called 'combat' and 'support' officers are not recognized as such in all the services, but officers themselves draw the distinction when they talk about the ease of transferring military skills to civilian life. As they perceive it, line or combat officers have fewer transferable skills; support or technical branch officers 'can always find a job'. Upon examination, however, the typical advantage of a technical military speciality is in getting interviews for jobs, rather than in performing them.

'Administration', whether public or private, commercial or professional, has become so broad a term that it is nearly meaningless for a retiree's evaluation of his skills. Along with his 'command' ability, the retiree's notion of his administrative skills offers hope, confusion, and despair – often in that order – to the retiree looking for something gainful to occupy the rest of his life. The middle-grade retirees who have been found to be most influential in administrative jobs have been those with specific active duty experience in finance and accounting and those who are willing to undertake procedural reform tasks for civilian employers. Another clear finding is that civilian employers tend to weigh retiree's personality characteristics heavily in hiring, but show less concern about matching up military skills with job assignments.

The importance of a public service aspect to a second career can hardly be overestimated. The notion of performing a public service helps officers through many of the frustrations and rough spots of a military career, and it is an ego-satisfying criterion for retirement employment. As many as 25 per cent of middle-grade retirees fulfill the criterion by working for the federal government as civilians, most of them in the Department of Defense. Far fewer find jobs with state and local governments, mostly because state and local bureaucracies and entrance requirements are biassed against military retirees. Civil defense interest among retired officers, or lack of it, is interesting because civil defense would seem to offer a chance to perform public service, frequently some income, and above all activity related to military experience. More than half of interviewed retired officers say they would be willing to help with local civil defense, but one in four rejects it; as one said, 'there's too much politics', that is, local civilian politicians. Next to federal government employment, teaching and educational administration appear to be the fast-rising public service areas that retirees aim for. As educational standards in the services have climbed, including the bachelor's degree requirement for all officers, more retirees have earned primary and secondary school teaching certification and advanced degrees, with the result that between 5 and 10 per cent of retirees in the 1970s will find their way to schools, including premilitary institutions. A much smaller percentage will find jobs in higher education, and most of the jobs they find there will be administrative. The exceptions are officers who earned master's degrees on active duty and help staff small four-year, junior and community colleges.

In interviews in the early 1960s (hereafter called the 1964 sample), we expected a positive relationship between employment dissatisfaction and discontent along specific and general political issue dimensions. We did not find it. Jobless or luckless retirees were discontented, to be sure, but even by approaching potential relationships from several angles over an extended interview, we could not discern a spillover from second-career dissatisfaction to political issues except on the salient 'recomputation' issue and Congressional behavior. The quantifiable results for 1971 resembled 1964, but the quality of their responses differed. For one thing, the 1971 sample on the whole had found stable second careers sooner and more satisfactorily. However, whereas 1964 respondents expressed discontents of various sorts and the 1971 group were vocal about discontents on various process and political issues, the 1971 group were better informed about how their jobs could be affected by political action and had reached this level of information sooner in retirement than the 1964 sample. Of particular interest in 1971 was the correspondence between the level of government policy the retiree was most interested in, and the level of government policy most directly related to his job. For example, the broker was more interested in national economic regulation, the contractor and school administrator in local bonds and rezoning, the defense systems analyst and diplomatic historian in international politics. This correspondence could also be expected among a civilian white collar population, but is interesting among retired officers since they might have had more than the average reasons to be concerned with internal issues.

Social, Community, Political Organization. Military life rivals, if it does not exceed, any other social behavior pattern in its complete organization. The military environment has been called a 'total' environment compared with the civilian 'open' environment. The military environment more nearly unites the basic human activities of work, recreation, and rest under a single system of rules than any non-military institution of its size. The military environment can be explained in terms of the military mission, and it can often be described in terms of the hierarchies that support the mission.

Retirement strips the officer of many of these organizing hierarchies. In civilian life, a male breadwinner's existence is usually organized by what he does for a living; his job regulates his residence, his business, and many social associations, and many of his important attitudes towards politics. Military life does not totally constrain political attitudes, by any means, but it does supply other organizing devices, such as the most reliable single indicator, military rank. Military rank or grade grows out of the military mission, and is a key to authority, predictability, and efficient communication. When an officer retires, military title and other hierarchic symbols that help to organize so much of his active duty life may or may not operate similarly in a civilian community, depending largely on the cultural and political tone of the community. Surveys suggest that somewhat more than half of all middle-grade retirees use their military title sometime in the years after active duty. It is a declining percentage, however. As usage declines, channels of communication among retirees will doubtless be even weaker than they are today and another structural support for retiree satisfaction, or dissatisfaction, will have disappeared.

Many retired officers, in different words, express a dissatisfaction that boils down to a discomfiture, a feeling that civilian life lacks a node or stable center from which rules and assignments stem. From the civilian's perspective, the retiree's discomfiture appears to be over-attachment to the military. From the former officer's standpoint, however, what he misses is not the military mission but the emotions and security that were associated with the mission. The distinction goes far to explain why the 125,000-member Retired Officers Association, a conservatively governed all-services organization, is politically almost impotent but socially rewarding for retirees who gather periodically for meetings of its local affiliates.

Clearly, 1971 interviewees for this study maintained fewer personal and collective associations with other retired officers than the 1964 sample. Several 1971 respondents had to pause for a minute to think of any retired military they interact with once a month or oftener. However, they were not so compulsive about avoiding other retired officers as the 1964 sample had been. For 1964 retirees, avoidance of military peers was a much more deliberate, self-conscious act, as if avoiding other retirees might be the secret of successful adjustment. We were also interested in measures of cohesion between careerists and the ever larger percentage of the population with brief military duty. Both 1964 and 1971 samples, as expected, dismissed such organizations as the American Legion and the Veterans of Forign Wars as irrelevant to their own situations. However, 1971 respondents seemed much more ready than 1964 retirees to talk about military life and affairs as equals with business associates and friends who had been draftees or short-term officers. As one 1971 respondent said: 'It's something in common to talk about. Maybe he's been an aircraft mechanic in the service, or airborne. A lot of times it doesn't mean you agree on things, but it's something to talk about.'

Retirees' social and psychological isolation in their communities remains a key variable. Middle-grade retired officers have not been found to be any more or less 'joiners' than their white-collar civilian contemporaries. At the Rotary-Lions Club level, few retirees find satisfaction or companionship in these activities if they were not already taking part in them during their military years. As for overall social satisfaction, including some measures of political 'belongingness', middle-grade retirees are more likely than not to find civilian life at middle age less satisfying than active duty. Only about one in four finds he is 'as satisfied' or 'more satisfied' in retirement, and about one in eight – particularly higher ranking and regular retirees – considers the two situations incomparable.

Contrary to the Colonel Blimp stereotype, middle-grade officer retirees defy easy classification by militant or otherwise consistent issue opinions. Although we were primarily interested in intensity of orientation rather than direction of opinions on specific issues, interviews almost invariably included issue discussions. Moreover, two minimum issues were routinely introduced into the 1971 interviews:

the volunteer army, and the services' current image, roles, and missions.

Interviewees in the early 1960s displayed a lower level of information on the issues most often discussed with them at that time: post-Sputnik national priorities, defense reorganization, strategic missile forces and conventional forces, American East Asian (not yet really South-East Asian) policy, Kennedy Administration social policy. By contrast, 1971 retirees were better informed but less intense; on the other hand, they were more difficult to engage in discussions of local and especially non-local issues. Recent retirees, exposed for a longer time to fluctuating force levels and the contingencies of Cold War politics, were firmer than the 1964 sample about the necessity for flexibility in the size and capability of the armed forces. This position was associated with opposition to a volunteer army. Reflecting views among active officers, 1971 retired officers generally agreed that a volunteer army would not work, and even if it did work it should not work because international politics was not stable enough to permit a small, professional American cadre. Recent retirees did not typically broach the relationships between a volunteer army and broad social representation, but they were not hesitant about discussing it in those terms when it was raised.

It would be premature to say that the 1971 sample were basically less authoritarian in approaches to resolving social problems – most often expressed in the interviews as law-and-order, urban dilemmas, and campus disorders. It is probably more accurate to say that 1971 respondents, compared with 1964, were inclined to think that authoritarian solutions are impracticable, not that they are theoretically unsound. If indeed trends in authoritarianism can be discerned, it still begs the question of the relative effects of reduced authoritarianism within the modern military itself, or military men's reactions to changing patterns of authoritarianism in the larger civilian environment.

Summary: The Matrix of Retirement Politics

The massive military manpower levies of the past third of a century, combined with up-or-out careers and the traditional approach of lucrative retirement benefits to attract and keep leaders, created a sizable young retired military population in the United States. Traditional public uneasiness with the military and frustrations of protracted nuclear diplomacy and competing domestic values facilitated stereotypes of warriors unhorsed, Colonel Blimps inclined to mischief or malice towards civilian democracy.

The bulk of officers retired in field grades do not fit the stereotype. Moreover, the American military is too pervaded with civilian values and its retirees too diverse a product of pre-military and military socialization to presage a reasonable likelihood of their concerting effective political reaction. Their matrix for political reaction is too loose, their origins too varied, and the polity too pluralistic for sustained cohesive group response.

However, the military institution, properly defined by its unique combat mission, will always be more different from all other occupations in the polity than those occupations are different from each other. The fact that the institution can be more distinctive and perhaps anomalous than the human beings it comprises makes the disjunction between the military and military people especially poignant. Hence, the need for flexible, even radical policies of military careers and career compensation are as great as the inanity of legislating career military service as if it were just one more line of work. The social and financial costs of large-scale military retirement, present and future, are part of the costs of security. Military retirement costs and their peculiar problems of civilian-military relations offer a retrospective, crisis-free point from which to re-examine earlier commitments and to re-evaluate the promises of present commitments to military security.

NOTES TO CHAPTER 5

1. The supporting data for this summary of retiree behaviour patterns come from four principal sources: (1) lengthy personal interviews and follow-ups by the author with two hundred young retired field-grade officers from 1961 to 1972; (2) a national survey by the author during 1964-6 of state and local government experiences with military retired employees; (3) government and private opinion and attitude surveys among large retiree samples between 1960 and 1970; and (4) second-career choices as reported in Congressional hearings and in publications of the Retired Officers Association and the service press, primarily the *Journal of the Armed Forces* and

the weekly papers of the Army Times Publishing Co. Any discussion of modern military retirement must acknowledge the seminal, continuing initiative of Albert D. Biderman of the Bureau of Social Science Research, his associate Laure M. Sharpe, and actuarial consultant Joseph Glenn of the U.S. Department of Defense.

2. Ever since retirement pay raises were unhitched from active pay raises in 1958, retirees have been paid according to active scales in the years when they retired, with periodic raises for cost of living. Hence, a retiree who served through the Second World War and Korea from 1941 to 1961 started at lower retirement pay and stayed financially behind a careerist of equal rank who missed the Second World War and served, for example, from 1946 to 1966. The pay scales in this table do not reflect tax benefits for retirees with disability allowances, or the deductions from retirement pay for regular officers who take federal government jobs. Career reservists are not subject to such deductions.

3. The size of the permanent officer corps, that is, officers holding regular commissions, is fixed by statute. Therefore, remaining officer needs are filled by reservists who spend full careers on extended duty and perform identical duties with regular officers, albeit with much less chance of elite promotion or retention past twenty years. A separate class of retirees, those truer civilian reservists who earn retirement pay by attending drills and attaining the age of sixty with only limited active duty, are not considered career military in this study.

4. Albert D. Biderman, 'The Retired Military', in Roger W. Little (ed.), *Handbook of Military Institutions* (Beverly Hills, Calif.: Sage Publications, 1972), p. 550.

6 Strategic Ideas and Defense Policy: The Organizational Nexus

COLIN GRAY

There has been comparatively little attention in the literature on defense issues given to the relationship between the production and refinement of strategic ideas, and the production and deployment of weapons. Hardly any more concern has been given to those organizations that have the responsibility to relate the one with the other, thereby turning ideas into operational reality. The reasons for this lack of attention to the strategic theory/defense policy interface are not hard to find. Ideas are obscure in derivation and are soon widely diffused. Rarely is it possible to document the path of an idea from conception to military realization, particularly when an idea has served to affect the 'climate of opinion' rather than to determine some specific outcome.[1] Further, government departments, especially those responsible for defense matters, are not in the habit of opening their archives for outside investigation.

Among studies of strategy and defense policy can be found works that trace the momentum of the strategic theoretical debate, that highlight military technical developments, and which 'tell the story' of changes in defense policy. The importance of civilian strategic theorists in the United States has been widely acclaimed, yet the evidence for their importance is by no means overwhelming. There is a growing collection of studies of civilian strategists in non-profit advisory institutions and university-based groups, but these have been more concerned with the strategic theoretical output of these organizations, than with their influence and impact on defense policy formulation.

The purpose, therefore, of this paper is to explore some of the links between producers and the content of strategic ideas, and the formulation of defense policy. Problems of definition arise immediately. A strategic idea is understood to be one relating to the preparation, structuring and employment of the military power of a state for the goals set by policy.[2] The term 'defense policy' is taken here to mean those directing ideas and principles that are in fact embodied in the defense posture of the state. In other words, there is an important distinction to be drawn between operational and declaratory policy. It is assumed from this that the men, machines, organization and operational plans constitute the empirical referents for its defense policy. The prime consideration, however, is to relate the realm of ideas to the preparatory activities of those agencies of government that produce these tangible features of defense policy.

The concern here is only with the advanced industrial societies.[3] Discussion of the defense problems of those states which fall within this category is generally marked by an agreement among them that certain kinds of weapons and certain security issues are 'strategic'. Such issues are related to potential attacks upon, and the defense of, the homelands of these states; and because of the sophistication of modern weapons systems, and the exponential rise in the costs of their development, production and use, such attack or defense would, almost inevitably, involve atomic or thermonuclear devices.

The 'organizational nexus' referred to in the title is that agglomeration of government departments, executive agencies and service institutions that link ideas to policy through their responsibility for the development, direction and management of military forces. In short, for strategic theory to become strategy, it must be converted into men, machines, organization and operational plans. This is a function performed collectively, though not equally, by senior civilians and armed servicemen within a Ministry, or a Department, of Defense. The task will very probably be conducted in conjunction with other defense 'experts', located in the office of the chief executive, and in economic, technological and foreign policy agencies. Although all these other experts also come from intra-governmental organizations, they are likely to see the problems of defense in a totally different perspective than the military and civil defense department personnel immediately concerned.

It is not assumed *a priori* that all strategic ideas of importance originate outside the boundary of the organizational nexus. In theory, the organizations comprising the defense nexus are concerned only to establish the relevance and feasibility of strategic ideas. In practice, however, though they are meant to be impartial and objective, they tend to make value judgments upon the worth of strategic ideas well in advance of examining their feasibility or relevance. In addition, the organizations comprising the nexus have their own goals, possess organizational norms and operate in a fashion that may influence, or prejudice, their individual judgment. It is possible that any one of these sub-units of the defense nexus might pursue any number of very narrow internally derived goals that could frustrate defense objectives established by a higher executive agency, or prove to be dysfunctional to the efficiency and efficacy of the entire defense decision-making process.[4]

The analysis, however, is concerned also with the working of the defense community as a whole.[5] 'Defense community' is a term that refers both to those individuals and organizations that have a legal or customary responsibility for the formulation and execution of defense policy, i.e. the intra-governmental defense organizational nexus, and those who operate extra-governmentally, but who nonetheless are continuously concerned with it. The particular questions to be asked of the defense community, therefore, relate first to the sources and content of strategic ideas, and second to the relationship between these sources and the defense organizational nexus. In other words, it must be established what are the particular features of the nexus, and particularly of the military sections within it, that either hinder or facilitate the acceptance of strategic ideas as a basis for future policy.

In an advanced industrial society, the defense community is typically a large one. Conversely, the individuals who possess the qualifications and the interest to produce practicable strategic ideas are relatively small in number.[6] A useful distinction can be drawn here between the strategy generalist and the strategy specialist.[7] The former category would include those people with an interest and expertise in broad national security questions; the latter serves to identify and gather together the vast majority who have an interest and expertise in specific defense matters. For example, most of those working in advisory, or in 'line' positions within and outside government are concerned only with very narrow sectors of defense, such as the technical improvement of the 'hardware' or the 'software' bases of defense policy, or the specific problems of one of the branches of the armed services.

The strategy generalist is not to be found in all sectors of the defense community, nor is there equal distribution of their number. In order of importance as a source of strategic ideas on broad security issues there is first, executive defense agency affiliated and non-affiliated advisory organizations and universities. Second come the sections and agencies within the defense organizational nexus itself; and finally there is the relatively thin scattering of generalists in the ranks of dependent industries and among retired military officers.[8]

Two distinctions regarding the producers of general strategic ideas will assume importance in the analysis below: the first is between civilians and soldiers, and the second is between civilians within the organizational nexus and those who are principally outside it. The source and sponsor of a strategic idea may assume a greater importance than either its content or its implications. It is therefore necessary to examine systematically a number of hypotheses about the link between strategic ideas and their adoption by the defense organizational nexus in the formulation of, and as a basis for, future defense policy. This will be done by taking alternative hypotheses concerning the characteristics of this link and examining them separately. The first such hypothesis is that strategic ideas serve to rationalize defense policy decisions taken on other grounds, usually pragmatic, rather than to instigate and promote new developments.

The actual role of theory is one of the insoluble problems of strategic studies.[9] Historical evidence yields no proposition concerning the relationship between theory and technological change that is easily tenable.[10] There have been widely acknowledged occasions when an armed service has adopted and promoted a particular theory for the conduct of war, even though the theory itself was well in advance of the military-technological state-of-the-art. Early air force and air corps adherence to the strategic airpower doctrines of Trenchard, Douhet and Mitchell are a case in point.[11] Conversely, there have been instances of the adoption of a particular weapon by an armed service when that weapon does not clearly fit into existing ideas regarding the conduct of the war. For example, there have been occasions when a weapon was not developed for a specific military strategic or tactical end,[12] but because of an operational requirement which had been issued on the basis of imaginative, or optimistic, insights of the battlefield of the future. It might be argued that in the United States neither the atomic bomb nor the ballistic missile programs were initiated because of any profound concern for a specific military tactical or strategic purpose.

At times, some strategic ideas are welcomed either by a single service as, for example, was Mahan's doctrine of command of the seas,[13] or by particular interests within it, as for example the strategy of 'flexible response' by the U.S. Tactical Air Command.[14] There is, on the other hand, little evidence of a strategic idea being welcomed or adopted readily by the armed services as a whole. It is difficult to escape the conclusion from these observations alone that in most cases each military service has a dominant and traditional 'preferred strategy'. The 'preferred strategy' of a service can be seen as being either that which has been tried and has succeeded in the past, or that which seems to express the essence of the capability of that particular service.[15] Such 'preferred strategies' are understandable. They stress those kinds of combat situations in which the military professional is called upon to demonstrate the maximum of his professional expertise and quality of character; it also tends to be one that downplays the value of active assistance from other services. It is, in addition, one that could be pursued with the greatest chance of success because it assumes a situation favorable to the believed advantages of the service; that is, in the unlikely event of 'other things being equal'.

In order to present a contemporary image, particularly for reasons of the annual budgetary battle, military service will often adopt a strategic theory or idea simply in order to be in apparent accord with the 'spirit of the time'. The doctrinal justification for the development and procurement of the U.S. *Forrestal* class aircraft carriers, for example, shifted significantly over time.[16] It is comparatively easy to criticize a service for procuring its favoured weapon system and then adjusting the justification for its maintenance so as to comply with shifts in the strategic theoretical climate. It is a fortunate service whose procurement policy is a dominant influence on the nature of the strategic climate, as was, for example, the development of the U.S. navy early thinking on submarine-launched strategic missiles in 1956.[17] But it is a fact that nearly all past prognoses concerning the course of future wars have been significantly in error. Therefore, regardless of the doctrinal veneer put upon capability, it may be held that a service is wise to behave conservatively and to provide continually for a mix of operational strategies, some new, some traditional. The danger in this 'insurance' approach to future war, however, is that there is a tendency to succumb to the temptation to over-insure or to waste scarce resources in planning for every conceivable contingency.

Underlying this first hypothesis is the assumption that military organizations, as on-going concerns, have a traditional and well-understood set of strategic beliefs and doctrines. These 'institutionalized' doctrines are vital for the efficient working of the organization.[18] The weapons systems and operating command structures of these organizations evolve in a fashion that is often remote from the changing formulae and semantics of strategic theory. 'Massive retaliation', 'graduated deterrence', 'limited war', 'flexible response', and 'crisis management' come and go, but, for example, the ships and organization of the navy go on, apparently, for ever. To the extent that political expediency requires, strategic theory will be culled from a wide range of sources for arguments that both serve to justify a service's preferred activities, and implicitly or explicitly to cast doubts upon the activities of rivals. It is, of course, equally open to higher executive agencies to whom the services are responsible, to find strategic theories and ideas that serve the same purpose, in this case to justify imposing a common policy upon the whole of the military establishment.[19] It is not too misleading to state that rationality invites rationalization, through these two uses to which strategic theory can be put are not necessarily mutually exclusive.[20] Furthermore, they can also serve an educational function as well as having a 'significant causal force' in defense policy formulation.[21]

In-house strategic thought, generated from within the organizational nexus, has advantages over other sources. It is served by an ease of access to classified material; its mode and channels of expression are most likely to be in a manner calculated to induce acceptance; and it is probable that it would reflect a profound and necessary sympathy for the organizational and human consequences of new and untried strategic ideas. But the second hypothesis, here, is that in-house strategic thinking, for all these advantages, is unlikely to be an important stimulus to defense policy change. It would appear paradoxical that the very authorship and organizational locus of in-house strategic ideas and thinking are very often the fundamental reasons for poor results.

In the creation of new strategic ideas, there is a dichotomy between the immediate concerns of military and civilian bureaucratic organizations, and the long-term perspective. The requirements for creative thought would seem therefore to be extremely difficult within the defense organizational nexus where responsibility is unevenly divided between practical day-to-day management and operational planning, and forward thinking. The military profession, in for example the United States, could have relied less upon contracted strategic advice from outside, and could have encouraged more officers both to acquire and to employ a broad strategy expertise. But what must not be forgotten is that, regardless of such policies, the nature of the policy process within the organizational nexus and the nature of the military profession could not be rapidly altered.

Perhaps in an informal and uninstitutionalized way, some in-house strategic thinking may be put forward. The motives behind such action vary, though they would likely be the attempt of an individual or a group to comment on broad defense matters, more perhaps as an internal tactical move to upgrade their particular military function, or their particular 'pet' project, than as a serious proposal to improve the quality of strategic thinking. Two factors might be suggested in support of this thesis: the first is that any criticism of service or government thinking on strategic thinking – and new ideas in an organizational context are at least implied criticism – whether expressed implicitly or explicitly, is almost certain to be viewed as a form of disloyalty. Indeed such activity is likely to present to organizational rivals and to the general public a view of a service or of the defense organization nexus being divided within its own ranks.[22] The second, which is closely related to the first, relates to the structure of the defense departments in which relatively few personnel have the opportunity to see defense planning in a broad context and in political terms. When the opportunity does arrive, it is relatively late in the careers of most personnel and the process of career patterns and promotion within the organization will have played an important selective process.

A formal and institutionalized method of stimulating in-house strategic thinking would be the establishment of a group within the central defense department or in all or any of the armed services charged explicitly with the critical function to inquire into broad strategic questions and to test and formulate new strategic ideas. Such a definition of institutional responsibility is, however, unusual. The more typical delegation of intellectual task is that designed to facilitate an intensive, hostile analysis of another service.[23] The formation by Mr Healey of a Programmes Evaluation Group within the British Ministry of Defence would be an example of the attempt to establish a genuinely critical in-house intellectual effort.[24] It is perhaps significant to note, however, that this particular group was dissolved not long after its brave beginning.

A major constraint upon the intellectual activity of the military professional is precisely the fact that he is a military professional. There are hazards in proceeding on the basis of an ideal type, but it is important to note that the officer will have internalized the values not merely of the military profession, but also of his particular branch. Unlike the civilian, the officer is steeped in the strategic folklore of his service.[25] Deviant individuals can of course be cited, but these men are significant in that they point to the doctrinal norms of their service. The profound acceptance of the values and the strategic functions of a particular service should not, however, be demeaned. An intimate association of the individual with the goals of the military organization is essential for career satisfaction. It is difficult to deny, conversely, that long association with a restricted set of strategic concepts is likely, in his middle or late career, to inhibit an individual from an open assessment of arguments that bear upon the future well-being of his service. The quality, and content, of teaching in staff colleges is clearly a critical variable in this context.[26] Elementary career considerations must not be ignored either, nor within the context of military organizations must the factor of rank. The staff officer must be constrained in his analysis by his knowledge of the official 'position papers' of his service, and of the personal views of his chief of staff. In similar fashion, a chief of staff may not wish to 'rock the boat' for his subordinates in planning positions.[27]

These particular situations have been described in terms of their being 'prisoner problems'. A military officer who makes known his ideas on strategy, who is seen to be disloyal by declining to act sufficiently as a service representative in a joint planning office, or who is not thought to be putting his services' interests persuasively enough, faces the possibility of career restriction. For the military professional this is likely to be far more serious than for the civilian, especially those who are co-opted on an *ad hoc* basis from outside to advise the government on defense matters. The growing parallelism between military and civil employment as the military profession becomes more 'technocratic' should have an impact on this condition.[28]

Military officers, however, are increasingly acquiring the intellectual skills necessary for strategic speculation; and military organizations have appreciated the nature of the threat posed by unsympathetic extra-military defense experts both within and outside the organizational nexus. They have gone some way to having institutionalized, in-house, broadly defined planning units. In addition, in the United States, governments have sought to discipline defense expertise by establishing extra-organizational groups working under military supervision. Such organizations would count among their number the Institute for Defense Analyses (I.D.A.), and the Research Analysis Corporation (R.A.C.); both are very close to being in-house groups.

General observations on the features of in-house civilian strategic thinking are dangerous because of the circumstances peculiar to each country. For example, there is likely to be considerable difference in terms of independence of opinion and the willingness to express it, between a group of career civil servants on the one hand and co-opted defense experts from outside on the other. The career civil servant, with a concern for orderly administration and possibly with strong sympathies for a particular service that has grown out of a long association,[29] operates under many more constraints than the expert, who has neither of these concerns and who is probably on a short-term secondment from another occupation anyway. Many of these outside experts will have been seconded into the organizational nexus because their particular strategic thinking is already known, rather than as an unknown quantity.[30]

All organizations have regular, routine on-going business to conduct and no in-house strategic activity can long remain in isolation from the demands of such business.[31] In-house strategic thinking is therefore only likely to be effective because the communication lines will be short; it is 'wired in' to the needs of the organization as defined by the top executives. It is precisely because of this efficient communications network that any activity originally intended as strategic vision is more than likely to eventuate in perpetual 'fire-fighting'.[32] The stresses and strains of government life and departmental 'boundary maintenance' cannot be ignored; the bureaucratic battlefield has been the graveyard of many an ambitious and imaginative strategic idea.

In-house activity in strategic theory formulation has increased in importance throughout the 1960s. But, although this may have been the case, and there has been a rise in the sophistication of the arguments deriving from or adopted by the defense organizational nexus, it is important to note the essential function of these ideas to that of 'system (and more often sub-system) maintenance'. For there to be any real departure from this pattern in the near future there would have to be an unprecedented change, both in the time horizon of concern by those at the top, and in military organizations with respect to the kind of behavior appropriate to their members.

It can be argued, as with the third hypothesis, that strategic ideas are received by a military organization according to their anticipated impact upon its over-all authority and prestige. The fallacy of such a contention would derive from an over-concentration upon the domestic political processes particular to the defense politics of each country. A military organization must continually keep in mind, when considering which strategic idea it will support or adopt, the *raison d'être* for its very existence. This might well in turn depend upon the image of the service and its domestic standing relative to the other services. At the present time, prestige is customarily seen in terms of war-waging success or whether the service operates the principal deterrent role.

In practice, the criteria of public prestige and intra-defense organization politics rarely confront each other in an obvious way. It would be unusual for a military organization to be presented with a strategic idea which, although unimpeachable from the point of view of military effectiveness, would also harm its authority and prestige. It would be a rare strategic idea that did not involve a significant division of military opinion concerning its military value.[33] The fact that often considerations of authority and prestige coincide with judgments concerning the value of strategic ideas should not invite conclusions that parochial and traditional service judgments necessarily determine the outcome of a strategic debate.

A military organization has a domain of authority over certain military missions. This domain often implies, and equally often the services explicitly claim, the exclusive maintenance and use of some categories of weapons systems.[34] From its domain of authority, and from the consensus of opinion within the government and society at large, regarding the relative importance of its military mission, a services' prestige is derived. Military executives may be excused for thinking that authority and prestige are closely linked, but two diametrically opposed phenomena should be noted: first there is a positive feed-back effect, in that those granting authority enhance the prestige of one particular service and consequently are inclined to grant more. For example, a good record of technical foresight and management efficiency in one missile program may incline the government to 'reward' that service with a further program, irrespective of the marginal worth of the follow-up program.[35] The second phenomenon is that of 'fair shares'. This idea acknowledges that if one military organization, however deservedly, is starved of funds for prestige-producing programs, it is likely to engage in disruptive public relations activities.[36] Further, there is the tacit assumption between the services that there should be a rough norm establishing an equality of treatment between them. Harmony in a federal defense structure is difficult to obtain if one of the participants feels that there has been discrimination against its interests.

Since 1945 changes in the technology of war have posed serious threats to the authority and to the prestige of military organizations in advanced industrial societies. In the post 1945 period there has been, at least in the West, a growing inter-service consensus that the deterrence of major war by means of nuclear weapons is the primary mission of the armed forces. Such a consensus on one broad strategic concept has implied no agreement on the subordinate concepts concerning either the proper military posture to ensure an effective deterrence, or the relationship between deterrence and defense.[37] The pre-eminent broad strategic concepts of deterrence and limited war defense have cut across the traditional tri-service mission boundaries. The result, particularly in the United States, has been a doctrinal free-for-all. The stake in this competition is the allocation of funds for those weapon systems that are perceived to enhance authority and prestige, and to enlarge the domain of the service. A service might well be tempted to pursue this path of authority and prestige, even though it could run counter to the intellectual convictions predominant in the service, or within both the organizational nexus or the defense community at large. The 'guerrilla warfare boom' of the Kennedy years produced this effect, with the navy and air force joining the 'special forces' bandwagon. The reasoning behind such action is clear; a service may not favor a certain strategy, but for public relations reasons it may find it expedient.

Today, an armed service is unlikely to be a largely autonomous body; it is more likely to be a department within a federal defense structure, sharing common services with other departments. A reluctant, or recalcitrant, service may be told that a certain weapon system instrumental to a strategic concept will be developed and will be introduced into operational service.[38] The structure of the organizational nexus must therefore work to restrict the freedom of a service in adopting, or not adopting, a strategic idea. A service can no longer expect to be able to defend a particular strategic idea on grounds of related experience or of 'military judgment'.[39] Instead, a service must assume that its judgment will be challenged by rival analyses of other services, or by defense department civilian experts.

Considerations of authority and prestige are very important to a military organization when potentially radical strategic concepts are recommended. But these considerations must be tempered by some concern for the intrinsic merit of the formal goals of the organization. The authority of a military organization is limited. If an idea is rejected, and an alternative imposed from above, the service in question may well suffer loss of prestige and, more importantly, vital political advantage within the organizational nexus.

The fourth hypothesis is that strategic ideas will be received by a military organization according to their anticipated impact upon martial values and upon the internal allocation of prestige. And, in this context, the rise in importance of the manager and the technologist in the military organizations of advanced industrial countries cannot be overlooked. These skills are increasingly being welcomed in the ranks of the military service and defense departments. [40] However, the *ultima ratio* of an armed force is the fact that a country may find it necessary to fight. The project manager or the rocket fuel technologist, however skilled or necessary, does not embody the dominant virtues of the professional soldier. The ideal type of martial virtue would be manifest in the individual warrior whose success rested solely upon his individual skill and character, and who could be seen in action against opposing military forces. But it has been suggested that martial values have been declining in significance since the discovery of gunpowder.[41]

Contemporary military tasks are a challenge to widely held martial values, and are often at variance with the preferred strategies of the armed services. Service opposition to a military mission and its attendant weapons systems cannot be explained by reference to martial values; such a resistance would be correctly vilified as military romanticism. Nonetheless the 'permanent revolution' in military technology since 1945 offers numerous examples of the alienation of the professional soldier from his assigned task. One such example is the impact of the nuclear weapon upon traditional service roles.

One of the important consequences of nuclear weapons has been the extent to which civilian control has extended over those spheres previously deemed to have been exclusively military. One implication of the strategic concept of deterrence is that there will be close control of the military. Thus one source of neo-Clauswitzian[42] ideas of contemporary civilian strategies is the fact that these ideas require interpretation of the proper scope of military expertise on the one hand and civilian authority on the other. Largely autonomous general staffs no longer prepare war plans, nor conduct wars.

Strategic ideas may be judged by many military officers not on their merits but upon their likely impact on the relative standing of certain branches of the defense organization. This factor is closely tied to the notion of martial values. Strategic ideas that are likely to be harmful to martial values are likely to meet heavy military opposition if they appear to upgrade the importance of a branch of the armed forces that has distinctly 'unheroic' characteristics. Resistance will be fed by the career anxieties of officers whose expertise lies in the more traditional areas. There may well be fears that the elevation of one part of the armed services, and one which is new, technocratic and devoid of traditions, might well prove detrimental to the cohesion of the armed services as a whole. These fears of elitism might well give good cause to resist certain strategic ideas.[43]

The fifth and final hypothesis is that different ideas about the conduct of war will be reflected in the different demands that the organizational nexus would have to make of society. Strategic ideas are, in other words, examined in ecological perspective. The demands of the defense organizational nexus do not only take the form of financial requests but also of approval by society of the means and ends of national security. If the support of society were withheld, a situation of alienation would be confronted.[44] Society may temporarily withdraw its mandate as a consequence of an unsuccessful war, because of scandals, or because of widely challenged equipment decisions and wastage.

The adoption or neglect of a strategic idea may in some instances depend not upon the relative merits of the proposal, but upon the ecological problems facing the organization. There are innumerable examples of attempts by a military organization to structure the attitudes dominant in its environment.[45] Public relations activities, from comic strips to 'junkets' for legislators, have been employed to induce favourable attitudes towards the military, or more specifically military strategic ideas and programs. Retired military personnel have been used extensively to exert influence. The military are not alone in this sphere. Defense-orientated industries with stakes in specific strategic ideas are also heavily engaged in such exercises. Often they generate their own strategic ideas and try to sell them to both the military and the public. Indeed the term Military–Industrial Complex highlights the ecological problem. But, generally speaking, it is more likely that military organizations and its industrial, quasi-academic, and journalist supporters will respond to ecological dangers by manipulating the external threat.[46] Uncertainty over an adversary's intentions, and lack of evidence concerning future capabilities, allows a service facing budgetary contraction some leverage by stressing their national security role. It has been traditional for potentially hostile submarines to be sighted off-shore prior to debates on naval strategy and financial estimates.

Strategic concepts, when adopted by the defense organizational nexus, may require considerable changes in the pattern of conscription, force deployment, operational plans and budgetary demands; but the willingness of society to meet these requirements may be less than satisfactory. Save at times of obvious peril, a society and its defenders seldom march as one. The security benefits of a seemingly inactive military are hard to demonstrate; deterrrence cannot be seen to be done. Conversely, the military may be perceived to pose a threat to both civilian values and to civilian government. Strategic ideas that would enhance the operational effectiveness of military forces may appear barbaric, or at least detrimental to society in the eyes of civilians. Chemical and biological warfare research is a case in point. In peacetime, the inevitably parasitic characteristics of the defense organizational nexus provide a constant source of argument for those who resent vast sums of money being spent on defense and the conscription of youth.

The intention has been to explore areas of inquiry that serve to link the interests of strategic theorists and the user departments. The specific form of the organizational nexus in each advanced industrial state and the various sources and differing substance of strategic ideas combine to make any summary run the risk of distorting the general picture.

It would appear, however, that strategic ideas serve the political needs of military organizations as often as they serve as a guide to military technical progress. Strategic ideas produced by in-house groups also tend to serve 'current system supportive' functions. The nature of the military organization, the pressures of organizational life and the competitive features of the defense organizational nexus ensure that in-house activity will not produce ideas either of a radical or of a potentially disruptive kind. On the other hand, military organizations, i.e. the armed services, prefer to adopt, refine and support those concepts that promise to maximize their authority; in practice, however, they tend to temper such concepts because they have to provide the men and equipment for combat in both the long run and the short run.

The evidence for the close attention of an armed service to the preservation of traditional martial values and to the maintenance of an extant distribution of prestige among the different sections of the defense organization nexus is almost entirely inferential. Arguments over sophisticated technology, or over abstract strategic concepts, are not conducted in terms of fundamental qualities, despite the popular belief that 'in the last resort it is the man with the rifle that counts'.

Regarding the ecology of the defense nexus, it is clear that consideration has to be given to social considerations consequent upon the adoption of a strategic concept. But the ecological perspective is only one of many operating on the contemplation of a strategic idea. Military organizations may be directed by a higher authority, or may choose to ignore hostile pressures from society in the interests of maintaining a military capability necessary in the light of the perceived threat.

There is a paradox that, on the one hand, in-house strategic thought is likely to prove uncritical or over responsive to the needs of the moment, whilst on the other extra-military strategic thought would appear to be proceeding with a momentum of its own, largely unconcerned with the practical problems of the defense organizational nexus. Much of contemporary strategic thought should be viewed as being one stand in intellectual history, whereas military strategic thinking should be seen as an essential part of an on-going process for the making of defense policy.

By the very nature of his experience and skill, the civilian outside government is likely to stress the desirable, while the military or civilian expert within a defense organizational nexus will emphasize the necessary. A well-integrated defense community should provide transmission belts for ideas that have radical implications for the operating organizations. These belts may take the form of advisory units to service or civilian departments; of contractual agreements between individuals, for example academics or retired military officers, and government departments; of analytical groups within the defense-dependent industrial corporations; or of broadly educated military officers within the defense organizational nexus itself. The organizational nexus of military and related agencies must seek to adapt strategic ideas to the available technology, to its own need and capacity to change, and to the internal and external environment. Military complaints about the unworldlines of deterrence or limited war theory should be seen in conjunction with the knowledge that the fount of original strategic ideas is preserved because of its very distance from the immediate problem.

NOTES TO CHAPTER 6

1. Note the perceptive comments upon this matter in V. Davis, *The Admirals Lobby* (Chapel Hill, N. Carolina: The University of N. Carolina Press, 1967) pp. 181–2.
2. See U. Schwartz and L. Hadik, *Strategic Terminology* (New York: Praeger, 1966), pp. 94–5, 112; an interesting definition is offered in A. Wohlstetter, 'Strategy and the Natural Scientists' in R. Gilpin and C. Wright (eds) *Scientists and National Policy-making* (New York: Columbia

University Press, 1964) '... I use the words 'strategy' or 'strategic studies' mostly to describe research on the major and longer run alternatives in the design of conflict systems'. p. 205.

3. This is not to suggest, however, that the phenomena discussed in this paper is exclusive to advanced industrial societies; many facets of strategic policy formulation within the military/governmental organisational nexus can be seen among the emergent and developing states of the world.

4. A useful and brief comment upon the varieties of goal-orientation to be found in organizations is contained in A. Etzioni, *Modern Organizations* (Englewood Cliffs, New Jersey: Prentice-Hall, 1964.) Chap. 5.

5. A cartographic exercise upon a country's defense community should mark the following terrain features: executive agencies, the legislature, executive agency-affiliated advisory organizations, non-affiliated advisory bodies, dependent industries, universities, the press, retired military officers and the attentive general public.

6. B. Brodie, 'The McNamara Phenomenon', *World Politics* vol. 17, No 4, July 1965, pp. 672-86; also W. Posvar, 'Dispersion of the Strategy-Making Establishment' in M. E. Smith III, and C. J. Johns Jnr (Eds.) *American Defense Policy* (Baltimore: Johns Hopkins Press, 1968) pp. 342.

7. An illuminating study of the retired military professional is A. D. Biderman's 'Sequels to a Military Career: The Retired Military Professional' in M. Janowitz. (ed) *The New Military: Changing Patterns of Organisation* (New York: John Wiley, 1967) pp. 287-336.

8. W. Posvar, Dispersion of the Strategy-making Establishment', op. cit. p. 341 contains a useful distinction between the strategy 'generalist' and 'specialist'.

9. Sensible comment can be found in H. E. Eccles, *Military Concepts and Philosophy* (New Brunswick, N.J: Rutgers University Press, 1965) pp. vi, 26-7.

10. For an argument that stresses the complimentary nature of the strategic theory/technology relationship, and which refuses to assign a pre-eminence of importance to one or the other, see H. Brown, 'Planning our military forces' *Foreign Affairs* vol. 45 no. 2 (Jan 1967) pp. 281-2.

11. See W. Millis, *Armies and Men* (New York: Mentor, 1958) pp. 231-2. A similar example would be the production by the British Chiefs of Staff of the *Global Strategy* paper of 1952, advising an increased emphasis upon nuclear deterrence: R. Rosecrance, *Defense of the Realm* (New York: Columbia University Press, 1968) chap. 6.

12. It may be argued, for example, that in the United States neither the atomic bomb nor the ballistic missile programs were initiated because of a profound concern by the military.

13. Davis, op. cit. chap. 4; A. J. Marder, *From Dreadnought to Scapa Flow*. vol. 1, *The Road to War 1904-1914*. (London: Oxford University Press, 1961) chap. 1.

14. Congressional testimony by TAC officers from 1953 until Jan 1961 was distinguished by its difference in doctrinal emphasis from the Air Force's 'mainstream' focus upon 'massive retaliation'.

15. For example the British Army's 'Khyber Pass syndrome' in L. W. Martin 'British Defence Policy: The long recessional' *Adelphi Papers* No. 61, (London: Institute for Strategic Studies, Nov 1969) p. 7. Or the 'preventive war syndrome' of the U.S. and British Air Forces, see B. Brodie, *Strategy in the Missile Age* (Princeton: Princeton University Press, 1965, first pub. 1959) chaps. 3, 4, and 7.

16. Colin Gray, 'The Defence Policies of the Eisenhower Administrations 1953-1961' (Unpublished doctoral thesis, Oxford University, 1970) Chap. 10.
17. L. W. Martin, *The Sea in Modern Strategy* (London: Chatto and Windus 1967).
18. In the process of intra-executive bargaining, the responsible negotiating officers of a military organization must have some fixed points of doctrinal reference. Note the excellent analysis by L. B. Tatum, 'The Joint Chiefs of Staff and Defence Policy Formulation' in Smith and Johns op. cit pp. 377-92.
19. See W. P. Snyder, 'Policy-oriented Research: Contractors and Advisers' in A. A. Jordan Jnr (ed.) *Issues of National Security in the 1970s* (New York: Praeger, 1967) pp. 269, 303.
20. On the functions of strategic theory, see Eccles op. cit. pp. vi and 26.
21. The educative utility of strategic ideas as important instruments in conflict within the defense establishment has been well illustrated by Hedley Bull in a discussion of the U.S. armed forces force levels and doctrines in the mid-1960s. H. Bull, 'The Scope for Soviet-American Agreement' in *Soviet-American Relations and World Order*, Adelphi Papers No. 65 (London: Institute for Strategic Studies, Feb 1970) pp. 5-6.
22. Examples of the career consequences of radical innovating activity within an apathetic military organisation are offered by Davis, op. cit. pp. 41-7. Davis's examples relate to narrow technical matters. A classic example of prominent and fatal (to the challenger) 'disloyalty' is offered in the Fisher-Beresford dispute over the composition and the deployment of the Royal Navy: see Marder, op. cit., chaps 5 and 7.
23. For example, the Op-23 activity by the U.S. Navy in 1949 relating to the controversy over the value of the Air Force's B-36. See Davis, op. cit. chap. 8
24. M. Howard, *The Central Organisation of Defence* (London: The Royal United Services Institution, Apr 1970) pp. 41-2.
25. Invaluable guidance on the socialization of the professional soldier has been provided by J. P. Lovell 'The Professional Socialization of the West Point Cadet' in Janotitz, op. cit. pp. 119-57.
26. See M. Janowitz, *The Professional Soldier* (New York: The Free Press. 1964) pp. 139-45.
27. Tatum, op. cit. pp. 389-90.
28. One need not go so far as to hold that the content of policy is influenced by the architecture of government buildings, but as a variation on this theme, there is little doubt that physical proximity to the Pentagon has been intended to militate against any secessionist tendencies in IDA. The U.S. /RAC contractual relationship reflects the Army's previous unhappy experiences with a group based on Johns Hopkins University, and also the lesson learnt from some of the Air Force's troubles with RAND.
29. For example, the situation in the British Ministry of Defence in the 1960s. Also note S. Huntington, 'Power, Expertise and the Military Profession', in Posvar op. cit. p. 189. and P. Nailor's contribution to this volume, 'The Military Bureaucracy: a Case Study of a Civilian Contribution'.
30. For example, the experts brought into the U.S. Department of Defense from the RAND Corporation in 1961 by Mr McNamara, and the experts brought in to serve under Professor Kissinger in the rejuvenated National Security Council structure.
31. See H. Kissinger, 'Bureaucracy and Policy Making: the effect of Insiders and Outsiders on the Policy Process' in H. Kissinger and B. Brodie

(eds) *Bureaucracy, Politics and Strategy* (Los Angeles: University of California, Security Studies Paper No. 17) particularly p. 3.

32. Useful comment is to be found in Posvar, op. cit. p. 344.

33. For examples, consider the divided military opinion on such projects and policies as: the deployment of aircraft carriers (see Davis, op. cit. chap. 3; of a strategic air arm, see J. M. Spaight, *Air Power in the Next War* (London: Geoffrey Bles, 1938) and R. Higham, *The Military Intellectuals in Britain* (New Brunswick, N.J.: Rutgers University Press, 1966, chaps 6–8) and of the development of armoured forces (see Liddell Hart, *Memoirs* 2 vols (London: Cassell, 1965).

34. This is to some extent reflected in the administrative divisions between the armed services in the form of departments for the army, navy and air force, and their strong resistance to the idea of a central organization for defense, during the 1940s and 50s. Even now, in both the Defense Department in the United States, and the Ministry of Defence in Britain, the procurement of advanced weapons systems for the armed services is still a separate service responsibility though provision for coordination and consultation has been improved. Procurement is still far from being an integrated service function.

35. In the Second World War the U.S. Army was rewarded for appearing to be more sympathetic to scientific advance by the award of the Manhattan Project.

36. For excellent case studies of inter-service conflict resulting from some very unwelcome disclosures, see P. Y. Hammond, 'Super Carriers and B-36 Bombers, Appropriations Strategy and Politics' in H. Stein, *American Civil-Military Decisions* (Birmingham: University of Alabama Press, 1963) pp. 467–567. Also M. Armacost, *The Politics of Weapons Innovation* (New York: Columbia University Press, 1969).

37. For example, see the U.S. Air Force denial of the validity of limited war theory; see U.S. Congress Senate, Committee on Appropriations, Subcommittee on the Department of Defense, *Department of Defense Appropriations, F.Y. 1958, Hearings: General Twining* (U.S. Government Printing Office, Washington, D.C. 85/1, 1957) p. 329.

38. At a strictly tactical level the story of the resistance by the U.S. Army to the AR15 (M16) rifle is instructive. See J. Tompkins, *The Weapons of World War III* (London: Robert Hale, 1967) pp. 122–8.

39. R. N. Ginsburgh, 'The challenge to military professionalism', *Foreign Affairs*, vol. 42, no. 2. (Jan 1964) pp. 258–9.

40. K. Lang, 'Technology and career management in the military establishment' in Janowitz, *The New Military*, op. cit. pp. 39–81.

41. This point has been made forcefully in S. Andrejewski, *Military Organisation and Society* (London: Routledge and Kegan Paul, 1968, first pub. 1954) p. 222.

42. This somewhat pejorative term has been employed in A. Rapoport, 'Introduction' to C. von Clausewitz *On War* (London: Penguin 1968, first pub. 1832) pp. 11–80.

43. One of the best illustrations of the political dangers to a state and the disruptive potential within a military organization posed by elite forces is to be found in a novel about *les paras*. See J. Larteguy, *The Lost Command* (London: Arrow, 1966).

44. Notes the title given by Schlesinger to the section of his book in which he discusses the impact of the new civilian strategists upon the Department of Defense: 'The occupation of the Pentagon', in *A Thousand Days* (London:

Andre Deutsch, 1965) pp. 283–7. See also M. Edmonds's introductory essay to this volume.

45. Informative discussion of public relations activity may be found in the following: S. Huntington, *The Common Defense* (New York: Columbia University Press, 1961) pp. 381–402; M. Janowitz, *The Professional Soldier* chaps 18–19.

46. Sharp criticism of 'threat analyses' may be found in W. Proxmire, *Report from Wasteland* (New York: Praeger, 1970) chap. 9.

7 Militia in the Seventies: A Conflict Paradigm

PHILIP S. KRONENBERG*

A Peacefare Alternative

The world has turned many times since John Dryden penned these words:

> The country rings around with loud alarms,
> And raw in fields the rude militia swarms;
> Mouths without hands; maintained at vast expense,
> In peace a change, in war a weak defense;
> Stout once a month they march, a blistering band,
> And ever, but in times of need, at hand;
> This was the morn when, issuing on the guard,
> Drawn up in rank and file they stood prepared
> Of seeming arms to make a short essay.
> Then hasten to be drunk, the business of the day.[1]

Similarly unflattering comments about militia forces have persisted to this day. My purpose is not to add to the debate on militia effectiveness, but to explore the opportunities the militia affords to experiment in 'peacefare' outside the traditional military role.

* Without creating accomplices, I wish to acknowledge with appreciation the critical reactions to an earlier draft by several colleagues at Indiana University, New York University, and Vanderbilt University.

The problems raised by domestic unrest at all levels are perplexing for citizens and public authorities alike. We can, however, improve our ability to cope with these problems by discriminating between the uses of state action for warfare and peacefare. Peacefare is defined herein as the organization and application of social resources by the state with the objectives of inreased social justice, the reduction of violence, and the development of harmonious social relationships, in the spirit evoked by Henry S. Kariel when he pointed to America's need to become alert to unfulfilled needs and underdeveloped capacities, to extend the sphere of the country, add to its diversity, enrich its public existence, and enlarge the range of *manageable* conflict.[2] Peacefare also includes government determination of peace policy and in judgments about peace strategy and tactics. Although the concept of peacefare is applicable to international relations, my focus is on the domestic condition.

Peacefare is a 'developmental construct' similar to Harold D. Lasswell's perception of the garrison state, a construct to aid the timing of inquiry and to stimulate 'both planned observation of the future and renewed interest in whatever past events are of greatest probable pertinence to the emerging future'.[3] It presumes a need for reducing domestic violence consistent with the norms of an open society, and the desirability of exploring the implications of peacefare in the operations of public instrumentalities like the militia.

Little serious thought has been given to peacefare. There has been only passing attention to the use of military or para-military formations for anything other than threat, repression and destruction. Coercive uses of state power may be necessary in dealing with internal and external threats. Options for peace other than state violence, however, should also be investigated.

Violent Disorder and Creative Conflict

Widespread violence and aggressive behaviour are characteristic of life in several nations, industrially advanced and developing. Labor strife, child abuse, disturbances in schools, slavery, organized crime, terrorism, racial violence, and civil and external warfare are all contemporary expressions of the inability of man to cope with conflict in non-violent ways.

Personal violence – between husband and wife, parent and child, citizen and criminal – is ubiquitous in our society, as is military confrontation between nations. Such manifestations of violence have been traditional features of the terrain of history. Large-scale collective violence that emerged during the 1960s in America in the form of civil disorder in our cities and university campuses, led to the establishment of several public inquiry groups, such as The National Advisory Commission on Civil Disorders, The National Commission on the Causes and Prevention of Violence, and The President's Commission on Campus Unrest. Although there is reason to question the relevance, quality of analysis, and influence of such commissions in helping to resolve the problems of violence,[4] they have reflected concern for large-scale violence. In Canada, Ireland, Uganda, West Germany, Britain and other places throughout the world, violence has also erupted.

Any assessment of the role of the militia in large-scale civil disturbances must be preceded by an examination of the political characteristics of such violence and implications for the operation of government. It has become popular among some public officials, especially law enforcement personnel, to refer to civil disorders as *criminal* disorders. While criminal acts may be committed during violent disorders, this fact may obscure the point that these disturbances are often profoundly political phenomena. Amidst the hatred, fear, criminality and exultation of a major disorder, one finds some critical issues being raised about the authoritative allocation of values in society – the political issues of who gets what, how, and why. The political nature of these disturbances allows the role of public instrumentalities such as the militia to be given some analytical perspective.

Public concern with violent disturbances focus on three groups of actors: students, urban poor, and economically insecure members of the working class. A torrent of analysis and opinion has been produced regarding these first two groups. The student revolt in 1964 at the University of California at Berkeley exemplifies the first group, and the 1965 riots in the Watts district of Los Angeles characterizes the second. Disturbances involving the third group of actors which do not concern trade union strife are more recent and have occurred much less frequently, e.g. the 'hard-hat' counter-demonstrations against anti-war protest demonstrations in New York City in 1970. The key to understanding the political characteristics of these three groups during disturbances is that they are all *marginal* participants in the American political process. There are, of course, many important socio-economic and political differences between the three groups. All share uncertainty in trying to participate in the political process. The nature of the uncertainty in these groups can be suggested by the observations of several commentators.

The student revolt at Berkeley was analyzed by Sheldon S. Wolin and John H. Schaar. Wolin and Schaar concluded that the students were insisting on the same political rights on campus that accrued to them as citizens off the campus and that the legality of off-campus actions of students should be judged by the courts rather than by the university administration. Students also were arguing that the university administration was justifying its denial of students' right to engage in political activity not involving the name of the university on the basis of constitutional provisions which were intended to protect the political neutrality of the university as an institution. Finally, the students felt the university administration had been quite arbitrary in the application of rules concerning the day-to-day conduct of students.[5]

H. Edward Ransford performed research on attitudes and participation by blacks during the Watts riots. Ransford found that blacks who were isolated or who had intense feelings of powerlessness and dissatisfaction were more likely to undertake violent action than those who were less alienated. Also, isolation had its greatest impact upon the tendency to violence when racial dissatisfaction was intense or when individuals felt powerless to control events in society.[6]

Michael M. Schneider, a white electrician with twenty years of experience on building-trades jobs, has commented on the frustration of the white working class in 'middle America'. He felt that much of the frustration of the white working class derives from rising prices and taxes. He also concluded that the draft was another source of anger for the white worker who sees his own sons drafted while draft-exempt college students demonstrated against institutions that he feels obliged to revere. 'These people want to be recognized, they want to be told that they exist, and not only as a negative force in American life. They are not happy, because they don't know what to do with their lives. They are fearful. The fear can produce fury in the absence of direction.'[7]

These several observations reveal aspects of the marginality and uncertainty of the political roles in the three groups which help explain their propensity for unrest and violence. (Although the vote is denied to many students, many dimensions of the political process germane to understanding violent disorder lie outside of the matter of voting.) The most critical aspects of the political process concern decisions about the ordering of norms or values, how and by whom such decisions will be made, and how scarce resources will be allocated in order to implement these decisions. The Berkeley, Watts, and 'middle America' illustrations suggest how marginal political participation involves a sense of alienation from the norms of the dominant community and second, a sense of powerlessness and frustration.

Many students reject the materialistic work norms of the adult middle class and find repugnant the conduct of a costly and protracted war in Indochina which they perceive to be without strategic and moral justification. They also find limited chances of having an influence on the political judgments made within the university or in broader jurisdictions. Poor blacks and browns in the central cities see racial discrimination of increasing visibility and find few opportunities to influence their social condition. Working-class citizens who accept the principal norms of the middle class find themselves absorbing more social and economic burdens with decreasing capacity to shape these decisions.

This growing alienation and powerlessness due to the marginal political roles of these citizens represents a basic challenge to the legitimacy of the dominant community and the institutions which sustain it. Their questioning of the legitimacy of middle- and upper middle-class America leads to the formation of alternative life-styles or counter-communities. These alternative relationships with the dominant community range in form from those involving apathy and disengagement from specific types of participation in the life of the society to general withdrawal of cooperation (as in some communal movements) to – at an extreme limit – violent hostility toward the dominant community. The point at which any given citizen would be located on this continuum appears to be a function of his feelings of frustration and dissatisfaction and the extent to which he feels threatened by economic, political and social conditions.

Inasmuch as the marginal and uncertain role of an individual in the political process shapes his propensity to engage in violent disorder, then a reduction in such propensity can occur only when he is both motivated and able to become integrated into *some* viable political community and to define with some certainty his political role in that community. *Motivation* implies that there must be opportunities for socialization to the norms and role definitions of alternative communities, presuming that socialization to middle-class norms is unacceptable. *Ability* implies the existence of viable alternative communities, whose existence implies conflict with the larger community. If the dominant community tolerates this conflict then the alienation and powerlessness felt by an individual will soon be replaced by effective political participation. There may be brief surges of what H. L. Nieburg calls 'frictional violence'[8] which quickly subside as grievances are forced by broadly legitimate state coercion into non-violent channels for successful resolution. 'Successful' here does not mean absorption or repression by the dominant community but resolution in which the emergent challenger can satisfy his principal political objectives without encountering prohibitive costs.

The ability to replace alienation and powerlessness with effective participation is a definition of political change. Toleration of appropriate levels of social conflict is therefore necessary for change. Lewis A. Coser has developed a number of propositions to support the notion that social conflict is useful: 'Our concern is mainly with the functions, rather than the dysfunctions, of social conflict, that is to say, with those consequences of social conflict which make for an increase rather than a decrease in the adaptation or adjustment of particular social relationships or groups.'[9]

The bitter violence found in any nation under such stress suggests an absence of the tolerance of graded levels of conflict that is required to accommodate demands for political change expressed by these social groups. Instead of frictional violence, these societies face what Nieburg has called 'political violence', an upward spiral of escalation and counter-escalation of violence.[10]

Three strategies appear open to political decision-makers in these cases: repression, decision-avoidance, or creative conflict. A repressive strategy by the state is hardly fitting in an open political system. Since repressive regimes tend to apply coercion indiscriminately, the numbers of those who would require repressing is usually too large to handle with this strategy beyond the very short term. A strategy of decision-avoidance in the hopes of the problem wearing itself down puts a heavy conflict burden on non-governmental institutions without providing them with the support of legitimate authoritative action.

Creative conflict is perhaps the only ultimately viable strategy in cases of growing violent disorder. It draws marginal participants into the political system by supporting their non-violent but authentic aggression through building alternative political communities which are distinctive but not separated from the rest of society. Such a strategy requires tolerance by public authorities of broader social conflict.

Public authorities seeking to avoid repression have frequently relied on decision-avoidance in the face of collective violence, often by misapplying rules to avoid recognition of the actual problem, as in the case of a university teaching assistant suspended from teaching duties on grounds of professional inadequacy when suspension is due to militant political activities. Decision-avoidance may also occur when decision-makers delegate discretion to low-level officials in order to avoid public controversy. This emphasis on decision-avoidance seems to be undergoing a gradual transformation in various parts of the world, reflected by a growing capability and conviction to use repressive measures by public authorities, matched to a degree by dissident groups' ability to counter-escalate.

It should be stressed that the creative conflict strategy is based on a judgment that reliance on the other two strategies is inappropriate (in contemporary disorder), i.e. creative conflict is presumed to have greater general social utility for the society. Specific situations may, of course, warrant coercive response. An individual about to blow up a classroom filled with students must be prevented from implementing his plan.

There are several methods for enlarging the capacity of public instrumentalities, including the militia, for creative conflict, first by organizing groups around the emergent norms of alternative communities. This will assist alienated citizens in acquiring access to groups which, while they reflect and support political norms other than those of the dominant middle-class community, provide greater identity and cohesion.

Second, the enhancement of access to political influence by these alternative communities improves the political bargaining position of these groups *vis-à-vis* important units in their environment and reduces the powerlessness of the participants. Without greater power these groups will always be in the position of supplicants in the political process.

Third, expanded tolerance by the dominant community of non-violent conflict, thus reducing the use of conflicting groups of violence as a means for handling differences.

Fourth, facilitating the communication of grievances from citizens to public officials in a position to correct the problems will improve the access of frustrated citizens and groups to effective solutions.

Fifth, non-violent confrontations can provide conflicting groups with experiences in constructive aggression. Since the aggressive exchange of authentic information about the sources of threat and frustration inhibits mutually fruitful bargaining, the outcome of constructive aggression is tension relief or catharsis and mutual goal change or adjustment of differences which prevented non-violent conflict resolution among groups.[11] These constructive aggression experiences could draw upon techniques developed in sensitivity training and in encounter and confrontation groups.[12]

Sixth, an emphasis on conflict management and problem-solving service to citizens, especially disadvantaged citizens, rather than the functions of law enforcement or conflict suppression would increase confidence among alienated citizens that such public agencies are a 'friend in court' who will not exploit their relative powerlessness or manipulate them on behalf of the interests of the dominant community.

Finally, recruiting personnel for public instrumentalities from groups with alternative political norms and socializing them to values of creative conflict and service to multiple political communities enhances the sensitivity of agencies to the problems and life styles of multiple communities, increasing the chance that alienated citizens will see these agencies as sources of help.

Militia And Civil Disorder

In the past half decade the United States, for example, experienced a rash of violent civil disorders across the land which strained the social and institutional fabric of the country. These disorders levied a heavy cost on human life and property. From 1965 to 1972 there were some two hundred disturbances responded to by public authorities, including the call-up of a quarter million National Guardsmen. In the two-week period between 5 and 20 April 1968 alone, following the murder of Dr Martin Luther King, Jr., over 120,000 National Guardsmen in twenty-five states were ordered to duty in response to civil disorder incidents or potential incidents.

During May 1970, following an announcement of the movement of an American military expeditionary force into Cambodia, a rash of campus disturbances spread across the country. National Guard units were called to active duty on twenty-four occasions at twenty-one universities in sixteen states.[13] At one of the universities, Kent State, several students were killed by Guardsmen during their attempt to quell the disturbances on that campus. The death of these students provoked widespread criticism of the National Guard and was a contributing factor to the establishment of the President's Commission on Campus Unrest in June 1970.

These numerous large-scale responses of National Guard units to civil disorder generally took the form of acting as a standby reserve force to supplement state and local police or, when directly committed, as an infantry formation engaged in clearing and securing streets. Whether serving as a deterrent or directly involved in crowd control or security patrol operations, the organization and doctrine of the Guard were clearly those of an infantry structure performing a military function.

The planning, equipment, and training of Guard units reflect this orientation toward the military function. The six-month basic training for Guardsmen is the same as that received by regular army personnel. Only military policemen in the Guards have received special civil disturbance training. When Guardsmen join their units following basic training, they receive only limited training for civil disturbance duty.[14] Up until the mid-1960s there was a very small amount of Guard training devoted to riot control or civil disorder. The main focus was on being prepared to react on a mobilization date to be available for combat duty in support of the regular army and air force. The object of training was tactical preparation for all field-type operations with almost no planning or training directed toward civil disorder. After the Detroit riot in 1967, thirty-three hours of riot control training were included into Guard programs. The next year saw the addition of twenty-four hours of unit training plus an increased amount of staff training for civil disturbances. Presently, about 30 per cent of Guard training at company and staff levels is on civil disorder, with the remaining 70 per cent devoted to training for mobilization for combat missions in federal service. The entire annual two-week Guard summer camp is spent in regular combat training.[15] Civil disorder training directives are issued by full-time Military Support to Civil Authorities Plans Officers assigned to each state adjutant general's office. These directives are based upon guidelines provided to each plans officer by his National Guard Bureau counterpart in the Pentagon. Commanders of the Guard units in each state may alter these training directives to emphasize certain aspects of particular importance to the mission of their units. But this is done on the premise that units will be deployed as infantry.[16]

The training doctrine and techniques used by the Guard are incorporated in the Civil Disturbance Orientation Course (SEADOC) conducted by the U.S. Army Military Police School at Fort Gordon,

Georgia. From the establishment of SEADOC in February 1968 through mid-1969, 971 senior Guard officers completed the course. The fifty-six classes conducted during this period also included several thousand civilian police and officials and other active and reserve military personnel who completed the four and a half day SEADOC program.[17]

The strong orientation of the Guard toward its combat military function even inhibits its ability to support and perform the police function during disturbances. Roger A. Beaumont argues that 'an armed force organized and equipped for ground combat is not an efficient mechanism for police activity.... Standards of police personnel selection, training, discipline, communications and operating rules are quite different from the army's. The amount of duplicate, heavy and expensive equipment designed for military field employment does not meet police needs.'[18] Beaumont calls for the consideration of alternatives that will allow the Guard to concentrate on its primary task of supporting the combat mission of the active army. It would appear that only military police units in the Guard are well prepared to perform the law enforcement activities of the police function.

This suggests that the use of the National Guard is appropriate only in circumstances where the suppression of domestic violence by infantry formations in indicated. At best, the use of the Guard for the police function is inefficient. There is also reason to conclude that the selective use of the Guard in a show of force may be useful when its presence may serve a deterrent function when violence threatens. This preventive role was successfully played by the Guard in New Haven in May 1970 according to the President's Commission on Campus Unrest.[19] But there is no basis to expect that the Guard would contribute to the successful application of the creative conflict strategy which was outlined in the preceding section, other than as a deterrent. As presently constituted, the Guard is an instrument of the repressive strategy. Its technology, structure and doctrine, rooted in the use of coercive force, are inconsistent with the criteria of creative conflict and the concept of peacefare.

A New Militia Concept

A new concept of the militia is needed to reorient it toward a peacefare function. Such a New Militia would require enlarging the militia's role to include implementation of the creative conflict strategy in addition to the traditional militia activities of emergency law enforcement and disaster relief. A New Militia concept could well entail abandonment by the militia of its traditional role as a reserve of the active armed forces.

Contemporary problems of social unrest call for a broadly based application of the creative conflict strategy by governmental jurisdictions. The implementation of this strategy would involve public instrumentalities in all three branches of government with responsibilities in public education, safety, health and welfare. A New Militia anticipates a central role for the state Guard forces in this endeavor. But why should the militia/Guard assume a leadership role instead of some other state agency? The answer lies in the traditional premises of the militia/Guard and in its relative advantages over two other alternatives: incorporation of the creative conflict strategy into the mission of an existing agency, or creation of a new agency to implement the strategy.

The image of the militia conveyed by National Guardsmen shooting down unarmed students at Kent State University in May 1970 is misleading. That tragic event was more a statement about the poor training and fire discipline of those particular Guardsmen than it was an accurate reflection of the traditional service premises of the militia. The determination of community goals, their implementation, and the management of conflict generated by those goals have traditionally been the responsibility of local government in the United States, with state government in a supporting role. The traditional premise of the state militia has been to supplement the efforts of local government to manage social conflict and maintain the orderly conduct of community affairs when their disruption was threatened. At the core of this premise is the idea embodied in the Constitution that state government will organize a militia of local citizens and resources from local communities. These militia units are expected to come to the aid of their particular communites in the event of conflict or of a breakdown of essential public services. Thus, the *raison d'être* of the militia has not been to perform military or police services *per se*. Rather, the militia has been intended to perform extraordinary community service on behalf of the maintenance of order and the management of conflict.

Over the years, the form in which these extraordinary community services were performed tended to emphasize reliance on physical enforcement of order. The forerunner of the militia in ninth-century England alternated between military defense against invading Danes and service in the shire as a *posse comitatus* in enforcing local customs, traditions and law. Jim Dan Hill comments on the role of the Volunteer Militia during the American colonial period:

> Everyone knew they were there, prepared to respond to any emergency, be it to aid the volunteer fire brigade; to provide flood relief; to assist the police in law enforcement; to man the harbor forts against pirates or other raiders from the sea; or to march or ride, if on the forest frontier, to drive Indians from a beleaguered settlement.[20]

The militia was a decisive element in achieving victory for the rebels under George Washington against the British Crown.[21] The American Civil War and the two World Wars reinforced and sharpened the military dimensions of the militia's role. By the mid-twentieth century the core commitment to broader community service remained a recurring feature of the militia. Bennet M. Rich and Philip H. Burch, Jr., in a study published in the mid-1950s, argued that the domestic role of the National Guard had undergone a subtle but radical transformation in the preceding ten years. While acknowledging the continuing law enforcement mission of the Guard, they concluded that 'the policing function has been progressively overshadowed by the development of the state military bodies as community service organizations'.[22] This community service orientation involved a shift from the emphasis on patrol duty to more extensive participation in disaster relief activities. Rich and Burch found that this shift toward community service was quite satisfying to the Guard's self-image.

Militia in the Seventies: a Conflict Paradigm

This sort of record of community service in recent years is an important factor in the increased prestige which the Guard has come to enjoy. The role of the individual members has been in large measure reversed. Guardsmen now are called upon principally to help their neighbors, in marked contrast with their former all-too-frequent duty of being arrayed, in battle garb, against the people of their own communities.[23]

State agencies that are currently existing offer the advantage of having relatively established bases of political, economic, and clientele support for their programs. But these bases of support represent a substantial weakness in terms of an innovation like creative conflict. Established bases of support imply obligations for these agencies to give priority to certain goals and strategies for their implementation to the exclusion of other goals and implementation strategies. The more stable and successful an agency is, the more disinclined it is to adopt innovations. Personnel within a successful agency as well as outsiders who receive its services or support its programs have commitments to its current purposes and modes of doing business. They are reluctant to introduce innovations into agency programs unless they are dissatisfied with the way the agency is functioning.[24] Another major inhibition on innovation in existing agencies is their tendency to develop rather persistent specialized notions of their goals and the nature and identity of their clientele with which they routinely interact. For example, urban police departments have had difficulty in achieving success in their community relations programs with inner-city youth. The specialized orientation of police agencies to criminal investigations and law enforcement tends to promote the use of these programs for acquiring criminal intelligence on youth gangs. This tendency undermines the initial objectives of these programs to develop respect for law and reduce gang violence.[25] Only in an agency free of such dominant commitments is it likely that creative conflict goals could be insulated from co-optation from within the agency.

New agencies are free from most of the entrenched commitments to means and ends that characterize existing agencies. They could choose to pursue an innovative program strategy like creative conflict. But the virtue in adopting an innovation appears as a shortcoming when viewed from the perspective of implementation. New agencies rarely begin life with political and economic foundations necessary to support their goal aspirations.[26] A new agency might build support by defining its goals and the nature of its clientele narrowly. In this way it would endeavor to become a protector of this special interest and, assuming that it faced little competition over clientele, could draw rather quickly upon the backing of its natural allies. The problem with this narrow approach is that, even if it did not compete with other public agencies concerned with students or workers or the urban poor, a specialized focus on, say, student affairs, would force it to ignore the other problematic groups contemplated by the broad terms of the creative conflict strategy. A second approach available to a new agency is to assume a creative conflict responsibility *vis-à-vis* all three groups. While more satisfactory than a specialized focus in terms of the clientele premises of creative conflict, it would place a new agency in stiff competition with a number of established agencies concerned with education, welfare, labor and urban programs.

The strategy of creative conflict is sufficiently innovative when compared with the orthodox program assumptions of most public agencies that its implementation requires nourishment in the form of distinctive institutional arrangements. The creation of a new agency or the grafting of creative conflict premises onto the commitments of existing agencies pose major problems. The militia, while no panacea, offers several relative advantages. First, the militia draws on a strong base of public legitimacy that is above partisan political considerations due to its traditional community service orientation and its identification with patriotic and community symbols. Second, in many countries it is a multi-purpose organization which comprehends such diverse activities as law enforement, relief in major natural disasters, mercy flights, search for lost or marooned persons, and holiday traffic control. It generates substantial economies of scale due to the size of its operation. This multi-functionality more readily accommodates innovation than is possible in more specialized agencies. Third, the militia includes an impressive array of different manpower skills due to myriad operational tasks – the variety of civilian professional, managerial, and technical skills that its largely part-time personnel bring to their militia duties. Fourth, unlike orthodox civilian agencies, the military style of discipline in the militia increases the probability that program innovations will be enforced. This was the experience when the active army initiated racial integration in the late 1940s.[27] Fifth, the militia has a large volunteer manpower pool of part-time participants, a relatively low-cost manpower resource available to state and local communities. Since its members are engaged in civilian occupations, the character of the militia is rooted in public-service volunteerism based on citizen participation.

Reconstituting the militia as a peacefare force involves two major organizational revisions: (1) separation into two components: national reserve and state militia; and (2) subsequent reorganization of the militia component into security units, disaster relief units, and Ombudsman units.

The separation of the United States militia, the National Guard, into a national reserve and a state militia has precedent in the historical debate surrounding the role of the Guard. The dual federal-state role of the Guard has been an important factor in the political survival of the National Guard but has seemed to contribute little to its effectiveness as a combat-ready reserve force. The assignment of parts of the Guard to a national reserve force, together with the present reserve forces of the several military services, would add to the integrity of the federal preparedness mission of all military reserve forces and complete the drift of the National Guard toward federal control.[28]

The retention of a part of the present Guard membership in state militia units would allow state governments to give priority to natural disasters and civil disturbances. This would reduce the deployment of forces trained primarily for combat operations and allow the new state militia to consider means of disorder control more appropriate for dealing with *citizens* and to specialize in techniques for creative conflict resolution.

The new state militia would consist of the three basic types of operational units under the general direction of the state adjutant general (see figure). Security units would perform basic military

126 *War in the Next Decade*

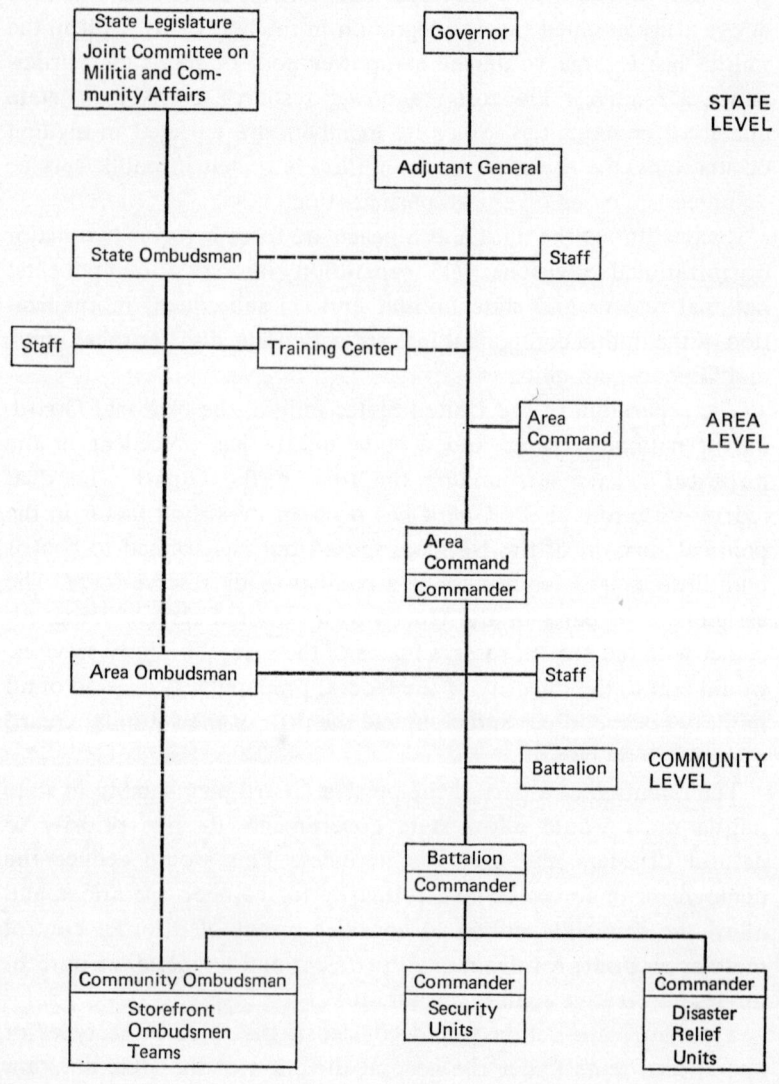

police functions and would be armed, equipped, and trained to apply coercive force to suppress violent disorders in support of local authorities and the state police. These units would be issued protective equipment, non-lethal weapons for crowd control, and sidearms. Anti-sniper teams would be established in each unit with appropriate equipment; shoulder and automatic weapons would not be issued routinely to security unit personnel. Their primary mission of disorder control would be guided by doctrine developed by the U.S. army. The secondary mission of security units would be to support the operations of disaster relief units.

Disaster relief units would be primarily engineering, heavy equipment, medical, and food services organizations trained and equipped to cope with floods, earthquakes, gas explosions and similar conditions; to restore essential public facilities; and to provide relief actions for victims of such disasters. They would have a secondary mission to provide engineering upport to security units and handle refugee or relocation problems in the event of a major civil disturbance.

The primary peacefare innovation in the new state militia is the Ombudsmen unit. These units would serve as bases for implementing the creative conflict strategy in local communities. The basic operational unit is the Ombudsman team working out of a storefront office in the local community. The several teams in a community would be under the supervision of the Community Ombudsman. Storefront offices would be located in sections of the community where clientele (students, urban poor, laborers) live or work with the expectation that teams would specialize on one of the clientele groups in larger communities.

The purpose of the Ombudsman teams are to identify and resolve grievances, improve the performances and equity of governmental administration, and enhance legislative oversight of governmental programs, all in support of the creative conflict strategy. There are three general types of problem with which the Ombudsmen will deal: citizen grievances caused by the exercise of lawful discretion by public officials; grievances prompted by the actions of officials which go beyond what lawful policies authorize or should reasonably be interpreted as authorizing; and complaints to the failure of public agencies to deliver services which citizens have a lawful right to expect.[29] The methods for performing the Ombudsman function include the organization of sensitivity training and encounter groups for joint sessions among complaining citizens, leaders of clientele groups, and public officials; and the conduct of impartial investigation, followed by negotiation and, where required, publication of findings in some public medium.[30]

The structure of the militia is organized into state, area, and community levels, as depicted on page 126. Recruitment, appointment, command authority, and the reporting function for units other than Ombudsman conform to traditional militia practice. Appointment of the state Ombudsman is done by selection by a Joint Committee on Militia and Community Affairs from a register of nominees proposed by the governor. (In addition to its characteristic legislative role, the Joint Committee determines policy for Ombudsmen units.) The state Ombudsman nominates area Ombudsmen candidates who are then appointed by the several area commanders who are responsible for militia activities in the principal regions of the state. Area Ombudsmen nominate a register of Ombudsmen for the community level; battalion commanders make the appointments from this register. The selection of community Ombudsmen and of battalion commanders and subordinate officers of security and disaster relief units are to be made on the basis of elections conducted by the personnel in each respective command. This practice contributes to the democratic and voluntaristic ethic of the militia and is consistent with its historical custom of popular election of officers. Recruitment of personnel into Ombudsmen units would draw upon professionals and pre-professionals from, among others, the law, psychiatry, clinical psychology, social work, the community organization field, and the clergy. The exercise of command authority and coordination over Ombudsmen at each level would be the responsibility of unit commanders. Ombudsmen would be accountable to unit commanders for their activities, subject to the proviso that no unit commander can direct an Ombudsman to act in contradiction to the operating policies enunciated by the state Ombudsman. Ombudsmen make reports of their activities directly to area and state Ombudsmen. The state Ombudsman would make periodic reports to the Joint Committee on Militia and Community Affairs along with his recommendations for action by the state legislature. The state Ombudsman would organize a state-wide training center for personnel in Ombudsmen units.

This essay may seem to some to be an exercise in social science fiction. But the need for non-violent management of social conflict is of such compelling urgency that we must be willing to speculate about alternative futures and means to those futures, even though they may transcend the *art of the possible*, as currently defined.

The New Militia Concept matches the criteria suggested for use of the creative conflict strategy. The Ombudsmen units, with a broad mandate to investigate, report, and draw contesting parties into potentially fruitful confrontations, involving constructive aggression, together with their direct access to the legislative institution, could stimulate the formation of alternative communities and improve their effectiveness in the political bargaining process. Abuses of power within and outside of government would be made visible and increase the probability that the political disadvantaged will not have to bear their legitimate grievances as mere supplicants to the powerful. They will have a non-manipulative friend in court who can insure that their complaints are carried even beyond the executive mansion. How would the tolerance of the dominant community for non-violent conflict be increased? It would require an act of faith by both dominant and alternative communities. As in the criterion concerning representative recruitment policy, success will depend upon the quality of skills and the nature of commitments brought to these tasks by the people who operate the new militia. It will also require a major effort by the militia to educate the public about the implications of peacefare and creative conflict.

The problems of implementing the New Militia Concept are substantial. First, the storefront Ombudsmen offer a seductive tool of manipulation to the elites of the dominant political community. The relationship between the legislature and the Ombudsmen units help reduce this problem but it is not eliminated. Paul Dolan correctly points to the problem of 'pseudo-Ombudsmen', Ombudsmen whose effectiveness is limited either because his office has been used as a means to protect the executive's political position and image in the community or because he was viewed as an 'interloper in the executive-legislative relationship'.[31] Second, there is the likelihood that the Guard and its lobby, the National Guard Association, would mount a fierce attack on any efforts to strip the militia of its visible military function and its legislatively mandated claim to be 'an integral part of the first line defense of the United States'.[32] The Guard has long defended itself against incorporation into the reserve components of the active armed forces without the protections of federal-state dualism. But the present realities of dominant federal influence might ease the effort to wean the Guard from its state roots. The extent to which individual Guardsmen could exercise discretion in deciding whether to transfer into the federal reserves or remain in the new state militia would have a strong bearing on the intensity of resistance. Third, there is the danger that the more traditionally oriented security and disaster relief units under the new system might co-opt and undermine the creative conflict function of Ombudsmen units. The ties of the latter units with the legislature could ease this problem. But the outcome would rest rather heavily on the composition of the proposed Joint Committee on Militia and Community Affairs. Fourth, the Ombudsmen units will be faced continuously with the possibility of co-optation by the citizen groups with which they interact. Indeed, a degree of reciprocal co-optation is an essential factor in building the minimum bonds of trust between the militia and its multiple clientele. The danger is that cynical leaders will exploit the co-optation process and compromise the constructive payoffs of creative conflict. These exploitative tendencies are as likely to occur within the militia as in the clientele groups. Fifth, can authority patterns which are military in origin actually be made to accommodate the style of the New Militia Concept? The corporate bureaucracy of the military profession is rooted deeply in the need to sustain the dignity of the profession of arms and to operate on the basis of discipline and predictability. One hopeful indicator is the changing pattern of military authority which Morris Janowitz cites.[33] His conclusion that the use of entrepreneurial and manipulative social skills in the officer corps has been growing is supportive of the operative style of the new militia, especially in Ombudsmen units. Finally, how will the operations of the new state militia be financed? Even with substantial reliance on unpaid volunteers, the personnel and equipment costs of the new militia will surely exceed the contribution which the states make to the current operations of the National Guard. The growing disposition of the federal government to redistribute tax revenues back to the states is an encouraging sign.

RESEARCH SUGGESTIONS

Each of the problems of implementing the peacefare function and the New Militia Concept imply several important research problems. Several beyond these can be suggested.

(1) There may be great merit in ending the traditional use of the military garb and other symbols of force and repressive authority under a New Militia Concept. Research into the effects of symbolic innovations would be useful.

(2) We know very little about the political attitudes and activities of attitudes towards minority groups and social innovation warrants study.

(3) Much of the activity anticipated by the New Militia Concept involves interacting clusters of organizations. At present we have only modest theoretical grounds of predicting patterns of interorganizational behavior. Further conceptual development is called for in this area.

(4) Related to the proposed strategy of creative conflict is what Arthur I. Waskow calls 'controlled creative disorder'.[34] The development of new methods to foster creative conflict which move beyond the present capabilities of sensitivity training and encounter techniques is appropriate and calls for further study.

(5) The activities of Ombudsmen units will be very stressful in social-psychological terms. We need further research on the limits to which conflict and ambiguity can be tolerated and utilized for useful social purposes.

NOTES TO CHAPTER 7

1. John Dryden, 'Cymon and Iphigenia', in C. H. Herford (ed) *English Tales in Verse* (London: Blackie, 1902) p. 134.
2. Henry S. Kariel, comment in 'Responses to the Idea of a New Constitution', *The Centre Magazine*, III (Nov/Dec 1970) 6, p. 77.

3. Harold D. Lasswell, 'The Garrison State', *American Journal of Sociology*, XLVI (Jan 1941) pp. 455–68.
4. Michael Lipsky and David J. Olson assess the limitations of riot commissions in 'Riot Commission Politics', *Trans-action*, VI (Jul/Aug 1969) 9, 9–19.
5. Sheldon S. Wolin and John H. Schaar, 'The Abuses of the Muliversity', in Seymour Martin Lipset and Sheldon S. Wolin (eds) *The Berkeley Student Revolt* (Garden City, N.Y.: Doubleday Anchor Books, 1965) p. 352.
6. H. Edward Ransford, 'Isolation, Powerlessness, and Violence: A Study of Attitudes and Participation in the Watts Riot', *American Journal of Sociology*, LXXIII (1968), pp. 581–91.
7. Michael M. Schneider, 'Middle America: Study in Frustration', *The Center Magazine*, III (Nov/Dec 1970) 6, pp. 2–3.
8. H. L. Nieburg, *Political Violence: The Behavioral Process* (New York: St Martin's Press, 1969) p. 134.
9. Lewis A. Coser, *The Functions of Social Conflict* (Glencoe, Ill.: The Free Press, 1956) p. 8.
10. Nieburg, *Political Violence*, p. 135.
11. This concept of constructive aggression is based on a modification of Bach's impact theory of aggression which he developed from his research on conflict in intimate dyads. See his 'The Impact Theory of Aggression: A Conceptual and Semantic Clarification', in George R. Bach and Peter Wyden, *The Intimate Enemy* (New York: Avon Books, 1968) pp. 364–9.
12. Several relevant sources are: Arthur Burton (ed.) *Encounter: The Theory and Practice of Encounter Groups* (San Francisco: Jossey-Bass, Inc., 1970); Erving Goffman, *Interaction Ritual* (Garden City, N.Y.: Doubleday Anchor Books, 1967); and Paul R. Lawrence and Jay W. Lorsch, *Developing Organizations: Diagnosis and Action* (Reading, Mass.: Addison-Wesley, 1969).
13. *Report of the President's Commission on Campus Unrest* (New York: Commerce Clearing House, Inc., College and University Reports, No. 277, Sep 29, 1970), pp. 5–43.
14. Ibid., pp. 5–44.
15. Ibid.
16. Philip S. Kronenberg, Organizational Response to Civil Disorder'. (Bloomington Ind.: Department of Political Science, Indiana University, 1 May 1970 (mimeographed) pp. 61–2.
17. Thomas E. O'Malley and Donald A. Lund, 'SEADOC: An Overview', *Military Police Journal*, XX (Oct 1970) pp. 4–10.
18. Roger A. Beaumont, 'Must the Guard Be a Police Force?', *Army* (Sep 1970) pp. 35–7.
19. *Report of the President's Commission*, op. cit. pp. 5–52.
20. Jim Dan Hill, 'The National Guard in Civil Disorders: Historical Precedents', in Robin Higham (ed.) *Bayonets in the Streets* (Lawrence, Kans.: The University Press of Kansas, 1969) p. 65.
21. Walter Millis, *Arms and Men* (New York: Mentor Books, 1956) p. 30.
22. Bennet M. Rich and Philip H. Burch, Jr, 'The Changing Role of the National Guard', *American Political Science Review*, L (Sep 1956) p. 702.
23. Ibid. p. 705.
24. James G. March and Herbert A. Simon, *Organizations* (New York: Wiley, 1958) chap. 7.
25. Kronenberg, op. cit., p. 31.

26. Truman points to the problem of 'unadministerable' programs: programs that lack the support of potential clientele and interest groups which are pushed through Congress by the president, but which then atrophy in their implementation when the president dies, leaves office, or otherwise turns his attention to other priorities. David B. Truman, *The Governmental Process* (New York: Alfred A. Knopf, 1951) pp. 441–2.

27. Richard J. Stillman, II, *Integration of the Negro in the U.S. Armed Forces* (New York: Praeger, 1968) chap. 3.

28. Derthick points to the dramatic shift in the size and financial support of the Guard in the 1930s, when it was larger than the active army with the states paying for one-third of its support, and indicates the changes manifested in the early 1960s: 'Thirty years later, following the enormous growth of the United States military force during the Cold War, the role of the states in national defense was unimportant. The National Guard constituted a small portion of the total of United States military manpower. The active army and air force included 1,934,000 men, the army and air guard only 450,000. The states' share of support of the National Guard had dwindled to about 6 per cent. Armory maintenance and their share (25 per cent) of the cost of new armories are the only substantial functions with respect to the Guard that remain in financial responsibility of the states. Even though the federal government provides the Guard with a far larger share of its support than ever before, expenditures for the Guard have become a small share of total federal expenditures for military purposes. . . . As of 1963, when the federal share of Guard support was over 90 per cent, expenditures for the Guard ($683,600,000) were only 4 per cent of all army and air force expenditures for personnel and operation and maintenance, and as a share of the total military budget, they were insignificant. The Guard, in brief, has been transformed from the largest military force in the country – in principle the mainstay of United States military strength – into a relatively small force, of peripheral significance.' Martha Derthick, *The National Guard in Politics* (Cambridge, Mass.: Harvard University Press, 1965) pp. 109–10.

29. Geoffrey Sawer, *Ombudsmen* (Carlton, Australia: Melbourne University Press, 1964) pp. 3–4.

30. These last three methods are proposed by John Carey of New York University School of Law. Referenced in Stanley V. Anderson, *Ombudsman Papers: American Experience and Proposals* (Berkeley, Calif.: Institute of Governmental Studies, University of California, 1969) p. 1.

31. Paul Dolan, 'Pseudo-Ombudsmen', *National Civic Review*, LVIII (July 1969) pp. 298, 306.

32. Derthick, op. cit., p. 171.

33. Morris Janowitz, 'Changing Patterns of Organizational Authority: The Military Establishment', *Administrative Science Quarterly*, III (March 1959) pp. 473–93.

34. Arthur I. Waskow, *From Race Riot to Sit-In* (Garden City, N.Y.: Doubleday Anchor Books, 1967) p. 288.

SELECTED BIBLIOGRAPHY

Rex Applegate, *Riot Control—Material and Techniques* (Harrisburg: The Stackpole Company, 1969).

R. Beckhard, *Organization Development: Strategies and Models* (Addison-Wesley, 1969).

W. G. Bennis, *Organization Development: Its Nature, Origins, and Prospects* (Addison-Wesley, 1969).

W. G. Bennis, K. D. Benne, and R. Chin, *The Planning of Change*, 2nd ed. (New York: Holt, Rinehart and Winston, 1969).

A. Burton (ed.), *Encounter: The Theory and Practice of Encounter Groups* (San Francisco: Jossey-Bass, 1970).

M. Derthick, *The National Guard in Politics* (Cambridge, Mass.: Harvard University Press, 1965).

Hearings before Special Subcommittee to Inquire into the Capability of the National Guard to Cope with Civil Disturbances, August 10, 11, 15, 22, 23, 24, 25, and October 3, 1967 (Washington: U.S. Government Printing Office, 1967).

Robin Higham, *Bayonets in the Streets: The use of Troops in Civil Disturbances* (University Press of Kansas, 1969).

P. R. Lawrence and J. W. Lorsch. *Developing Organizations: Diagnosis and Action* (Addison-Wesley, 1969).

Priscilla Long (ed.), *The New Left: A Collection of Essays* (F. Porter Sargent, 1969).

W. Millis, *Arms and Men* (Mentor Books, 1956).

W. H. Riker, *Soliders of the States* (Washington, D.C.: Public Affairs Press, 1957).

Geoffrey Sawer, *Ombudsmen* (Melbourne: Melbourne University Press, 1968).

Willian G. Scott. *The Management of Conflict: Appeal Systems in Organizations* (Richard D. Irwin, 1965).

J. G. Starke, *An Introduction to the Science of Peace (Irenology)* (Leyden: A. W. Sijthoff, 1968).

The Report of the President's Commission on Campus Unrest. College and University Reports, Number 277, 29 September 1970 (Commerce Clearing House, 1970).

The Report of the National Advisory Commission on Civil Disorders (Washington: U.S. Government Printing Office, 1968).

U.S. Department of the Army, *Civil Disturbances and Disasters* (Washington, D.C.: March 1968).

R. E. Walton, *Interpersonal Peacemaking: Confrontations and Third-Party Consultations* (Addison-Wesley, 1969).

Arthur I. Waskow, *From Race Riot to Sit-In* (New York: Doubleday, 1966).

8 The Burgeoning Arsenal: Developments and Projections

ROBERT SNOWDEN FICKS

'The means of destruction are approaching perfection with frightful rapidity' Jomini, *Précis de l'Art de la Guerre* (1838).

Throughout history technology has been a factor in the equation of warfare, providing the tools of combat, altering and introducing new tactics and strategies, and together with politics creating new forms of war. Until the United States Civil War, the pace of technology, like that of civilization, had been gradual. The most revolutionary development of that time, gunpowder, took centuries to grow from a curiosity to an essential component of an effective weapon. After 1750 the pace changed, man's ability to wage war on a broad scale increased rapidly and military technology grew more in the years from the Civil War to the Second World War than it had from pre-history to 1860. Since the end of the Second World War, military technology has continued to develop in a new third quantum. Since future wars will be conflicts of opposing ideologically guided technologies, it must be pointed out that while this chapter deals primarily with weapons, the total scope of military technology is infinitely broader, ranging from the 'nuts and bolts' of weapons and equipment to organization structure, computer design, communications and transportation. Because of the sheer mass of the subject and the blurring effects of secrecy, recent developments in various areas of weapons will be treated selectively.

The Assault Rifle and Beyond

Today the world standard in individual combat arms is the assault rifle. Whether it is designated M–16, AK–47 or CETME, it is essentially an assault rifle, a shoulder weapon whose configuration and design permit its user to deliver a massive volume of fire. The days of 'well-aimed rounds' have been replaced with the doctrine of massive, suppressing fire and the assault rifle is the tool.

The first true assault rifle was produced in Germany toward the end of the Second World War. Designated the MP–44, this weapon was just starting to appear on the Eastern and Western fronts as the war came to an end. Soviet forces captured large stocks of the rifle, placed it in use and copied its engineering for their subsequent family of assault rifles.

For the decade of the 1970s, it seems likely that the assault rifle will continue its role of small arms preeminence, but programs have been initiated in the United States armed forces and in other military establishments to seek a replacement.

Modifications to the assault rifle in the near future will probably include such features as burst-limiters and a single-point sighting system. The burst-limiter is a modification to the weapon's action allowing only a predetermined number of rounds to be discharged with each squeeze of the trigger, to conserve ammunition and improve the balance between suppressive fire and marksmanship. Such a mechanism was first seen on a forerunner of the assault rifle, an Italian automatic rifle designated the Breda PG, manufactured in 1935. Such devices, set for somewhat greater bursts, are also being installed on certain rapid-fire guns mounted on aircraft to conserve the relatively small supply of ammunition they carry.

The single-point sighting system is a device invented by a Nils Ruder of Sweden and is being manufactured by Singlepoint Ltd of Great Britain. Currently being tested by a number of armed forces as a replacement for traditional iron sight, the single-point sight produces a small point of light within its cylinder mounted over the rifle's receiver. One eye of the shooter looks at the point of light which seems to appear at infinity while the other eye looks at the target. With the natural process of binocular vision the brain sees

The Burgeoning Arsenal: Developments and Projections   137

the image of the light source superimposed on the target. Evaluations of this device show it to be effective for both day and night firing and on a variety of infantry weapons.

Beyond this generation of shoulder arms are a number of emerging possibilities. The traditional bullet might be replaced with what is called a flechette, a barbed projectile approximately one inch long with the diameter of a pencil lead. A weapon that fires the flechette, designated the SPIW (special purpose individual weapon), has been tested by the United States army.

It is also possible that small arms of the future may be rocket launchers, firing small missiles. The development of caseless ammunition by the U.S. firm of Smith & Wesson points in this direction. With this system, the propellant is affixed to the base of the bullet and fired by an electrical charge.

Even farther down the road of weapons development is the use of individual portable lasers. Experiments are currently taking place to develop these high-intensity coherent light producers, already in field use as range-finders, into a 'death ray' type of weapon. At the U.S. air force weapons laboratory, Kirtland Air Force Base, New Mexico, at ranges in excess of 150 yards, armor has been penetrated and flying drones have been shot down with the use of laser devices. Other refinements have been anticipated in strategic counter-missile roles.

Artillery

Napoleon I once said, 'It is with artillery that war is made.' Artillery has been consistently the greatest producer of casualties in war since it became a serious weapon. Artillery's history can be traced back to pre-gunpowder days, to its forerunners, such siege machines as the onager, trebuchet, ballista, catapult, *et al.* It is not known when the first primitive gunpowder cannons were made, but the earliest documented account of their use in action comes at the Battle of Crecy in 1346. The British employed small wooden cannons against the French forces with no effect except shock.

Today's artillery has much more than shock value and despite some disparaging post-Second World War remarks about it being made obsolete with the advent and proliferation of missiles, it has continued to be an important tool of war. Artillery offers levels of accuracy, reliability, ruggedness and economy that no other mass strike weapon can.

In the early 1950s, nuclear artillery shells were developed for the specially designed United States 280 mm 'Atomic Cannon' (T131) and the existing 8-inch howitzer. A nuclear round was made available for the 155 mm howitzer in 1963 and more recently for the 105 mm howitzer. The Soviet Union has also done work on small tactical nuclear weapons and has such rounds available for its standard artillery pieces.

Additional work on artillery ammunition has yielded self-consuming casings. That portion of the round that remains after firing is made out of material that would burn up as the charge is fired. Such an arrangement is extremely efficient and lightens the overall weight of the round.

A special projectile has been developed and used by the United States forces in South-East Asia to defend artillery positions. The round is packed with thousands of flechettes (small barbed arrowlike projectiles), the number varying with shell size. When fired, it fills the air with the flechettes, with grisly thoroughness.

Increase in range is another area of development. The Germans did work in the Second World War on large caliber rocket-assisted artillery rounds with the idea of increasing the effective range of their artillery. The Russians captured much of this work at the end of the war and it can be assumed that they have continued to advance the idea. In the same vein, a joint United States and Canadian project of recent years, called HARP (high altitude research project), has proved the concept of the assisted round capable of shooting objects into earths orbit. Using old 16-inch naval rifles and other tubes down to the size of the 120 mm tank gun, remarkable ranges have been achieved. The barrels are bored smooth so that the lands and groves of the rifling do not impede the velocity of the projectile. When the initial velocity, imparted by the gun's charge, weakens, the sabot* which surrounds the projectile

---

* A surrounding jacket that makes the projectile conform to the diameter of the gun's bore.

falls away and the rocket motor ignites. Altitudes of 125 miles have been reached with this system and implications for practical weapons development are several. A weapon based on this concept would be cheaper and less complicated than any missile with comparable range and would provide excellent accuracy with a high volume of fire.

Similar to the HARP idea is a project being worked on by the United States army. The DICORAP (directional control rocket projectile) program involves the firing of a small missile with a sophisticated internal guidance system from a conventional artillery piece. The existing prototype missile in this program is the 105 mm.

New designs of artillery pieces themselves have also appeared in the past decade in several countries. The desire to make the equipment easier to handle and air-mobile has led to the development of lighter pieces such as the U.S. M102, a 105 mm howitzer which makes liberal use of aluminum and alloys in its construction, as well as the Italian-designed NATO light 105.

The most revolutionary development in the design of artillery is the U.S. army FOOB (firing out of battery) project, in which the recoil process is reversed. In principle the system functions by an accelerating force being applied in the direction of firing to the recoil mechanism. When the desired velocity is reached, firing occurs, returning the tube to its original position, cocked and its spring re-energized. Weapons utilizing this system will be extremely mobile and much reduced in weight due to the elimination of the conventional hydropneumatic recoil mechanism, FOOB also offers the possibilities of higher rates of fire, faster 'time on target' (T.O.T.) and improved accuracy. Currently tests are being conducted on a 105 mm prototype, but larger caliber configurations are projected.

Tanks

References to 'chariots of iron' can be found in the Book of Judges and the twelfth-century Chinese developed chariots covered with leather for warfare. Not inappropriately, Leonardo da Vinci proposed a fighting vehicle whose appearance strongly resembled a coolie hat and Voltaire suggested armored horse-drawn wagons to be used to fight the Prussians.

It was not until the First World War that an effective machine-driven armored fighting vehicle appeared. While British and French tanks might have been much more decisive in that conflict, there was a great deal of reluctance to accept them. In the Second World War the tank finally came of age as a tool of war, with the Germans bringing the state of the art to a very high level.

The future of tanks as an effective battlefield weapon is assured for the same reasons that they became a major force in ground combat: mobility, great shock effect, massive fire power and a high level of survivability.

This last quality has taken on special importance with the advent of tactical nuclear weapons. Tanks and other armored vehicles, such as personnel carriers, can operate on the nuclear battlefield providing a relatively high level of protection from both blast and flash effects of tactical atomic weapons with life support systems installed. Armored vehicles also afford safety to the crew from post-blast radiation and chemical and biological agents.

Future directions of tank design are reflected in recently developed German *Leopard* and French AMX tanks. Mobility and first-shot kill capability are increasingly regarded as better protection than additional armor. The need for thicker armor has also been reduced by improved ballistic configuration, more powerful tank guns and anti-tank weapons. Guns in both tanks are high performance 105 mm models that are coupled to computer-based fire control systems and infra-red sighting eye.

The most radical tank design currently is the Swedish 'S' tank. This extremely low configuration lacks the traditional turrret, the gun is mounted fixed in the tank body, greatly reducing the mobility of the 105 mm gun. Traversing is achieved by turning the entire vehicle and elevation is controlled by altering the pitch of the tank's hull with the suspension system.

In attempts to improve the scope of the tank gun, France and the United States have produced combination weapons. The U.S. 152 mm 'Shillelagh' and France's 142 mm ACRA fire either conventional ammunition or a guided missile. 'Shillelagh' is currently mounted on the U.S. M551 *Sheridan*, a light (17-ton) airmobile reconnaissance vehicle, as well as in a heavier version, the intended

The Burgeoning Arsenal: Developments and Projections

weapon of the MBT 70.* At the present level of development, these role. Additional drawbacks to the systems are the cost of the missiles weapons have the serious drawback of being neither good missile launchers or guns due to compromises necessary to achieve the dual role. Additional drawbacks to the systems are the cost of the missiles – $3,000 in the case of 'Shillelagh' – and the complexity of the over-all system.

The Soviet Union is taking a somewhat different approach. For the main gun of its T–62 tank a smooth-bore barrel is employed to fire a fin-stabilized kinetic round. By eliminating rifling and employing a smooth tube, the Soviets think they can achieve higher round velocities. There has been some doubt expressed as to the level of accuracy of this weapon.

Future generations of tanks will probably follow the lead of the German *Leopard* and the French AMX with weights of less than forty tons, with improved protection being afforded by developments of aluminum and fiber glass as armor material. The application of gas turbine engines to tanks is being investigated by Avco Lycoming. Turbine units offer potentially greater power than current diesel and multi-fuel engines in a smaller, lighter package. Armament will continue to be the tank gun, coupled with automatic loading systems, advanced fire control equipment and laser range finders.

Great Britain and France have developed vehicles that can be described as light tanks. The British *Scorpion* and the French L.F.U. (light fighting unit) are compact track-laying vehicles that weigh less than ten tons. The French unit is perhaps the most powerfully armed vehicle in its class ever made. The standard configuration carries a 90 mm gun. Both may be modified for carrying and launching missiles. The L.F.U. by replacement of its gun turret is designed to carry and fire the Nord SS.11 wire guided missile. *Scorpion* can be armed with the English Swingfire missile in attached launchers.

Vehicles of this type are well suited to liaison work, support of tanks in operations and combat in built up areas. Further, due to

---

* MBT 70 (Main Battle Tank 70) originally a joint U.S.-German project to produce and advance battle tank for this decade, has been plagued with cost overruns, and its future is somewhat indefinite.

their weight they are easily air-transported and can operate on terrain that is denied to the much heavier tanks.

Aircushion Vehicles

Aircushion vehicles (A.C.V.), also called hovercraft and ground effect machines, are a relatively new development in the field of transportation. The British pioneered in the area under the leadership of Christopher Cockerell who produced the first practical models in the mid-1950s, with the first Channel crossing occurring in 1959.

The A.C.V. is basically a vehicle that rides on a cushion of air created by horizontally mounted fans located in its hull. Horizontal movement is achieved by directing the flow of air that forms the cushion or by aviation propellers powered by the main engine or by motors mounted specifically for that purpose.

The potential application of the hovercraft are numerous in both civilian and military spheres due to a number of unique characteristics. A.C.V.s can operate over most forms of terrain, limited only by the degree of slope or obstacle. Capable of high speeds, current types exceed 100 miles per hour. Other qualities make it well suited to military operations – low maintenance needs, moderate level of training for crews, and low operating costs. A.C.V.s also leave little wake or heat trail, making them difcult to spot, and they have good stability for employment as weapons platforms, There are, however, drawbacks, some of which can be corrected over time. They are extremely noisy, produce large volumes of dust on overland runs and are unable to toe or push through obstacles. Fuel consumption is a major problem with current configurations but the application of advanced gas turbines could reduce this.

Both the United States and Great Britain have employed hovercraft in military operations, the British in Borneo and the United States in South Vietnam. Several other nations, such as Iran and Saudi Arabia, have them in their catalog of hardware. The Soviet Union has produced a number of prototypes for civilian use and military evaluation. The number of missions that these craft can perform is extremely wide, ranging from medical evacuation and logistical support to reconnaissance and fast attack. A wide variety of weapons are suited for use on hovercraft. The Americans have mounted .50 cal. and 7.62 mm machine guns and 40 mm and M5 grenade launchers, capable of firing over 200 explosive projectiles per minute. Rotary weapons such as the U.S. 7.62 mm mini-gun and small millimeter cannons can also be employed. For even greater punch the possibility of installing missile systems such as the compact British ship-to-ship missile 'Seacat' exists.

At the present time there is a large variety of A.C.V. configurations under development and exploration. Bell Aerosystems is working on a large A.C.V. assault landing craft for the United States navy, due for introduction in the late 1970s. This 160-ton craft will carry a load of up to 400 troops or other military equipment for distances up to several hundred miles at speeds of 50 knots. Other suggestions have been advanced to construct larger A.C.V.s that would be in the class – both in size and firing power – of destroyers and cruisers. It is thought that these craft could be a reality by the 1980s.

The Helicopter

The concept of the helicopter is not a recent one. Leonardo da Vinci designed a number of model helicopters, some of which it is reported took to the air powered by small spring motors. In the nineteenth century as many rotor-based plans were put forth to conquer the air as fixed-wing designs. One rotor design built into a twenty pound steam-powered model by W. H. Phillips of England flew successfully several times.

Military applications of the helicopter were first proposed in the American Civil War by parties of both sides. Luther C. Crowell of Massachusetts patented the first U.S. helicopter design in 1862. It was extremely advanced for the time and was closer to a V.T.O.L. (vertical take off and landing) configuration than to a helicopter. Crowell's plan called for wings and rotors that moved from vertical to horizontal as the direction of flight changed. The inventor suggested that it would be of value in dropping 'shells' on the enemy. In the South, Captain William Powers suggested a helicopter with two vertical spiralling screws as a method of resupply to overcome the Union blockade. Both configurations called for propulsion by means of steam engines, but neither designer was more specific.

Flying helicopter prototypes were built in the early 1900s but the First World War ended all work except in Austro-Hungary where a plan to use a tethered helicopter for observation work was proposed. A three-engine, two-rotor experimental example was built, but it crashed in tests and the program was cancelled.

Helicopter development continued in a number of countries between the World Wars and in the Second World War there was limited service by helicopters in medical and utility roles. In the late 1940s, the United States marines started to develop tactics using the helicopter for fast troop movement and airborne assaults, Several years later it was learned that the Soviet Union had been doing similar work.

Korea saw the helicopter employed in roles of medical evacuation and rescue. The French first used the helicopter as a combat attack vehicle in Algeria. But it was not until the Vietnam affair and the deployment of the U.S. army's air cavalry division created in 1965, and the smaller marine corps' air units that it assumed a major operational role of assault vehicle and weapon. In these capacities the helicopter has been successful and responsible more than once for turning the tide of battle against N.V.N. and N.L.F. forces. It has also been highly valuable in its traditional role as ambulance – in Vietnam 81 per cent of the army's wounded survive. Despite the loss of more than 4,150 of them it is thought by many military men that the helicopter is the coming weapon in conventional warfare. Army chief-of-staff William C. Westmoreland has strongly favored continued development of the helicopter tactically. Others in the U.S. military have suggested that the troop-carrying helicopter will take the place of the paratrooper in future conflicts. To airdrop men requires them to be jump-trained, while regular infantry can be deployed with nearly identical speed by helicopter. However, not everyone is so optimistic, especially in Europe. They point out that the helicopter has not faced an enemy with a true air defense capability or an air force of its own. They further point out that there is no combat military experience with helicopters over terrain other than that of South-East Asia. This whole area of helicopter surviva-

The Burgeoning Arsenal: Developments and Projections 145

bility in unfamiliar and hostile environments is being examined by the United States military. This includes the possibility of aerial combat with jet aircraft. The outcome of this debate is yet to be decided, but the use and development of the helicopter continues.

Four general classes of helicopters have emerged from Vietnam experience: heavy transport, light transport, liaison and communications, and attack. It is less than ten years since the arrival of the attack helicopter on the battlefield, and third generation prototypes are being developed. The first generation of attack helicopter was Bell Aircraft's UH–1E, nicknamed 'Huey', a modification of an existing utility and transport helicopter, the UH–1. Armament was combinations of the 7.62 mm M–60 machine guns, various size air-to-ground rockets and 40 mm automatic grenade launchers. This craft proved highly successful, filling a gap in close air support.

A second generation model was also produced by Bell, the AH–1G, 'Huey-Cobra'. This helicopter was designed solely for the role of attack. Much more compact than the original 'Huey', only 36 inches wide, with a very narrow profile, the 'Cobra is also faster, having a dive speed in excess of 200 miles per hour. It carries a crew of two and is capable of carrying an extremely wide assortment of arms: the 7.62 mm rotary 'mini-gun', the 20 mm Vulcan rotary cannon, the three-barreled 20 and 30 rotary cannons, plus various unguided rockets and the T.O.W. missile system in various combinations. The 'Cobra' has also been equipped with a 'see-kill' device and an infra-red night vision system.

Third-generation examples are under development by both Lockheed and Sikorsky. Lockheed's model, designated the AH–56A, 'Cheyenne', has been plagued with development problems and cost overruns. With a 250 miles an hour plus speed, and carrying basically the same weapons as the 'Cobra', the 'Cheyenne' is larger than its predecessors with small wings and a pusher as well as a stabilizing rotor mounted in the tail. Sikorsky's S–67 is similar in configuration and performance to the 'Cheyenne' but possibly more realistic in terms of cost, a point which Sikorsky is stressing.

Other projected forms of the helicopter include Sikorsky's plan for an armored reconnaissance helicopter to withstand a high volume of small arms fire, the A.A.R.V. (aerial armored reconnaissance vehicle) to be constructed from relatively light-weight armor material with thick rotor and extremely low impact transparent material for windows.

V/STOL Fighter Aircraft

The value of an aircraft that could land and take off vertically or in extremely short distances and still possess a high level of performance has long been recognized. A VTOL craft called the 'Triebflugel' was studied in Germany during the Second World War but it never reached prototype stage.

In the 1950s a number of V/STOL configurations were produced in various countries, such as England with its 'Flying Bedstead', an experimental vehicle so called because of its appearance. The United States developed and tested several propeller-driven and one pure jet prototypes, but none of them evolved into production aircraft.

Currently joint V/STOL projects exist between the United States and West Germany and between Italy and West Germany. France has what is thought to be a practical V/STOL in the Mirage IIIV but no production plans exist. Soviet Russia has worked on the Yakovlev V/STOL (NATO code-name 'Freehand'), that first appeared in 1967 which Western observers consider purely experimental.

The honor of producing the first operational V/STOL fighter goes to the Hawker-Siddeley firm of Great Britain whose 'Harrier' vectored-thrust* jet is operational with the Royal Air Force. A single-seat strike reconnaissance aircraft, the 'Harrier' can carry air-to-air and air-to-ground missiles, homing torpedoes, rockets or cannon. It can operate from remote locations with a minimal amount of support equipment. In order to reduce potential fuel problems in the field, work is being done on the Rolls Royce *Pegasus* jet engine to enable it to burn the same grade fuel as that used by armored vehicles.

---

* A system to produce V/STOL flight by aiming the thrust of a plane's jet engines by means of nozzles. The Harrier' has four such nozzles, two per side.

The Burgeoning Arsenal: Developments and Projections 147

Interest in the 'Harrier' is high both in Europe and in the United States. It may be noted that the United States marine corps is planning to purchase at least 110 of the planes for close air support.

V/STOL aircraft offer a number of distinct advantages. They can be dispersed over an operational theater providing quick response to both close air support requests and interdiction missions behind enemy lines. Once dispersed, V/STOLs would be difficult for the enemy to locate and knock out, especially if sophisticated camouflage techniques are employed.

Application of V/STOLs in the naval sphere offers air capabilities to a wide variety of warships. The 'Harrier' has successfully operated from a number of naval vessels, the smallest being the 6,500-ton Italian escort cruiser *Andrea Doria*. V/STOLs also offer an alternative to nations that desire sea-going airpower but do not wish or cannot afford to build a conventional aircraft carrier. The Royal Navy is planning a new class of naval vessel for the 'Harrier' and its successors. Due in the late 1970s, these 15,000-ton 'through deck cruisers' will have missiles mounted forward and a flight deck to accommodate its aircraft on the aft section. This design is similar to the existing Soviet 'Moskva' class cruisers which carry helicopters for anti-submarine warfare and for landing of naval infantry.

Future development of the 'Harrier' include further technical refinements and the installation of a more powerful engine, and it is possible that it will be the first generation of a family of Hawker V/STOL fighters. What course the other projects will follow can only be guessed, but the 'Harrier' has introduced a new element on the battlefield.

Missiles

Since the end of the Second World War the weapons experiencing the most rapid growth and development are the missiles, for they have become a symbol of national status, not only to the 'Superpowers' but to many nations with far more modest military needs. Such countries as Brazil, the Union of South Africa, Israel and Norway are involved in missile development projects. Egypt belonged to this family of embryonic missile powers in the 1960s but quit when their program turned into an embarrassing and expensive failure.

Rockets were first used in warfare by the Chinese in the thirteenth century. They were primitive things that had changed very little by the eighteenth century when nearly every European army had a rocket corps. By the late nineteenth century these rocket forces had been abandoned. England was the last in 1885. Although the rockets were quite impressive when fired, the results weren't. Their initial shock value soon wore off, and they were far too inaccurate to be considered effective.

In the First World War an unsuccessful attempt was made to unite rockets and aircraft as an anti-balloon weapon. Between the world conflicts England and the United States had projects involving explosive-laden, radio-controlled aircraft, but these efforts were not followed through. It was not until the Germans refined the liquid fuel rocket motor and developed basic guidance systems that missiles became a practical weapon. Even though the V-2 was not decisive, and many aimed for England went smashing into Swedish forests, it introduced a radically new element to both the military and to international politics.

Postwar development of the missile concept has been incredible. Today there are scores of missiles and rockets built and designed for a wide variety of missions. The following general taxonomic breakdown of missile types in operation and development suggests the elaborate proliferation since 1944:

Ship launched

Anti-aircraft
 Short-range
 Medium-range

Ship-to-ship (surface)
 Short-range
 Medium-range

Anti-submarine

Strategic (primarily submarine launched)
I.R.B.M. (intermediate range ballistic missile)
I.C.B.M. (intercontinental ballistic missile)

Air launched

Anti-craft

Air-to-surface
Long-range
Medium-range
Short-range
Direct-fire rockets

Surface launched

Anti-aircraft
Man portable, unit self-defense
Low-level
Medium-range
Long-range

Anti-I.C.B.M.
Medium-range
Long-range

Tactical surface
Anti-tank
Light, man portable
Heavy, vehicle transported

Short-range
Guided
Unguided

Medium-range guided

Strategic
I.R.B.M.
I.C.B.M.

While most missiles will generally fit into one of the outlined groups, some may overlap into others. Anti-tank missiles like the U.S. T.O.W. (tube-launched, optically-tracked, wire-guided) and the Soviet 'Snapper' can also be employed against fortifications and ground targets. The tactical short-range surface types can with modifications be used from aircraft, ships and A.C.V.s.

The possibility of multi- or dual-mission ability has been explored for the largest of the missile family, the I.C.B.M. A 1969 U.S. air force project called 'Janus' investigated developing or adapting an existing strategic missile to have the capability of performing as either an I.C.B.M. or as an A.B.M. (anti-ballistic missile).

It is not clear at present whether missiles will continue to develop, especially at the current rate, or if some technological plateau has been reached.

Personnel Detection Systems

In the United States, General Electric has developed a device that smells the enemy, the E–63 personnel detector, called the 'People Sniffer', which operates on atmospheric measurement techniques of submicroscopic agents and particles given off by human bodies. The 'People Sniffer' consists of a detector head that can be mounted on the bayonet stud of a rifle and is connected by means of tubing to the man-carried backpack. This model and a more powerful aircraft unit have both been used in Vietnam. Further work is under way.

Other systems for detection, using both laser beams and infra-red, have been developed in the United States and Great Britain. These devices produce an alarm signal when their respective beams are violated. They may be employed to provide security for both permanent and temporary defense perimeters. Short-range surveillance radars which can be either vehicle-mounted or man-carried have been developed for detection operations. Such systems are effective to ranges of 5,000 yards for the larger vehicle models, and 2,000 yards for the man-carried radars.

Tactical night vision devices is another burgeoning field. These items, which have been pioneered by the United States army, utilize

The Burgeoning Arsenal: Developments and Projections 151

light from sources such as the moon, starlight and skyglow, and intensify it by means of photocathodes (a device similar to the television tube) and phosphor screens to provide an illuminated view of the areas of observation. Night vision devices are a direct outgrowth of the infra-red sniperscope of the Second World War and Korea, and range in size from the compact AN/PVS-2 'Starlight Scope' designed for use on infantry weapons with an illuminating range of up to 440 yards, to the AN/TVS-4 Night Observation Device (N.O.D.), effective to 1,300 yards.

In addition, application of television to armored vehicles has been suggested. Miniaturized units could be utilized for weapons aiming and operation of the vehicle while it is 'buttoned up', offering much improved visibility than is possible with current periscope installation.

Chemical and Biological Warfare

Chemical and biological warfare is a shadowy, unpleasant and little-known subject since most people are reluctant to consider them as possible weapons in any future war. Yet, ironically, limited CB warfare has practical advantages over both conventional and nuclear forms. With the use of nuclear weapons there is massive destruction and the distinct possibility that the real estate attacked will be uninhabitable for a long time. Even in a conventional conflict the level of destruction and the loss of life would be extremely high. With the employment of CB weapons destruction could be minimal and the loss of life could be small since some forms of these weapons are designed to incapacitate rather than to kill. To use any highly deadly CB agent massively, however, would be to create a body disposal problem of incredible proportions. It is the potential escalation from limited to advanced forms that has caused misgivings.

Chemical agents can be divided into four groups: blister, nerve, harassing and incapacitating. The first, the blister agents, is the family including the First World War's mustard gas. Such agents generally are fatal only if inhaled and produce extremely painful and difficult to heal burns on contact with the skin.

Nerve agents are the descendants of a German Second World War development named 'Tabum' and are extremely deadly. The development center for this was captured by the Russians at the end of the war. These compounds attack a chemical in the human body, acetycholine, which is involved in the nerve control of muscles. Nerve agents cause tightness in the chest, blurred vision followed by difficult breathing, and the loss of muscle control. Death occurs by asphyxiation as the muscles which control breathing cease to function.

The third group is the harassing agents like CN (tear gas) and CS which produce watering eyes, coughing, choking and with some compounds like Adamsite nausea. The effects last only a short time. These agents have come into prominence recently in their employment in riot control.

The incapacitating agent is a relatively new development and is currently represented only by the United States developed BZ, a brain agent that reduces the victim's mental and physical powers. Under this compound's effects, consciousness is not lost but the victim hallucinates and loses the ability for rational thought. Effects wear off in several days and no reoccurrences are experienced. This compound's drawback is that it affects people differently and these effects cannot be determined in advance. Delusions of grandeur are commonly experienced by people subjected to this chemical.

Biological weapons are divided into two classes, viral and bacterial. The first, viral, represented by such diseases as small pox, rabies and dengue fever, do not respond to antibiotics, whereas the bacterial diseases such as anthrax, cholera and plague do respond.

Chemical agents can be disseminated by aircraft, missiles or artillery. In the case of biological weapons the process is more difficult. Contaminated animals could be introduced to the target area or the compounds could be added to the sources of food or water. The most effective method would be by inhalation. This would mean spraying the target from aircraft in a manner similar to chemical weapons. This is much more complicated in the case of biological weapons since agents can be effectively destroyed by sunlight or dissipated by air currents.

Both the United States and the Soviet Union have done a great deal of work in these fields, although the former is rapidly trying to disassociate itself from the whole field of CB warfare. Two other leading nations in this work are Sweden and Great Britain. Since 1962 the British have been extremely active in attempting to organize international bans on biological and chemical warfare, which has led to speculation that they may have achieved a breakthrough of major proportions in this field due to their persistent efforts.

Cosmic Warfare

Although the Outer Space Treaty of 1967, to which both the United States and Soviet Russia are signators, forbids the use of outer space for military purposes such as weapons stationing, the technology and ideas exist today to include this area in the overall pattern of conflict in any future war.

While it may take a number of years before Buck Rogers-like space combat could take place, the ability to launch orbiting bomb platforms is estimated to be within the reach of the Superpowers. Such a delivery system would have a great time factor advantage over existing intercontinental missile systems, and a form of this concept, called FOBS (fractional orbiting bombardment systems) is known to be under development by the Soviet Union.

Further indication of the Soviets' interest in the military uses of outer space came in the mid 1960s when they established with the P.B.O., the anti-aircraft branch of the military, a unit designated the P.K.O. This is the anti-cosmic component of their air defense system, described in the Soviet military dictionary as being established 'for destroying the enemies' cosmic means of fighting'. Their mission is to be accomplished with 'special space ships, satellite fighters and other flying apparatuses with rockets and radio-electric apparatuses'. And in November of 1968 and October of 1970, the Soviet Union tested a 'killer satellite', observed by radar to move in on other Russian satellites and by some 'means' blow them apart While the precise method of these destructions is not known, it is generally felt that it was not done by firing a missile or weapon but rather with 'radio-electric' methods.

At the present time the United States does not have such a program under development overtly, but a 'killer satellite' system could probably be produced for between 30 and 50 million dollars with existing technology.

It is difficult to project what forms cosmic weaponry may take if they are developed – treaty or not.

Miscellaneous

In order to indicate the scope of current military technology and the level of innovation, here are briefly described certain new military hardware. Not all are weapons. Some are components of weapons, others are support equipment:

An inflatable bridge under development by the U.S. army that can span small rivers and provide support for vehicles up to the size of a medium tank.

A 'Flying Belt' being studied by Bell Aerosystems for the possibility of individual flight. Utilizing a compact turbojet for power, this unit when refined could fill both civilian and military roles.

Light-weight, rapid-fire naval guns that would provide new levels of fire power for patrol craft and increase that of larger ships. Configurations produced in both Italy and the United States are in various calibers and are highly automated.

'Instant Land' developed by the U.S. army can potentially be of value in construction over marshy and dusty terrain. It is made by combining two liquids which harden into a firm solid material.

Astrolite, a liquid explosive created by Explosive Corp. of America, offers possibilities in mine warfare. Poured onto the ground it produces a great upheaval when fired. It cannot be detected by conventional methods and dissipates after several days, thereby eliminating clearing operations.

Portable inflated field shelters, equipped with life support systems to protect occupants from radiation and biological and chemical agents are under development by the U.S. army.

The Burgeoning Arsenal: Developments and Projections 155

Gas turbine propulsion systems for naval vessels are becoming more popular due to low maintenance needs, weight and size advantage and high level of performance. Future Royal Navy frigates and destroyers will have gas turbine units as will the new United States Spruance class destroyers.

MTVs (marginal terrain vehicles) are in development throughout the world for such military application as logistical support, troop transport and weapons platform.

Riverine craft, developed for the U.S. navy to fight in shallow river waters, is a compact vessel utilizing fiber-glass construction, waterjet propulsion systems and carry arms ranging from machine guns to 105 mm howitzers and flame throwers.

Final Comments

Continued growth of military technology can be expected in the coming decade. Efforts in the direction of disarmament will be made, but it is unrealistic to think that their impact will be profound. Weapons development will most likely, as it has in the past ten years, be comprehensive with no single class of weapons being overemphasized. The vigorous competition in arms sales seems likely to increase.

The design considerations of mobility and simplicity seem likely to be stressed over the entire range of weaponry. Mobility, in and out of vogue throughout military history, is now receiving increased attention. Growth of the helicopter as a military tool and the increase of weapons with airmobile capability points this out.

Of greater importance is simplicity in design. Weapons have become increasingly complex, leading to higher costs, highly trained and technically oriented crews, increased probability of systems failure and greater levels of support, facts demonstrated in India–Pakistan, the Middle East and Vietnam. And in the preparation of defense or in the fighting of a war, error is not an effective **ally**.

SOURCE NOTES

All the material in this chapter came from published sources such as *Armor*, the *International Defense Review*, *Military Review*, *The Marine Corps Gazette*, *United States Naval Institute Proceedings*, *Ordnance* and *Aviation Week and Space Technology*.

Several excellent volumes that should be consulted in any study of military technology are '*Weapons of the World War III*' by John S. Tompkins, published by Doubleday, *Jane's Weapons Systems*, first edition, edited by R. T. Pretty and D. H. R. Archer, *Jane's All the Worlds Aircraft*, edited by John W. R. Taylor and *Jane's Fighting Ships*, edited by Raymond V. Blackman, all published by McGraw-Hill Books. Tompkins's book, while dated, provides an excellent background on contemporary weaponry with emphasis on the United States hardware. *Jane's Weapons Systems* is the only existing comprehensive study on the world's weapons and weapons systems, and the other two *Jane's* volumes are definitive in their fields.

9 Science, Technology, and the Future of Warfare

ROGER WILLIAMS

The relationship between science and war is so disturbing that there seems every justification for reflecting again and again on the terrible contents of the military Pandora's Box which science has opened up. The discussion which follows therefore deals with 'science' and 'warfare', though both are imprecise terms in this context. Strictly defined, science is a systematic, and typically empirical, explanation of natural phenomena, but in common usage the word 'science' refers not only to this but also to technology, development work and even invention. Similarly, 'warfare' must be construed to cover possibilities as well as actualities, since a chief characteristic of the impact of 'science' on 'warfare' has in fact been the phenomenon of technical obsolescence before operational use. Below, considerations of style have made it necessary to talk of 'progress', 'advances' and 'improvements' in weapons development. It is ironic that no more suitable modes of expression present themselves. The author's belief, shared with most people, that the less war the better, absolves neither him nor them from considering its likely future shape. Indeed, it demands especially that adequate attention be given to any characteristic of the weapons acquisition process which encourages the threat, precipitates the outbreak, or worsens the consequences of war.

It is well worth pausing at the outset to remember just where we are so far as the science/warfare interaction is concerned. This is sensible in that it provides the best foundation for talking about the future.[1] As regards military personnel, there is undoubtedly a good deal of truth in the criticism that, at least until recent years, their professional appreciation has generally lagged behind technical development substantially, and in many cases seriously. Nor is the suggestion that this reflects a contrast between the military and the scientific approaches meant as a compliment to the military. Fortunately for them, history demonstrates that other professions, including the scientific one, have often failed to anticipate and adjust to change. Certainly it is change, formerly slow, now frighteningly rapid, which lies at the heart of the science war symbiosis, and the record suggests at least five senses in which the former has contributed to the latter, all five therefore requiring to be considered here.

Three of these senses are mainly specific to weapons systems and relate to fire power, mobility and communications. Science has made the fire power available to modern forces stupendous in historical comparison, and of remarkable accuracy. It has dramatically improved land, sea, and air mobility, and it has fostered spectacular advances in the precision, speed and richness of communication. Independent developments in each of these three dimensions have led both to changes in the others and also constantly altered the military field as a whole. It is with this field as a whole that science has been concerned in a fourth way. The argument here has been that if the complexities continually being introduced into the military environment by modern technology are to be reduced to the point where effective choices and decisions can still be made, then the scientific method itself must be used to ensure this. Variants of, or perhaps approximations to, this method have as a result come to be applied, again primarily during and since the Second World War, to the conduct of most military affairs, from stock control and tactical questions right up to grand strategy. Finally, since science has also transformed the non-military sectors of society, the corresponding economic, demographic, political and technical changes constitute, to the extent that they have military importance, a fifth aspect of the science/war theme. In discussing the future of conflict it is not therefore likely to be sufficient to confine study to the obviously military. The net must be cast much wider than that. Political changes produced in the world as a direct or indirect result of science and technology may in the end prove far more crucial determinants of military requirements than narrower developments in military or associated technology. After all, we have hardly yet begun to exploit the capacity of science to modify the world at large, and whereas we may hope to reduce the causes of war, we need to be aware constantly of any new tensions we simultaneously create.

With these five categories in mind, what does the future seem to hold in terms of atomic, biological, chemical, conventional and exotic warfare?

Looking first at atomic warfare, here it appears that nature has already been persuaded to give up all the necessary secrets. Technology has made nuclear bombs or warheads available with yields ranging from a fraction of a kiloton to 60 megatons and more. They are capable of delivery at distances from less than a mile up to half way round the earth, or further. They can be constructed as extremely dirty or as relatively clean weapons. We have fission and fusion devices: there is no good reason for supposing that a new explosive process of comparative violence is likely to be discovered. Most possibilities, matter/anti-matter annihilation for example, seem to belong firmly in the realm of science fiction. If they did not, it would be hard to imagine a military requirement for them. What is to be feared is the development of an alternative or uranium fission as a standard fusion trigger. Even though, on current knowledge, the alternative might be expected to be at least as complex to construct as an uranium trigger, it would be prudent not to ignore the dangers of a simpler mechanism eventually becoming available. As it is, with alternatives to gaseous diffusion now being proved for uranium enrichment, obtaining a supply of U235 may in the next decade present few more difficulties than now arise in establishing a plutonium stock. Already enough plutonium is being produced throughout the world to make possible the manufacture of some 1,500 plutonium bombs per annum, and this is predicted as likely to rise to some 15,000 by 1980. Of course, this is almost entirely civil production, but the plain fact remains that it is becoming easier year by year, both technically and economically, for a nation to arm itself with nuclear weapons.[2] Since over the long term the political inducements in favor of going nuclear seem likely, in the case of several countries, despite international agreements, to outweigh the restraints, there would seem to be a high risk of a world with more than the present five nuclear powers. There is a general suspicion that the step to the sixth is the most significant, and that if this occurs it may in fairly quick succession prompt the seventh, eighth, etc. Apart from whether horizontal proliferation of itself automatically decreases international stability – it is sometimes claimed that only possession of nuclear weapons ensures full national responsibility – what is certain is that the nuclear weapons which some powers might choose to develop would be maintained under much less secure safeguards than those instituted by at least four of the present five nuclear countries.

If horizontal proliferation is the greatest of the nuclear questions, then vertical proliferation and the problem of China are the second and third. Each of the two Superpowers has in recent years perceived the other as presenting a serious and/or growing threat to its strategic deterrent. Partly each to deny the other a position from which it could destroy its opponent's retaliatory capacity in a first strike, and partly for reasons of general defense, both the United States and the Soviet Union have pursued the development of the antiballistic missile. There is no doubt that the gross uncertainties associated with the A.B.M., and with its counterparts, the multiple independently-targeted re-entry vehicle, the fractional orbital bomb and other offense-aiding systems, have together already introduced a new element of instability in the balance between the Superpowers.[3] The SALT talks in progress at the time of writing may check this decay; on the evidence of the past it would be unrealistic to expect them to reverse it. Technology is too good at creating uncertainty. In any case, some pretty fundamental assumptions seem certain to receive a major challenge from technology over the next decade or so. For instance, it is acknowledged now that even hardened missile silos may have only a limited lifetime.[4] To quote an American ex-Director of Defense Research and Engineering: '... there is no technical solution to the dilemma of the steady decrease in our national security that has for more than 20 years accompanied the steady increase in our military power.'5

The more complex the strategic balance becomes, the greater the scope for misunderstanding of intentions or miscalculation of capability. However, there are no grounds for supposing that the technological nuclear stalemate between the United States and the Soviet Union will really be broken technically in the coming decades, still less for believing that a situation is imminent in which either will again be permitted by the other to establish a first strike capability. The urgent question for both is rather at what level of cost the stalemate is to be held, and this in turn depends to an important degree on American and Soviet interpretations of the motives and policies of China. The advent of a third Superpower, at least in the nuclear sense, has a distressing parallel in the world of mathematics. There, while the equations of motion of a two body system are fully determinate, only approximate solutions are obtainable for a three body system. For a quarter of a century the United States and the Soviet Union have contrived to stay in stable equilibrium with each other, in spite of apparent incompatibilities. It is still to be shown that the dynamics of a three Superpower system will lend themselves to an equally tolerable solution over time.

If this is an imponderable, so too, if we are honest, is the true military utility of tactical nuclear weapons. The short-term, long-term and genetic effects of these weapons are well enough known to be taken for granted here. Military formations are naturally expected to be able to operate on a nuclear battlefield, and special training and equipment for this purpose can be provided. The underlying premises here are that the situation does not deteriorate into a strategic exchange, and that, in addition, the use even of battlefield nuclear weapons by both sides is fairly discriminate. Where an essentially continuous spectrum of nuclear weapons is to hand these premises cannot be relied upon to hold. In addition to the appalling destructiveness of even small nuclear weapons, and the absence of an unequivocal firebreak between a tactical and a strategic nuclear exchange, a third risk attends the use of tactical nuclear weapons. This derives from the mystique of nuclear weapons in general and could easily mean that tactical nuclear weapons were called upon to perform a role for which they were very unsuited, thereby inviting local military failure as well as strategic escalation. In fact, nuclear weapons of all kinds, as instruments of indiscriminate annihilation, have no natural place in the evolution of military doctrine. In particular, responsibility for the bee-sting deterrent is an extremely abnormal military function. The human mechanics of it – the personnel in missile silos and Polaris submarines especially – have received much attention from psychologists and others. The human element will presumably demand still further study if, as seems likely, new technology eventually makes necessary yet more stringent standby conditions. At higher levels in the military organization, Kahn *et al.* notwithstanding, those with the decisions to make will be ill-advised to repose confidence in any single calculus of nuclear use.

If the future of nuclear weapons is more politically than technically unpredictable, that of biological (B) and chemical (C) weapons is perhaps both. As noted in chapter 8 of this volume, an extensive range of weapons of both types has now been tested and developed. These weapons also have a major drawback – uncertainty of control and effect. The user has the taxing problem of ensuring that his own defenses are adequate; each substance has its own specific disadvantages; and most troubling of all are the possible long-term effects, perhaps stretching from devastating local pollution with chemical weapons to a major ecological disturbance, or even to a massive human epidemic from biological weapons. Certainly it must be anticipated that continuing research will lead to still more deadly products than those now to hand. For instance, some of the chemical weapons are directed against basic life cycles which tend to be very complicated and delicate, therefore affording plenty of opportunity for fatal interference. The power of these chemical weapons may then be expected to grow not only as a result of direct research, but also as an indirect consequence of the greater understanding of such life cycles, the latter being a legitimate concern of medical science.

Delivery systems for B and C weapons are somewhat less straightforward than those for conventional or nuclear explosives but, while refinements will no doubt continue to be made, the advanced powers have already investigated most of the feasible options very thoroughly, and a large range of munitions for chemical warfare are known to have been manufactured. Aerosol delivery of B weapons has also been greatly improved, if not perfected.

There are several general points about B and C weapons which need emphasizing. First, on grounds of cost and ease of manufacture, non-nuclear countries, the poorer ones particularly, may find them quite irresistible, not only to stockpile but also, in certain circumstances, to use. Second, it is tacitly assumed that the nuclear powers would also resort to them in any general nuclear war. Third, in spite of these two probabilities, B and C weapons seem to have received very little attention from strategic analysts. Fourth, with biological agents the possibility of covert attack must always be borne in mind. Finally, it seems right to regard both B and C weapons as bringing to war only a new style of lethality: the speculation that certain B and C agents could ultimately make possible war without killing can safely be forgotten.

B and C weapons might be employed against civil populations or against military units. Very much more could be done to protect the former were governments to think the effort worthwhile. Nevertheless, it must be confessed that a comprehensive defense of a large population would be prohibitively expensive and would also require constant revision as potential enemies amended their B and C threats. Furthermore, certain countries or regions would continue to manifest a special vulnerability, and all would remain vulnerable to surprise attack. The position with regard to military units is much less hopeless. Here, several programs of defensive measures can usefully be contemplated. Much depends upon adequate detection and warning systems. These problems are much more severe with B than with C attacks, and with B attacks there may be extra difficulties involved in identifying the agent. The first line of defense here in situations of doubt will be the working assumption that a B or C attack has already occurred or is likely soon to occur. A reliable source states that 'the weapons of C.B.W. are the only ones against which protection of a high order can be effected on the battlefield without severe restriction of fighting capabilities; and C.B. defensive equipment is either issued or held in reserve for most of the major armies of the world.'[6] Such equipment will include antidotes, vaccinations, specific antisera, masks, permeable and impermeable protective clothing, protection arrangements such as special shelters or vehicles, and decontamination systems.

The problems of mounting a B.C. defense are complex, and are exacerbated by shortness of time; the problems confronting the attack are scarcely formidable. B.C. weapons may seem to promise exceptionally high utility for certain missions, but the attacker will not be able to predict, except approximately, the effect he will produce in practice. Skilled analyses of atmospheric and meteorological conditions will necessarily precede all but the crudest attack, the choice of the most appropriate agent must then be made, and in the end the attacker must properly make only the most pessimistic assumptions. He must also weigh the risk of escalation. In the words of the recent United Nations Report: '[C.B.W.] could open the door to hostilities which could become less controlled, and less controllable, than any war in the past. Uncontrollable hostilities cannot be reconciled with the concept of military security.'[7] B and C weapons are different in principle from nuclear or conventional ones in that conventional wars are fought and nuclear ones are imaginable, but B.C. war seems likely only as an adjunct to one or both of these. It is evidently not very suitable against the dispersed forces of a nuclear battlefield, or against guerrillas where these are indistinguishable from friendly forces or non-combatants. Against concentrated units or cornered insurgents it might be thought an ideal form of attack. Those who reserve a particular abhorrence for B.C. weapons will hope that Dedijer is right:

> ... if some highly lethal new weapon, such as a nerve gas or an infectious micro-organism, were used effectively against the guerrillas, that local victory of the regular forces would be bought at a price of moral catastrophe which would make political victory utterly impossible.[8]

Bearing in mind the part played in war by expediency, they will perhaps be less sure that Meselson is right: 'The general problem of preventing chemical and biological warfare is to a large extent a psychological one.'[9]

In spite of the brevity of this summary of B.C. weaponry, reference inevitably must be made to Vietnam. The lessons to be drawn from the use of C weapons in the First World War are extremely suspect. Nor is it easy to draw valid conclusions from the occasions between that war and the Vietnam War on which C (and B) weapons were used or were alleged to have been used. In Vietnam, chemical warfare has taken two forms. (The use of napalm is excluded here.) These are (1) the use of harassing and riot control agents, which can kill of course, though rarely; and (2) herbicides, defoliants and anti-crop agents. Three and four respectively of these agents are acknowledged as having been used. Although this represents a comparatively mild form of chemical warfare, its political repercussions have been very damaging for the United States in the world at large, and in South Vietnam itself it appears to have promoted resentment and hostility on the part of the population. On the other hand:

> The military is emphatic about the effectiveness of defoliation in reducing American casualties.... The demand for the ... 12th Air Commando Squadron greatly exceeds their ability to supply them ... military experts [generally agree] that defoliation is a potent weapon in guerilla warfare ... [and] that in any future [limited] wars ... extensive use will be made of it.[10]

The same authors conclude a competent and notably unbiassed account by observing that in their judgment the ecological consequences of defoliation are severe and extend far beyond actual target areas. The military usefulness of defoliation is naturally challenged by other authors, and the practical utility of harassing agents, except in situations of limited violence, seems to be an open question even within the military.

With regard to atomic, biological and chemical warfare one must theorize almost from the first: since the Second World War, conventional warfare of one kind or another has unfortunately been virtually continuous somewhere in the world. There have been lightning wars, prolonged struggles and guerrilla wars: no doubt other types could be identified. Nor, unhappily, does a change for the better appear in prospect. The business of compromise and adjustment between the United States and the Soviet Union seems far from complete, and the role of China is still almost wholly undefined. Then, quite apart from these major issues, occasions for war persist elsewhere, mainly between and within particular states of the developing world. It seems most useful here to discuss conventional warfare in terms of the refinements in it being sought by the most advanced powers, since the evidence of the past suggests strongly that most, if not all, of the developments these powers accomplish will become available, sooner or later, to countries of the second and other ranks.[11] The advanced countries might well feel in the future that it was in their interests to slow down this transfer, and they might even agree upon ways of doing this, but artificial technology gaps are still best regarded as temporary and unstable.

The quite rapid developments in conventional warfare capabilities which have been obtained in the advanced countries in recent years have derived from two principal sources. These are, first, the military exploitation of the computer and electronic equipment generally, and second, a much more concentrated effort than ever before to ensure that conventional weapons systems fully reflect the current state of technology. According to Sir Solly Zuckerman:

> ... computers can take over jobs done at 'middle management levels which, till now, have been manned by specialist officers ... of greater interest is the possibility ... that ... computers and rapid communications could put distant military operations under immediate central control. ... It is difficult to see what effect this ... could have on ... 'generalship...'[12]

We are clearly likely to witness a continuing electronic battle between offensive and defensive systems with respect to land, sea and air fighting, and at any future stage a major war between technically advanced powers, excluding the use of A.B.C. weapons, could only be, in General Beaufre's words, a 'truly enormous experiment'.[13] And, we may add, an extremely grim one.

The upper limits, as presently conceived, on what may be achieved are well indicated in the following quotation from an article written by Leonard Sullivan in 1968 when he headed the special office in the

Pentagon set up to expedite research and development (R and D) activities of relevance to the South-East Asia War.

> ... we can detect anything that perspires, moves, carries metal, makes a noise, or is hotter or colder than its surroundings.... Eventually we will be able to tell when anybody shoots, what he is shooting at, and where he was shooting from. You begin to get a 'Year 2000' vision of an electronic map with little lights that flash....[14]

Sullivan added that this kind of development was what was needed for 'porous war', where the friendly and the enemy were mixed together. H felt that R and D had already demonstrated the possibility of providing, with the appropriate instrumentation, real time surveillance of the battlefield round the clock, and had even shown that in the end there would be little difference between fighting at night and during the day, though this he admitted would be the toughest challenge. On the latter point, an authoritative British source is less optimistic:

> Although the prospect of making ground combat fully as efficient by night as by day remains remote, there are now becoming available a wide range of experimental techniques . . . which should go far to remove many of the current limitations.[15]

In fact, the true modernity of modern armies is apparently wide open to argument. In his book, *Machine Age Armies*, John Wheldon makes some penetrating comments on this subject.[16] He believes that modernity in armies should be measured not by comparing their past performances with their present capabilities 'but by comparing the army's degree of sophistication in organization and communication with the best contemporary civil practice.' In particular, he feels that army vehicles compare very badly with civil ones, having evolved too slowly by contrast with developments in the lethal apparatus they carry. 'If fighting ships and aircraft must have mobility far superior to the common norms of the civilian world, why not military land vehicles?' He holds that full integration of air and land activity is a highly significant trend, and he states that 'the first military organization to rationalize this process, accelerate it, and ruthlessly prune the dead wood from it will place itself in the forefront of military competence.' He would like to see the military cast off what he considers to be an 'obsession with simple destruction', aiming instead at paralyzing resistance through 'swifter reaction and superior mobility'. His conclusions go to the heart of the relationship between societies, their armed forces and technology:

> The modernization ... of ideas is a task not just for ... soldiers ... but for the nation as a whole ... military concepts are strongly bound to the military social organization, and both ... are more subject to ... potentially disastrous collision with new knowledge and ... artefacts ... than any other type of human society. ...

He may be right. Certainly the military susceptibility to change and capacity for innovation receive very little attention from organizational analysts compared with that which they lavish on civil and commercial organizations. In his study of the contribution of science and engineering in the Second World War,[17] Guy Hartcup concludes in a similar vein that technical ingenuity counted for less than did the integration of the military and scientific disciplines.

Whatever the current state of this integration, it is difficult to think of a weapon or aspect of conventional warfare which has not in the last few years been subjected to determined up-dating and improvement. Beginning with espionage, here the specialist aircraft has already been for many purposes superseded by the new spy satellite and, while taking much of the James Bond technology with a pinch of salt, on this front too there are known to have been quite technical advances. In field warfare, Vietnam especially has accelerated the introduction of new conventional weapons and has led to striking increases in the killing power of the old. And killing power naturally remains a chief ingredient of military success. Much more savage anti-personnel bombs and mines have thus come forward and considerable evidence has been gathered about the comparative effectiveness of various types of gun and rifle. At the same time an old lesson has had to be relearned, namely that while the technical frontier moves ever on, not everything it leaves behind becomes obsolete or redundant. To cite an embarrassing example, the best of air launched missiles do not necessarily remove the need for aircraft to be provided with old-fashioned cannon. Too great a commitment to technical advance can easily mean neglect of the more elementary means needed to counter the methods and equipment of less sophisticated forces, e.g. the Israeli's use of the 'obsolete' M–4 Sherman.

It has now been demonstrated unequivocally in Vietnam that engineering development, coupled with operational analysis of battlefield conditions, can steadily raise the kill or casualty-inflicting capacity of a military force, nor has any definite limit to this trend yet revealed itself. Speaking of the gap between conventional and tactical nuclear power, one author points out that 'the gap may never be completely closed, but we already have so-called conventional munitions that are in the same league with nuclear when it comes to killing power'.[18] It might therefore come about that in a standard conventional war between advanced countries battlefield operations could be made prohibitively expensive in terms of material and/or personnel. In the limit, conventional war might even become as 'unthinkable', being almost as devastating as nuclear war, while the upper limit on the destructiveness of conventional war might not be very different from that with which we are already familiar. Continued refinement of equipment and methods might show diminishing returns on the battlefield as the technical demands on the individual, perhaps at low levels in the military hierarchy, began to approach the limits of his abilities. Appalling levels of attrition might even be accepted again as they have so often been in the past. Alternatively, with the battlefield an anachronism, surgical attacks on nerve centers might lead to quite disproportionate success. It is impossible to know and, if one hopes for conventional stalemate, one should still fear conventional attrition. In any case, the argument may never hold for guerrilla wars....

What progress to be looked for in strategic and tactical mobility? The constraints likely on tactical mobility are perhaps the most difficult to foresee. In this category the helicopter (or airmobile) division has claims to being the most striking curiosity. A relatively long time after its introduction an astonishing number of roles have now been discovered for it, as transport, as command post, in reconnaissance, as a weapons platform, and so on. A revelation in Vietnam, General Wheeler has said of them: 'In my judgment, the introduction of the airmobile concepts ... has put back into the military arsenal a capability which went out with the disappearance of horse cavalry'.[19] In situations similar to those encountered in Vietnam the helicopter can hardly in future be denied an important part, sometimes perhaps even a decisive one. However, the helicopter has an intrinsic vulnerability and against a defense of equal technical competence, provided with specific anti-helicopter weapons, it might well, in at least the most dangerous of its roles, go the way of the horse. Even if that happened, the helicopter would still have to be regarded as having for long exemplified poor appreciation of exploitable potential. Air-portable tanks might conceivably be another example of the same thing.

Other very vulnerable military facilities are airfields and aircraft carriers. The acute problems of defense here have for some time indicated a switch to STOL and VTOL aircraft, each one in the limit capable of sustained independent action. As the same time, the complexity, and therefore cost, of conventional fighters has been forcing a move from special purpose to multi-role aircraft, functions as different as continental air defense and interdiction being demanded of what is basically the same airplane.[20] With so many design compromises having therefore to be made, and made easily, there is a new high premium on the right choices, a premium measured in terms of development time, cost and value-in-use of the aircraft.

Important strides in strategic mobility seem certain to occur for some time yet. Aircraft larger than the C5A, very high-speed hydrofoil or hovercraft transport ships, and large submarine transports may all one day become realities for the strategic planner. Actions to forestall the outbreak of hostilities has been possible several times since 1945, and enhanced strategic mobility may in the future make this politically desirable option more frequently available.

Given the confusion, richness of technical choice likely to obtain indefinitely across the whole military field, it must be assumed that the scientific analysis of decision-making will expand from its already notable status. In the formulation[21] of the then American assistant secretary for defense, Alain Enthoven, one has: operational analysis for the evaluation of military effectiveness in specific situations; weapons systems analysis for the examination of alternative feasible weapons systems in a range of uncertain applications; force requirement studies to probe the variety of force postures; and strategic studies for the major policy problems involving a military, political, technical and economic mix. Scientists – natural and social – are essential to such studies, but it would be a mistake to assume either that the quality of work in this field is always high, or that analyses are free of aberration or bias. For a long time to come those with real decisions to make will need to examine cautiously the premises, the conduct and the conclusions of any studies of the foregoing type. Such studies are naturally ideal ground for the computer. This can increase the reliability of the results, but can also make sound criticism more difficult for those who lack time, facilities or competence to check the analytical procedures. In the military field as in the civil, we must expect a constant struggle to ensure that the computer remains firmly the servant of its users.

A summary of the state of the art of conventional warfare must note several things. First, the postwar neglect of this art, a neglect noticeable in the United States because of trust in the nuclear deterrent, has now been more than rectified. The art is currently in a state of uncertain flux and the outcome of conventional wars in future will be far less predictable as a result. Thirdly, since modern civilization has become dependent upon modern technology, selective conventional attacks on communication systems, power, supplies and transport facilities could go far towards paralyzing societies – militarily as effective as the crippling use of nuclear weapons. Finally, it is unwise to dismiss conventional wars as somehow safe: even partial conventional defeat may drive a non-nuclear country to develop nuclear arms, and certainly such a defeat gives a nuclear country a pressing temptation to threaten their use.

Turning next to exotic warfare, there are possibilities here, geological and meteorological warfare for instance, discussed by others but which seem too remote to be worth serious consideration. In such cases the human race does not as yet possess much of the basic science involved and it may never do so. In the meantime, each natural disaster, an earthquake say, brings forth from commentators the natural hope that science will make possible warning and better still, some remedy. However, a remedy at least could only be rendered possible by the kind of understanding and capability which might in other circumstances be used to cause a similar disaster. This deliberately far-fetched example makes that point very well, but it applies no less with more familiar scientific discoveries.

There are more detailed exotic concepts too, laser and acoustical weapons and plastic armor for instance, of which, at this stage, one can again do little more that take note. Under the same 'exotic' heading, there are, however, two new theaters of war which may be about to open up under the challenge of technology, namely the deep sea and seabed and near and planetary space.

True submarine warfare had to await the development of nuclear engines. A naval craft which operated by surface-effect rather than displacement, in consequence relatively small and very fast, would by itself quickly revolutionize surface naval strategy.[22] This apart, there are already strong reasons, both economic and military, for supposing that the conquest of the deep sea is about to begin in earnest, so that the submarine and a deep-ranging counterpart may pose much graver tactical and strategic problems than ever before. In the ocean depths electro-magnetic radiation cannot be used for surveillance and area cover must give way to monitored barrier lines. Such lines will not be cheap to establish or maintain, and away from friendly coasts, at depths and in uncomfortable conditions, might not be possible at all. A long battle between detection measures and evasion counter-measures may lie ahead: at the outset at least, the odds distinctly favor the latter.[23]

In spite of the remarkable steps which have been made in space exploration it is hard to imagine that conflict is about to be exported to near-earth space, still less to interplanetary space. As weapons platforms, the earth and seas are likely to retain distinct advantages for some time to come, and satellites are fundamentally vulnerable craft. On the other hand, satellites have a tremendous value for surveillance/communication, etc. and this could lead by gradual stages of their defensive armament and then to experiments with them as strategic weapons platforms. It seems that it is absence of military need rather than technology which is preventing this. With existing and immediately projected space propulsion systems, and their support hardware, extended contests in interplanetary space are not a real contingency.

Regardless of whether these more *outré* speculations ever materialize, it is apparent that there has been a permanent change in the relationship between the military and the scientists/engineers. In the words of Marshal Malinovsky: 'Tumultuous scientific-technical progress has evoked radical changes in the development of military technology. [Soldiers are now confronted] with the task of deep study of technology, to know how to exploit and adapt it.'[24]

There would have been grounds for predicting that the military technology of the last thirty years and the chronic international perils of that period together would have led to a widely mobilized citizenry, though 'the technological military acuteness of every level of the population' could never have been what Major-General Pokrovsky claimed it was for the Soviet Union in 1959,[25] namely 'the undeniable foundation of our national defense and of our preparation against any unexpected events'! Instead, the political natures of the Western democracies now leave no doubt but that they will rely permanently on professional forces. The standards demanded of these forces, and of all others undertaking to confront a technically advanced and determined foe, are already high and show every sign of rising further. They can be simply stated, but that is the only simple thing about them:

> A widely disseminated capability to improvise and reach accurate decisions will call for the highest possible educational level throughout; a willingness to take and act upon those decisions will call for a deep commitment to national goals.
>
> Military units will expect to enjoy maximum support from the agencies of psychological and political warfare.
>
> They will possibly need to be equipped and trained for widely

different sorts of warfare but, in spite of a nurtured competence to operate fast and flexibly, they will typically meet situations where the soundest tactics may be dangerously uncertain.

The exact configuration of their equipment will be the result of growing friction between the 'pull' of strategy and tactics and the 'push' of technical feasibility, and they will seek to maintain the closest contacts between military planning staff and defense scientists and engineers.

The two Superpowers are now on a relative technological plateau – relative only to the astonishing changes of the last century. Already in the mid-1960s, Erickson, in noting many signs that the military-technical revolution had slowed at the strategic level, pointed out also that it might actually be speeding up in the area of limited warfare.[26] It remains a possibility that a new scientific discovery could lead to a steep change in military thinking, similar in magnitude to that prompted by fission weapons, but the possibility is a remote one. But if the risks of either side producing a surprise ace are very low, the steady development of existing systems is a formidable challenge to both. They must choose ever more wisely from alternatives made mutually exclusive on cost grounds. They must both fear wrong choice. Already both have found their freedom of action restricted by earlier choices between technical options; and in spite of cost benefit analysis, such situations will recur. There are too many technical avenues for even the Superpowers to be able to explore them all. As long as both remain on the technological plateau, or, substituting metaphors, in the shadow of the deterrent, the outcome is more likely to be frustrating than critical. At the same time, the pressures for cooperative R and D between lesser powers will harden, and yet in spite of this they may commonly find themselves in situations for which they are not prepared technically.

But if the Superpowers are capable of ensuring that over-all strategic balance between them remains a dominant feature of the international environment, what happens beneath it? In many areas of the world the local situation resembles the world at large before the advent of nuclear weapons. Since the countries concerned tend to be selectively armed with equipment developed by the major powers, the wars that break out between them must in part resemble the Second World War, being more or less sophisticated depending upon local availability of the most modern conventional weapons, together with the ability to use them effectively. It is a first priority that such local wars be disconnected from the Superpower balance, and a second priority that such local conflicts should not be allowed to bring about the development, deployment and use of A B and C weapons. In this context one must describe as encouraging the apparent recognition by each Superpower that it cannot with safety act successfully in the back yard of the other. At the same time, it is vital to remember how much of the world falls in the back yard of neither.

It is usually said that the quality of man's politics is much lower than that of his science. As long as war is a characteristic of international behavior, then the application to it of science and engineering seems as politcally inevitable as it is technically logical. Thus the process of procuring military systems came to be the most important single pressure for technological development.[27] Our technology, and to a lesser extent our science, are so far predicated upon military demands that were these suddenly removed, we should undoubtedly find that the differentials between and rate of progress within the various technologies altered rapidly from familiar norms. The more our technology mirrors our military wants, the less it mirrors our economic ones. While hard to quantify, it already seems likely that in terms of economic growth, we lose more indirectly because we are not developing the right technologies fast enough than we lose through diverting production resources to military ends. The burden is heavier still because where there are considerations of national security the only tolerable risk is that of being caught with excess capacity.[28] The dove-tailing of military requirements, industrial interests and technological innovation has led to a serious social concern with 'the scientific-technological elite' and what Eisenhower described in the United States context as 'the military-industrial complex'.

In any event, military systems acquisition is not a normal market activity. The severe uncertainties of both demand and supply associated with military work put a very heavy strain on those R and D programs which increasingly call for ambitious state-of-the-art advances in situations of high military urgency.[29] One corollary of this is that, according to SIPRI, in countries such as Britain, the United States and France, the research input-output ratio is 'at least twelve times greater in the military field than in the civil'.[30] Arms races between advanced powers can now be said to consist of calculated responses to technical challenges that are more qualitative than quantitative. This happens in several ways. First, countries at similar levels in an area of technology can expect to make a particular advance in that technology at about the same time as each other. Then, following the so-called Action-Reaction Phenomenon, two such countries aiming at full security must not only counter the *actual* moves of the other, but because of the long time scale of military R and D, offset any other possible move which the other could make from its initial technical position. Further, so-called Worst Case Analysis requires that each country makes the most pessimistic assessment of its own research, development, deployment and operational efforts and the most pessimistic assumptions about those of its potential adversaries.

Still other complications can occur. For instance, R and D and deployment directed towards strictly defensive ends can, in certain circumstances, increase the actual probability of war. It is easy to see why the momentum and intrinsic instabilities of military technological innovation are seen as a threat to the preservation of the nuclear equation, a danger equal to and perhaps less controllable than premeditated, preemptive or accidental war.[31]

The activity of R and D is now carried on by armies of professionals. Genius is welcome but by no means essential. This, incidentally, diminishes one of the hopes sometimes expressed for disarmament, namely that the scientific community could be self-policing. The extent and density of research is now too vast for monitoring except at the highest levels where administrators need scarcely be aware of what appear to be essentially routine, though in fact extremely sophisticated, development programs. In any case, the scientific community is divided. One observer, confessing himself 'quite baffled by the mentality' of those who do biological warfare research, has reflected: 'How far this is a betrayal and perversion of the aims of science and medicine, probably only scientists and doctors would properly understand.'[32] Another admits disappointment when told by a laboratory, company or university that they did not feel it appropriate for them to participate in R and D for the Vietnam War. He added: 'I also find it personally embarrassing to find this nonconstructive attitude within the engineering and scientific community....'[33] Both are members of the scientific/ engineering community, broadly defined. The effort of some members of the community to persuade colleagues of responsibility for the consequences of their work, however commendable, encounters a very harsh political reality. It is, of course, possible still that the net effect of the application of science to warfare will in the long term be beneficial to the human race. It is usually conceded that nuclear weapons may have been largely responsible for the fact that there has been no major world war in the last quarter century. It must be hoped that nuclear war will be permanently eschewed, even though, as noted above, conventional warfare might one day be made to approach nuclear warfare in its lethality and therefore its 'unsuitability'. On the other hand, as McNamara observed, we do sometimes overlook the fact that every future age of man will be a nuclear one.[34] It follows that as long as leaders judge that there are certain international political problems best given over to military solution, then every day brings greater risks. As Konrad Lorenz has said:

> An unprejudiced observer from another planet, looking upon man as he is today, in his hand the atom bomb, the product of his intelligence, in his heart the aggression drive inherited from his anthropological ancestors, which this same intelligence cannot control, would not prophesy long life for the species.

It seems that we must wait to see whether in the case of our species the ethical neutrality of science is in the event a truly genuine one.

NOTES TO CHAPTER 9

1. It is also salutary in that we are forced to recognize that we may still be at quite an early stage of the process, this century, the Second World War above all, marking the critical take-off phase.* The development of weapons was extremely slow, in the majority of cases the pressures to innovate simply not being felt by those who might have stimulated development. And this in spite of the fact that technical superiority in weaponry had commonly led to victory in war, and was often recognized to have done so. Gradually, a distinct class of military engineers emerged, a status distinction came to be drawn between 'pure' and 'applied' science, and some scientists and engineers began to experience a moral repugnance against any warlike use of science. See, for instance, Bernard and Fawn Brodie, *From Crossbow to H-Bomb* (New York: Dell Publishing Co., 1962).
2. See, for instance, United Nations, *Report of the Secretary-General: Effects of the Possible Use of Nuclear Weapons and the Security and Economic Implications for States and the Acquisition and Further Development of these Weapons*, 1968, A/6858.
3. Two of many books on this subject are Abram Chayes and Jerome B. Weisner (eds), *ABM* (London: Macdonald, 1970) and Johan J. Holst and William Schneider Jnr (eds) *Why ABM?* (London: Pergamon Press, 1969).
4. G. W. Rathjens and G. B. Kistiakowsky, 'The Limitations of Strategic Arms', *Scientific American*, 222 (Jan 1970) p. 26 But see also the letters column in the same periodical for May 1970, p. 6.
5. Herbert F. York, 'Military Technology and National Security', *Scientific American*, 221 (Aug 1969) p. 29.
6. Stockholm International Peace Research Institute (SIPRI), *Yearbook of World Armaments and Disarmament 1968/9* (London: Gerald Duckworth and Co. Ltd, 1969) pp. 130–1.
7. United Nations, *Report of the Secretary-General on Chemical and Bacteriological (Biological) Weapons and the Effects of their Possible Use*, 1969, A/7575, para, 368.
8. Vladimir Dedijer, 'The Poor Man's Power', in Nigel Calder (ed.) *Unless Peace Comes* (London: Allen Lane, The Penguin Press, 1968) p. 36.
9. Mathew S. Meselson, 'Chemical and Biological Weapons', *Scientific American*, 220 (May 1970) p. 25.
10. Gordon H. Orians and E. W. Pfeiffer, 'Ecological Effects of the War in Vietnam', *Science* 168 (1970) p. 553.
11. See, for instance, George Thayer, *The War Business* (London: Weidenfeld and Nicolson, 1969) and Lewis A. Frank, *The Arms Trade in International Relations* (London: Praeger, 1969).
12. Sir Zolly Zuckerman, *Scientists and War* (London: Hamish Hamilton, 1966) pp. 88–90.
13. André Beaufre, 'Battlefields of the 1980s', in *Unless Peace Comes*, p. 20.
14. Leonard Sullivan Jnr, 'R & D for Vietnam', *Science and Technology*, (Oct 1968) p. 38.

* Before it, through most of history, one is surprised by the absence of a persisting corpus of knowledge about military equipment, weapons often being used once or twice and then forgotten. The history of science and war is thus in large measure one of invention and war, true science being a feature mainly of the last two or three centuries.

15. E. C. Cornford, 'Technology and the Battlefield', in *The Implications of Military Technology in the 1970s*, Institute for Strategic Studies Adelphi Papers No 46 (London, 1968) p. 52.
16. John Wheldon, *Machine Age Armies* (London: Abelard-Schuman, 1968), chap. 8.
17. Guy Hartcup, *The Challenge of War* (Newton Abbot: David and Charles, 1970), p. 274.
18. John S. Tompkins, *The Weapons of World War Three* (London: Robert Hale Ltd, 1967) pp. 112–13.
19. Ibid. p. 47. General Wheeler was at the time chairman of the U.S. Joint Chiefs of Staff.
20. See, for instance, Joseph Rees and Arnold Whitaker, 'The Next Generation of Fighter Aircraft', *Science and Technology* (Oct 1968).
21. 2nd Report from the Select Committee on Science and Technology, Session 1968–9, *Defence Research*, HC 213, Appendix 43.
22. See, for instance, William A. Nierenberg, 'Toward a Future Navy', *Science and Technology* (Oct 1968).
23. John P. Craven, 'Ocean Technology and Submarine Warfare', in Adelphi Papers no. 46.
24. Quoted in Raymond L. Garthoff, *Soviet Military Policy* (London: Faber and Faber, 1966) p. 106.
25. Major-Gen G. I. Pokrovsky, *Science and Technology in Contemporary War* (London: Stevens and Sons Ltd, 1959) p. 166.
26. John Erickson (ed.) *The Military-Technical Revolution* (London: Pall Mall Press, 1966) p. 14.
27. In the USA, 80 per cent of Federal R & D is concerned with the external challenge – OECD, *Reviews of National Science Policy: United States*, 1968, p 36. It has often been acknowledged in the Soviet Union that it is only in the 'priority' sectors, essentially those closely connected with defense, that planning has really worked – OECD, *Science Policy in the USSR*, 1969, p. 435.
28. Lt-Gen. A. W. Betts, then head of the U.S. Army R & D, interviewed in *Science and Technology* (Oct 1968) p. 95. See also in the same number John S. Foster Jnr, the Director of Defense Research and Engineering in the Pentagon, 'The Leading Edge of National Security', p. 18.
29. Merton J. Peck and F. M. Scherer, *The Weapons Acquisition Process: An Economic Analysis* (Cambridge, Mass: Harvard Business School Division of Research, 1962), especially the concluding chapter.
30. SIPRI Yearbook, p. 94.
31. See, for instance, Alastair Buchan, *War in Modern Society* (London: Collins, 1966) pp. 154–75.
32. John Cookson and Judith Nottingham, *A Survey of Chemical and Biological Warfare* (London: Sheed and Ward, 1969) p. 282.
33. L. Sullivan, *Science and Technology*, p. 32.
34. Robert S. McNamara, *The Essence of Security* (London: Hodder and Stoughton Ltd, 1968) p. 51.

10 The Military Bureaucracy: A Case Study of a Civilian Contribution

PETER NAILOR

The department of state that controlled the affairs of the Royal Navy, supported the exercise of policy in foreign parts, and had an interest too in mercantile marine affairs was – as everyone once knew – called the Admiralty. It was large, powerful and conceded to be effective. It was composed of a rather unusual balance of military and civilian expertise which, commentators and critics alleged, contributed to its confidence and efficacy. This essay tries, against a background of determinant factors in government operations generally, to account for some of the Admiralty's strengths and weaknesses.

I cannot deny, however, that this is also a requiem. It was faintly ridiculous, of course, in the middle of the twentieth century to receive a letter which began 'Sir, I am commanded by My Lords Commissioners of the Admiralty to inform you that....' and which ended 'I am, Sir, your obedient servant.' It made hardly more sense that instructions to Commanders-in-chief always ended (in capital letters) BY COMMAND OF THEIR LORDSHIPS. It was all rather unnecessary, and sometimes quite out of place. There must, however, have been a certain satisfaction in writing to the correspondent who wanted to know why the Admiralty flag was not half-masted on the death of King George VI, that it was a corporative flag, not a national or personal emblem and that 'even in so untoward an event as the simultaneous demise of all My Lords', the flag would stay close up. There was a certain charm too in receiving visitors in the room where Nelson's enspirited body had lain before its committal, or in being admitted on special occasions to the Board Room with its superb Grinling Gibbons decorations, and the wind indicator which showed if the French could get out of Brest (or the British out of Spithead). Was it true that the segment had been cut out of the table to accommodate a minister's belly, or was it his portfolio that overflowed normal limits?

The past, in the Admiralty, was a living past; a tradition, even a building, that provided a link with a fascinating heritage of practice, standards and beliefs that welcomed the newcomer and comforted the established practitioner. But if it was a comfort, it may also have been delusion; times change and needs vary. In the postwar world, the Admiralty tried hard to make the transition without surrendering the place it felt that the navy, and the Admiralty, should have. This essay does not pretend to be either complete or impartial; a number of topics, like manpower policy and dockyard organization are either not investigated at all or only touched upon briefly. Nevertheless, it does attempt to highlight major features which affected the performance and achievements of the Admiralty in recent times.

The fashioning of defense policy, like all other forms of government activity, shades into routine administration and is only intermittently exciting. It is at least as much concerned with the day-to-day management of existing resources as with the planning of future needs, and over a wide range of activities depends as much upon general managerial competence for effective results as upon specialist military knowledge. At one end of the spectrum, the broad issues of defense policy are virtually indistinguishable from foreign policy, but at the other end the mechanics of defense policy bear many of the hallmarks common to any large industrial activity.

Major decisions do, of course, arise, and sometimes are of a sort where the participants are aware of the fundamental nature of the occasion. Even then it sometimes happens that the *consequences* of the decision, the efforts and resources that will be required to support the decision, are not, or cannot be clearly perceived. A case in point was the decision by the British government in 1954 to commit a large element of the army to be stationed on the continent of Europe permanently, as an obligation under the Treaty of Brussels. This decision consciously broke a pattern hundreds of years old; it was instrumental in resolving a diplomatic situation which had threatened to divide the Western allies, and it acknowledged firmly what was thought to be an essential need of the system of common defense between allies in the atomic age, namely the prior commitment of forces. It is arguable, however, that the extensive significance of this decision – even though it was made at the highest ministerial levels – was not immediately realized and took some years to sink into the political and bureaucratic awareness of the government machine as a whole. It was not perhaps given due weight at the time – only some three years later – when another decision was taken to end compulsory military service in Britain; and it is open to question whether the problems involved in paying for this foreign-based army were fully evaluated. There can hardly be any doubt that the strategic implications of the decision for the remainder of Britain's security commitments, especially those she still sought to bear outside Europe, took more than a decade to work to the surface.

For most of the time, however, the processes of defense management and decision-making are neither so innovatory nor so important. The majority of events, so far from making ripples ten years or more hence, sink without any more trace than a transitory fleck of spume. 'Decision-making' as a description of the core of the administrative process has positive and dramatic overtones which belie what actually goes on (and ignores those other features which are also important, decision-evasion and decision-reversal).[1] It also tends to discount the routine and humdrum nature of most administrative tasks, which are not concerned to precipitate new decisions as much as to give continuing substance to old ones.

In government departments, like those concerned with defense, good record-keeping and consistency are prime and necessary virtues. The nature of the activity requires that public money is adequately accounted for and recorded and that regulations are applied to all causes and persons in a like fashion. This in turn imparts a certain ponderousness to the whole style of administration, that some forms of commercial activity can avoid, though by no means all do. Extra work may be done, and extra time taken, to produce a careful and documented answer, that may be only marginally more right (or true, or expedient) than the response which at the outset experience and the light of nature indicated would be appropriate. Nevertheless, the public service has a duty to be careful, and if this sometimes involves delay, the general sense of parliamentary and public reaction indicates that delay is an acceptable price to pay – provided that it is not unduly prolonged and the eventual answer is commendable.

The size of the operation has an effect both upon the timeliness and the rightness of the response. Kenneth Boulding has expressed the opinion[2] that there is a limit to the efficient size of an organization: 'Beyond a certain point, increase in the scale of an organization results in a breakdown of communications, in a lack of flexibility, in bureaucratic stagnation and insensitivity.' When this point has been passed, letters go unacknowledged, the small print more than the intention of a regulation is emphasized, bad supervision goes unpunished (or even unnoticed) and, as a culmination, bad decisions are not only made but persisted in and defended. It is not, however, a sudden or definite fall from grace; it takes time to occur and may only come to light as the result of a specific incident or complaint which puts ministers or senior staff on their guard. The gradual nature of the decline arises from two other inherent features of bureaucratic structures. The first is that all structures tend to grow in complexity and size; the second that any sizable organization can only be efficient if delegation and trust are exercised. The exact identification of Boulding's Point is probably only possible in retrospect.

The governmental machinery by which defense policy is controlled in Britain has gone through a number of evolutionary stages since the end of the Second World War, all of them tending to enhance the powers and position of a central department concerned with defense as an entity, at the expense of the departments which historically have controlled and managed either a single fighting service or the procurement of defense equipment.³ From one point of view – the impression gained by outside analysts and taxpayers – the development of new mechanisms of government is a slow and unwieldy game; expediency as much as efficiency seems to dominate the moves and there is no integral expectation that the fittest, rather than the toughest, will survive. Usually there is confusion about whether the purpose of the change is to achieve the same result at less cost or some better result at a different cost. The public expectation that there will be a better consequence at a smaller cost is not often achieved. From the inside, however, the effects of change are different. The broad statements of intention and general principle which are made in public are only the tip of the iceberg; below the surface, the departmental organization may be turned upside down, or at least sideways, so as to give institutional form and backing to the changes at more senior levels. These internal changes, though they may be secondary in scale and importance, have reverberative effects which may go on after the public effect of the major changes has subsided – in the belief that the new arrangements, having been announced, have also been completed. Hierarchies and departmental interrelationships are altered; new patterns of paper flow have to be devised; office locations are switched, and different personnel agglomerations are rationalized. All of these alterations absorb time and energy and may create new anomalies and structural nonsenses to replace those which it had been the purpose of the reorganization to eliminate. Many of the difficulties, of course, are transient and trivial; new patterns of work develop and, as in a disturbed anthill, the obstacles to day-to-day busy-ness are quickly overcome. Some difficulties remain however and are observed; if they cannot be eradicated by adjustment, they tend to become obscured by the necessity to carry on the governmental process, so that there may grow up a tacit acceptance of the fact that actual methods and responsibilities are somewhat different from the formal descriptions attached to them.

This tends to happen in all organizations. Sometimes it is caused by the interpolation of a dominant personality as well as by changes or weaknesses in structures. The phenomenon may expedite administration, but in the long run it usually causes trouble, when clever Mr X moves on or when, in a new reorganization, the actuality has at last to be identified.

The departments concerned with defense have for nearly twenty years been involved more or less continuously in the reorganization game. Sometimes the causation has been a relatively simple wish to eliminate archaisms and improve day-to-day efficiency; this has been reflected most frequently in internal restructuring, which has sometimes assumed major proportions.[4] On a number of occasions, however, most notably in 1957-8 and in 1963-4 major changes in ministerial and departmental responsibilities have imposed consequential effects within as well as between departments. There have also been other changes, less dramatic and longer drawn-out in their effect which have nevertheless been of considerable importance in shaping the way in which business is carried on; and of these the most notable in the postwar period has been the creation of the North Atlantic Treaty Organization. At the military as well as at the diplomatic level, the formulation and execution of national policy has had, however unwillingly, to take account of NATO; NATO has evolved its own bureaucratic forms and needs, like the rendering of periodic reports, on which NATO-wide assessments have to be based, and it has increasingly come to be the forum within which national perceptions have had to be reconciled with the interests of the alliance as a whole. It has also, at the single service level, created new patterns of relationship and faction, so that one could point, with some truth, to the closeness of the relationship between the Royal Navy and, say, the United States Navy, or the Royal Netherlands Navy, as a factor which can affect organizational form as well as institutional outlook. This can be illustrated, on the operational side, by the similarity of training patterns and the cooperation in, for example, anti-submarine techniques and execises, and in the institutional and administrative sphere, by the cordial and effective collaboration between the Royal Navy's Polaris Executive and the United States navy's Special Projects Office.

The position of the Admiralty in the postwar period has some special features of interest from a general institutional point of view as well as in the more specialist defense context. It was historically one of the major departments of state, going back, in something like its twentieth-century shape, to the first half of the seventeenth century, and having been a model for many important and even crucial bureaucratic innovations. The device of a board of commissioners was a precursor of the institutional form of boards of directors; this particular mode of organization was evolved to pay off the Duke of Buckingham's debt rather than deliberately to improve the state of the Stuart navy. Similarly, many techniques of good modern office practice were foreshadowed by Pepys and his like, though they were perhaps instituted to provide a defensive evidence against inquisition by Parliament or Treasury as much as to create the machine celebrated, in a famous passage, by Arthur Bryant:

> To obey orders punctually and without question and to hold the Regulations of the Admiralty as more sacred than the Ten Commandments, to do one's duty for one's bare wages without cavil and in the face of death, and to lay one's all in the keeping of the navy in the belief that somehow in this world or some other the service would care for and vindicate its own; such was the creed which the little scribe in the great wig taught the fighting men of the Stuart navy.[5]

It was a creed the substance of which lasted a very long time; the creed itself probably never existed anywhere in reality, but the sense of service, of obligation and of involvement was as lively in the Admiralty Office as anywhere else in the naval service. The Admiralty, as an institution, found it somewhat easier to stress the romance and the responsibility of the Royal Navy than the fleet always did; and there were a number of occasions, not all of them mutinies, which seemed to indicate that the naval service was not always being administered as intelligently and responsively as all would wish. Nevertheless, the durability and the continuity of what came to be thought of as the British 'naval tradition' had a considerable effect in giving to naval affairs and to naval administration an eminent standing. The Admiralty even after the primacy of the royal navy had passed away continued to be thought of, and to think of itself, as an important department of state, and it continued – as Pepys had sought – to run the navy firmly and, so far as in it lay, fairly. It was a centralized machine, the grip of which was tightened rather than relaxed by modern communication methods, and which in war was sometimes obtrusive. It had a way of responding quickly and well to major issues, but it could also be unimaginative on small problems.

It was predominantly civilian. The last secretary of the Admiralty was the thirty-second since Pepys; in the interval, 'sea-officers' had evolved, through the merging of seaman and gentleman, into a major and well indoctrinated profession, with distinctive attributes. But the proportion of naval personnel employed in the Admiralty remained small, both absolutely and by comparison with the War Office and Air Ministry; and although the organizational form of the other two service departments was consciously based on the Admiralty pattern, the relationship of the civilian component to the service component remained unique in some important ways and was, some observers thought, more effective.[6]

The function of the naval officer in the Admiralty was to be the expert, the professional consultant, whose knowledge, whose opinion and, in some areas, whose decision, was essential for the formulation of a sensible policy. Clearly there were fields where this expertise was dominant; the direction of operations, tactical doctrine, discipline, equipment characteristics. There were other areas where specialist knowledge of sea-life and sea-fighting was not so crucial, though, of course, it was still highly relevant to an activity whose main purpose was servicing the fleet. The organization for the supply of stores, food and spare parts was only partially under naval supervision; a rough line of demarcation was that logistic support in ships and fleet establishments was naval-manned, on shore civilian-manned. A major part in determining logistic philosophy was taken by civilian specialists. The dockyards too were predominantly civilian in their staffing and management. But perhaps most important of all over the years, the responsibility of managing the business of the Admiralty Office, and of communicating with the outside world, was firmly in the hands of the Admiralty secretariat, the heirs and assigns of 'the little scribe in the great wig'.

Although there is evidence to support the belief that at various times – usually of crisis in interdepartmental wrangles – some naval opinion chafed at the large element of civilian participation,[7] in general the relationship between the naval and civilian managerial components was easy and beneficial. In the first place, both believed that the work they were engaged on was important, and there were as many civilians as there were naval officers who went further and would assert that their involvement was vocational as well as professional. In the second place, there was usually a general consensus about the necessity for the importance of the task to be reflected in a strong, well-equipped, well-trained and well-supplied navy; as strong and efficient as the nation could be willed to provide. There were naturally a number of contributory elements in this commonly shared desire, and it would be wrong to discount the benefits which it was perceived would flow from success. Not only would there be more ships to command, more establishments to superintend, but there would also be more senior civilian posts to be filled. It would, however, be at least as wrong to suppose that bureaucratic aggrandizement was a prime (or even often a conscious) objective of policy; the important thing was to do well by the navy.

The third major factor was that the partnership between service and civilian elements was of long standing; it was what both sides had come to expect, it was what they had come to learn how to manipulate, and it was generally a successful and prestigious partnership. As Snyder explains it:

> There is a very high degree of confidence and trust between [civil and naval personnel].... An officer's up-to-date knowledge of problems in the fleet enables him to act as an innovator or catalyst, continually confronting his civil-servant colleague with the new problems that need attention. The role of the civil servant is that of critic and manager, improving and refining the proposal and engineering its approval in the Admiralty or the defense establishment generally.[8]

There was a fourth factor too, which was important, although its effect was uneven. This was that the civilians provided continuity, and a stability in the techniques and tactics of interdepartmental negotiation, which would buttress – and, as Snyder suggests, supplement – the views brought in regularly by the naval officers from the fleet. Naval officers normally only served two, or at the most three, years in a headquarters appointment, and the majority of them began to get Admiralty experience only when they had already reached the rank of commander. They might subsequently acquire a sizable headquarters expertise of their own, if they also achieved a better than average career, to captain or above; but initially they were at a disadvantage in deploying their professional expertise in a headquarters environment. This deficiency was not always abrogated by staff or command office experience; the navy's attitude to staff training and the concomitant development of a staff doctrine and to the acquisition of administrative competence was uncertain. The highest form of naval excellence was sea service, and a command experience at sea was, quite rightly, held to be an invaluable prerequisite for flotilla or fleet command. This view was, however, pressed to an extreme, in the sense that it led to other forms of training for high rank being discounted. The reasons for this feeling are obscure; it was reflected in the long struggle to set up a naval staff, and it may have something to do with a belief that the civilian expertise at headquarters, and the excellence of the support given by the supply and secretariat specialists in commands, and at sea, could provide a surrogate for staff training. It certainly had something to do, in the postwar era, with the growing scarcity of sea billets as the number of ships, and the size of most major units, contracted; and there may too have been a reaction among some seaman officers to the erosion of their dominant position in the service as the status of other officers was improved (most notably in the formation of a 'General List' in 1956). Whatever the reason, a smaller proportion of naval officers were given formal staff course training than in the other two services; and the navy did not always send its brightest prospects to the higher level of military institution, like the Imperial Defense College. The element of continuity and experience at headquarters provided by civilians was therefore an important part of their contribution; but an examination of administrative class appointments in the period from 1952 to 1964 shows that, so far as this particular group was concerned, the average length of duty in any one post did not significantly exceed the normal naval tour of duty. The burden of continuity (even given the fact that the administrative group was small and cohesive) was therefore in the discrete components of the secretariat pushed down, as it were, to the executive class level, and to a dependence rather upon good records than a group-memory. There were exceptions, of course; one head of Commissions and Warrants Branch (which dealt among other things with the entry and training policy for officers) in the 1950s served for almost five years in the post, succeeding an assistant secretary whose tenure had been even longer, and one head of Military Branch (which provided secretariat support for the naval staff) served in the post for rather more than five years. In general, however, continuity — in the sense of long individual appointments — tended to be provided either at a level lower than assistant secretary or principal, or at a higher level. Undersecretaries, deputy secretaries, and most notably the permanent secretary stayed longer in post. These were naturally very important and influential positions, and provided the element of judicious review inherent in the contribution expected from civilian continuity at a level where it could be most helpful in large and broad issues of policy. The reverse side of the coin, however, was that to a certain extent these senior civil servants also had to provide continuity to their own oraganization as well as to the naval staff; and this put a premium upon their own depth of Admiralty experience, at a time when interdepartmental movement of senior civilian staff was beginning to be developed as a conscious Treasury technique for broadening civil servants' knowledge and equalizing promotion opportunities. Perhaps even more important at this particular time was the fact that for the most part the experience represented in this handful of men was of wartime and prewar conditions; the appropriateness to the conditions of the 1950s was not necessarily direct, and sometimes, in the view of some naval officers, became a brake on change in the face of the new problems which the Admiralty was experiencing. The relevance of continuity was, in fact, diminishing.

The civil service element of the Admiralty Office was drawn for the most part from the general service classes of the home civil service. There were in addition – as in several other departments – special departmental grades and classes, which were allotted special list roles.⁹ Recruitment, except for temporary or low-grade posts, was centrally controlled by the civil service commission, and allocation to a specific department, such as the Admiralty, depended upon a combination of preference, relative standing in the competitive entry procedure, and chance: thus, if one wished to be appointed to the Admiralty and came close to the top in the administrative class competition (and, of course, if a vacancy existed), gratification was more likely to be achieved than if one came low on the competition list. In postwar years, however, the number of administrative class entrants who specifically chose any of the defense departments was small; this arose partly from a perception that the home and social service departments were more likely to be good career bases than defense, and partly from a real or imagined disinclination to be concerned with topics that were becoming, at one and the same time, socially less fashionable and nationally less important. There was also something in the argument that new entrants knew so little of the details of the work of the expanded civil service that their preference for departments was usually based upon hearsay or fancy; thus the Treasury became the objective of self-defined mandarins, the Home Office or Education attracted those who felt they would like to do some as yet undefined good. The immediate consequence for the Admiralty was that a large proportion of new entrants felt no special receptivity to its traditions.

New entrants to the administrative class were usually, though by no means always, graduates. The class as a whole was a relatively small unit, oscillating in the postwar period between 2,200 and 3,000, whose duties were diverse; they were in theory concerned with policy-making, but in fact included a wide range of general managerial tasks. The ethos of the group was that they embodied intellectual gifts of a high order which enabled them – in the words of the Fulton Report – to take 'a practical view of any problem, irrespective of its subject matter, in the light of [their] knowledge and experience of the government machine'.¹⁰ The greater size and pervasiveness of the government machine, as it was developed during and since the Second World War, led to a substantial alteration in the historical function of the administrative class generally and to some alteration in its structure; intellectual power had to be supplemented to a greater extent by managerial capacity, and this included not only a new emphasis in the traditional open competition, but the admission of a large number of non-graduates and graduates who had proved their ability in other parts of the government service, either by a competition organized on a service-wide basis by the civil service commission, or by departmental reviews, in which the civil service commission was represented. So far as the Admiralty was concerned, these developments led to a strengthening of the Administrative class group by individuals who, though able, were rather less inclined to accept the assertions of Admiralty interest as dogma; either because they had a wide range of outside experience, or because they reflected more directly the attitudes of the postwar generations.

The new entrant to the Admiralty, in the late 1940s or 1950s, found himself in a group of no more than sixty or at the most seventy members of the administrative class (which inclded statisticians and actuaries), all working in the permanent secretary's department. The great majority worked in the London headquarters buildings, which at that time comprized principally the Admiralty building, in Whitehall, and Queen Anne's Mansions, looming disconsolately over St James's Park. A handful worked in Bath, whither one-third of the office had been dispatched in the government dispersal program of 1938, and whence, it seems, they are unlikely to be recalled. The group was divided pyramidically, with its own career structure, and at that time an insignificant amount of sideways movement between departments outside the Defense group occurred. The entry grade was an assistant principal (although a class-to-class promoted entrant might come in as a principal); this was essentially a training grade, and involved fairly frequent movement between a range of posts, and usually included some experience as a private secretary to a minister or to the permanent secretary, as well as short periods of attachment to the fleet, a dockyard and a major contractor's plant. After four or five years, the assistant principal would be promoted to the main grade level of principal, where he would take charge of a block of work, supported by executive and clerical staff who might number anything between four and forty, depending on the nature of the function. Promotion to the next grade of assistant secretary was by selection: merit tempered by seniority, and might take place at any age between about thirty-five and fifty, although usually it occurred after between nine and twelve years' experience as a principal. The pyramid narrowed rapidly towards the top; there might be perhaps about thirty principals and statisticians, and some twenty assistant secretaries, but above them there were only six undersecretary posts, and three higher posts. Luck, as much as merit or seniority, might take a turn at these levels; but even though the postwar situation might seem a little turgid, because the age structure of the group was unevenly layered, an ambitious man could not but be heartened by a comparison with the prewar case, when the total administrative class component had been no more than a round score, and when advancement had been a long haul indeed. Sir Henry Markham, who was secretary of the Admiralty during the Second World War, had been an assistant principal for more than eleven years; and even if he had then become a permanent secretary less than six years later, the combination of a World War and a most unusual, imported, predecessor who retired on the stroke of sixty, was unlikely often to recur. Sir Archibald Carter was brought across from the India Office in 1936 to replace the legendary figure of Sir Oswyn Murray, who caught a chill at the funeral of King George V after being the secretary of the Admiralty for nineteen years; the intrusion was initially resented not least because it was seen as an attempt to weaken the cohesion of the secretariat. Markham himself died prematurely towards the end of 1946 and his place was taken by Mr J. G. (late Sir John) Lang, who became as legendary in his time as Sir Oswyn Murray.

Sir John Lang was secretary of the Admiralty for rather more than fourteen years; long enough for him to have as colleagues on the Board of Admiralty at the end of his tenure, sea lords who had been junior captains or mere commanders when he first took office. (Earl Mountbatten was in this, as in so many other ways, a distinguished and unique exception.) Lang had joined the Admiralty as a second division clerk before the First World War, in which he served in the Royal Marine Artillery; after the war he continued to serve as what would now be called a junior and then middle-grade executive class officer, and was eventually (and rather belatedly) promoted into the administration class in 1930. During the Second World War he established a reputation first by organizing and controlling the vastly expanded communication and signals distribution system (the War Registry) and then in superintending naval manpower policy, both in regard to wartime usage and to planning for demobilization. When Sir Henry Markham died, he was preferred over older and more senior colleagues to act as secretary of the Admiralty, and then was confirmed in the appointment in February 1947.

By background, therefore, Sir John Lang did not conform to the stereotype of the permanent secretary; his career does however provide something of a corrective to the general impression that infers a close and narrow comparability between the backgrounds of members of the administrative class. His colleagues too were representative only insofar as they provided a reasonable cross-section of the administrative class as a group; if one takes the position in 1961 as an example, forty-one of the total sixty-nine were direct entrant graduates and sixteen were entrants from another class of the civil service. Twelve of the total were wartime entrants who had been attracted to remain in the Admiralty and who were, in quality even more markedly than in quantity, a significant force: three of this group had reached the equivalent rank of Undersecretary or better by 1961.[11]

The executive class civil servants in the Admiralty had a wider scope of employment than in the other two service departments insofar as they provided the managerial staff for the supply organizations dealing with general stores, armament stores and victuals. These, together with the contractual and accounting organizations, provided unusually good career opportunities in their own separate hierarchies, at the peak of which a director might be the equivalent, in pay, of an undersecretary and a major force in his own right within the office. By comparison, executive class staff in the secretariat led a more restricted, and secluded, life. Their promotion opportunites tapered off markedly above the equivalent of the administrative class principal, even after a number of the small and separate groups had been brought together into a 'Combined List' in the 1950s, and they did not enjoy (or were not subjected to, depending upon one's point of view) the opportunities for postings abroad which the supply and accounting department staff had, until the reorganization of the 1950s and 1960s closed most of the overseas bases down.

The general picture of the executive class to be derived from recruitment literature indicates a managerial function, implementing rather than determining policy (though doing that too at the more senior levels), and an educational background broadly of A-level (i.e. high-school) competence or better. There have been, for example, a growing number of graduate entrants to the class.

Although this picture seems to reflect not unfairly the structure of the supply and accounting departments which had always been regarded as 'special departmental classes', and had consciously recruited for managerial competence, the situation in the secretariat was more complex. The secretariat group of executive and clerical staff before the Second World War had been small, and direct executive recruitment had been spasmodic. During the wartime expansion, and again during the Korean rearmament period, the majority of executive class posts were filled by the promotion of clerical staff. Many of the personnel were of a good standard – since clerical recruitment before the war had also been genuinely competitive; but their career development had been largely unplanned, and the age structure was unevenly layered. Consequently, seniority was inclined to outweigh any but the most evident merit. Many small pockets of staff – for example, those directly servicing the naval staff divisions – remained as isolated units; they, and to a certain extent the secretariat branches, provided an inadequate training for the managerial functions which senior and chief executive officers had to perform. Pressure from below to maintain promotion outlets for clerical staff was intensified for a time by the 'executivization' of senior clerical positions in the early 1950s, and a trickle recruitment of direct entrants from the executive class competitions was not resumed until the later 1950s.

It is perhaps worth noting here a factor which, from interviews as well as from tracing individuals' records in such published material, seems to distinguish the postwar civil servant from his prewar counterpart: promotion is more important. Before the war promotion was slow but the work was responsible, well paid, and socially well regarded. A higher clerical officer on his three hundred pounds per annum was not a negligible figure. After the war, the level of work-responsibility seems to have been diluted and, comparatively, the pay as well as the status of civil servants declined. The way to maintain, let alone improve, one's standard of living (and perhaps self-regard too) was by promotion – the opportunities for which had anyway increased with the growth of all departments.

The effect of the wartime expansion, and the postwar maintenance of a large Admiralty, had the consequence (again to take the position in 1961 as an example) of giving an executive class structure to the supply and accounting departments which included between 25–30 per cent of staff who were not direct executive entrants; but the corresponding figure in the secretariat was more like 80 per cent, and at the senior levels nearer 90 per cent.[12]

One special feature of the secretariat (and Contract Department) executive lists, at this time, was that they included women. Women had been accepted in the Admiralty as reluctantly as the telephone; one of the nicer stories was that at the time of the outbreak of the First World War there had only been a few of each of these innovations in the office. The most accessible telephone was in the corridor outside the first lord's room; and the 'lady typewriters' were securely locked in their room and guarded by a messenger, a few doors away. More lady typewriters were introduced, as the habit grew up of typing rather than scribing routine correspondence, and more telephones. As late as 1936 however it was common practice to send a hand-written note to a colleague in another Ministry (by hand of messenger) rather than to telephone. And it was not until 1958 that a woman first reached the rank of senior executive officer. The argument against the use of women in senior positions was based upon the premise that all civil servants were liable to be transferred to outports establishments or abroad, or even on occasions to ships at sea, and that as women could not be expected to undertake some of these duties, and would not be acceptable to others, they should not be employed in grades where the likelihood of such postings was a real, rather than just a theoretical, possibility.

What was the substance behind the reputation which the Admiralty had? There are a number of factors which point to a conclusion that the reputation was not without some foundation, and a few that suggest that it was a waning asset. Almost all of them, unfortunately, are impressionistic, not merely because of the difficulty of documenting recent events, but also because most of the considerations are either subjectively comparative or episodic.

By way of a background to any general assessment, it undoubtedly helped that the Admiralty had a long history and a record of achievement that already existed; when you got involved in a fight with the Admiralty you knew you were taking on an opponent with experience and a reputation. If this encouraged some opponents to try harder, it discouraged others. It also meant that the Admiralty was not especially deterred by anybody else's reputation, and was not easily browbeaten. Thus, for example, the Treasury was regarded with respect but no awe; and the Air Ministry, though a disputatious southpaw that could not always be handled easily, boxed to the same code of rules and would usually settle for a drawn decision.

Secondly, the long history of collaboration between naval and civil personnel helped to establish both the reality and the appearance of unity. When there was an interdepartmental meeting, it was quite common for either a serving officer or a civilian to represent the Admiralty interest; the other service departments usually sent at least one of each. And when the Admiralty sent a pair, they would think it highly improper to disagree with each other before 'outsiders;' arguments were for internal consumption only. The Admiralty had a habit, however, of being the last department to reply in any interdepartmental correspondence. This does not seem to have been deliberate; it may have reflected a rather ponderous internal consultative process, but at least on occasions it seems to have been due to a genuine difficulty in establishing what the appropriate Admiralty-wide view should be. Although this usually gave rise to no special concern inside the Admiralty, it was nevertheless an irritating trait, which may on occasion have meant that the department lost ground which it need not have conceded. One other trait was quite common too; the Admiralty representatives at meetings were frequently junior – implying what was sometimes the case, that delegation and trust enabled work to be kept down to a reasonable level. To take one exotic example, the interdepartmental committee set up to make the preliminary arrangements for service participation in the Queen's Coronation in 1953 had, from the War Office, a deputy secretary; from the Air Ministry, an undersecretary, and from the Admiralty, a principal.

One circumstantial piece of evidence indicates that Whitehall still took the Admiralty reputation seriously enough in the 1960s to take also the opportunity which the reorganization of the Ministry of Defense and the service departments in 1963–4 offered to do something about it. The practice of interdepartmental transfers of staff which grew up in the late 1950s did not really begin to affect the secretariat until a couple of years or so before the major reorganization of 1964; but it had the effect of cracking the corporate identity of the administrative class group and, in the short term, of adversely affecting the assumptions of complete identification with the naval staff. In the medium and longer term this latter point was overcome in part, because the individuals concerned were almost all of a high and admirable quality; even so they were not 'born and bred' Admiralty men and however good they were (and however much they came to relish working in an atmosphere that was friendly and cooperative) they could not easily fulfill all of the requirements which, on the naval side, were regarded as integral parts of the bargain which had been struck over the years. In the period of the run-up to the implementation of the 1964 reorganization, and in the months thereafter, the cross-postings increased in number. This was only to be expected; it was necessary to demonstrate that a new organization was being set up, and there were restructurings and rationalizations being implemented which made some shuffling inevitable The impression was created among Admiralty administrative class staff, however, that a special effort was being made to split up their corporate sense of identity. This may, of course, have been due to hypersensitivity, and to an erroneous rationalization of the regret which they (and the staff of the other service departments) were inclined to feel at the down-grading of their Ministries; but they could point to the fact that, in April 1967, only three of the nine most senior posts in the secretariat were held by 'natives', and that in the comparable Central Ministry of Defense secretariat structure, only one out of thirteen posts was held by a 'born and bred' Admiralty man. What made the whole affair very much more suspicious was that the Air Ministry people had done significantly better!

It is difficult to esablish in this sort of matter where the balance of truth lies. It is at least conceivable that there was a deliberate intent to introduce a sizable infusion of new blood into the Admiralty structure; but cross-postings took place elsewhere too. It is at least possible that the policy was carried to a further extent in the Admiralty than in the other departments of the new Defense complex; but if the Admiralty failed to get 'fair shares' it is not beyond the bounds of possibility that this had something to do with the Admiralty's earlier attitudes to Ministry of Defense attempts to coordinate defense activities, and that some of the 'Air Ministry people' – head for head – were better qualified for key appointments or promotion. It is also just possible, though no 'Admiralty man' worth his salt would like to admit it, that there was a need to infuse new life into a mechanism that was running down.

It could be argued that in the postwar period the Admiralty came up against a series of issues that were inherently difficult but which, in the end, it failed to handle as well as its reputation implied could have been done. (Whether any organization could have done better is, of course, an open question.) A general survey of the issues confronting British defense policy-makers would be out of place in this essay; an admirable one already exists,[13] and a few examples will illustrate the point.

The attempts to create an acceptable balance between the demands for defense and deterrence in the dawn of a nuclear era that was also the sunset of empire led to some awkward compromises. During the Korean rearmament period for example, the navy had to juggle between refurbishing a fleet that was either pre-Second World War or of wartime origin, and preparing some new equipment plans against an emerging adversary whose scale of power had taken a great leap ahead in September 1949, with the first Soviet atom bomb test. It is perhaps a measure of the caution of the Admiralty that the naval threat was then conceived in rather traditional terms – though no one else was in a better case to prognosticate by how much future wars would change; nevertheless, it seems surprising now that so much effort was expended in developing a mine-sweeping and mine-hunting capability, that within a few years was recognized to be overdone.

A little later on, when the chiefs of staff had made an early, but perceptive, attempt to visualize what influence thermo-nuclear weapons would have upon both national and allied security[14] it could be argued that the Admiralty reacted either too quickly or too half-heartedly in unveiling in 1954 a concept of 'broken-backed war' that was tailored at least as much to existing capabilities and plans as to the admittedly speculative future.

Part of the difficulty undoubtedly arose from the feeling that in the 1950s, the navy was open to attack, and the significance of naval force was open to doubt, in a way that had never been experienced before. For the first time the Admiralty could understand what life had been like in the Air Ministry almost continually since the establishment of an independent air force in 1918. In this predicament, a certain amount of panic was understandable; but the day-to-day needs of managing the huge industrial complex that the dockyards, the bases and the supply organizations represented (and from part of which at least the other two service departments were freed) was a diversion, and the low priority given to the elucidation of doctrine in naval staff training was a disability. Moreover, the internal organization responded sluggishly. Even though Professor Parkinson's amusing (and inaccurate) account of the adversely changing ration between the size of the Admiralty and the size of the fleet[15] had not yet struck home, there was a sensitivity about the growth in staff numbers which had an effect in slowing down attempts to strengthen those parts of the organization that had to deal with the new challenges. These were the days of 'The Way Ahead' Committee and other attempts to reduce the ponderous 'tail', and in their train the Plans Division of the Naval Staff and the

Military Branch (to take two instances) made do much as they were; an odd accretion here and there, but most of the load was absorbed by longer hours of work, which sometimes assumed ridiculous consistency, and perversely came to be a matter of pride rather than concern. There may have been adverse consequences flowing from the quality of some of the staff; several factors which could have contributed to this have been mentioned, although the evidence is hardly conclusive.

All was not entirely black, however; L. W. Martin and W. P. Snyder have documented[16] how effectively, if unusually, the Admiralty contrived to put the substance of the doctrine it was evolving before influential circles in the aftermath of Duncan Sandys' Defense White Paper of 1957; by a specially staged conference and by press 'briefings' many of the points which had failed to weigh with Mr Sandys were given further airing. They were received sympathetically – partly because they were sensibly argued, partly because they came from the Admiralty, and partly because there was some feeling that whatever the alternative merits of Mr Sandys' position (itself not very fully developed), he had gone beyond acceptable limits in discounting the views of his professional advisers.

However starkly Mr Sandys tried to show the deterrent side of the security posture, there was a continuing need to strike some sort of balance between deterrence and conventional weapons which could both defend and help deter, and in the years after 1958 the Admiralty endeavored once again to plan the size and shape of a fleet that had some military credibility and was within the economic limits which increasingly determined policy. New organizational forms endeavored to maximize the potential of the Admiralty material departments and the dockyards, and new appreciations had to be made of the relative benefits to be gained from developing new weapons and techniques; VTOL, airborne early-warning anti-submarine weapons, nuclear propulsion (and all the complicated engineering that went with it) and guided weapons were only the most expensive possibilities coming along. It is at least as much a measure of this complexity and intractability as anything else that all of them remain on the policy-makers' agenda for the 1970s.

NOTES TO CHAPTER 10

1. See S. P. Huntington, 'Strategic Planning and the Political Process', *Foreign Affairs* (Jan 1960), for comments on some of these aspects, and the article by C. de Paula on 'A business man in Whitehall', in *The Times* (4 Aug 1970), p. 19.

2. K. E. Boulding, 'The Jungle of Hugeness: the second age of the brontosaurus', *The Saturday Review* (1 March 1958).

3. See Michael Howard, *The Central Organization of Defence* (London: Royal United Service Institution, 1970) for a perceptive and comprehensive analysis of the evolution.

4. For example, in the Admiralty, the reorganization of the Controller of the Navy's Departments in 1957–8, following from the investigation headed by Mr Justice Nihill; the reorganization extended to the royal dockyards as well as to headquarters departments, and involved the creation of new managerial structures grouped, at headquarters, in a way reminiscent of the U.S. Navy Department's Bureaux.

5. Arthur Bryant, *Samuel Pepys: The Saviour of the Navy* (London: Collins, 1938), chapter 5.

6. See, for example, the comments in chapter 7 of W. P. Snyder's *The Politics of British Defence Policy, 1945/62* (London: Benn, 1964).

7. Most recently in the disputes whether or not to begin building a new generation of aircraft carriers, which went on intermittently from 1959–65, and finally resulted in a government decision that the cost would be too great.

8. Snyder, *Politics of British Defence Policy*.

9. The titles and descriptions used here are going to be changed in the restructuring of the civil service proposed by the Fulton Committee Report (Cmnd. 3638, June 1968) and accepted by the government. For a full and interesting account of the recent predicaments of the civil service, see R. G. S. Brown, *The Administrative Process in Britain* (London: Methuen, 1970), especially chapters 2 and 3.

10. Fulton Report, chapter 1, para 15. Do not read this particular chapter of the Fulton Report without reading also the corrective gloss provided by Lord Simey (pp. 101–4).

11. See Brown, *The Administrative Process in Britain*, pp. 44–8, for an analysis of the composition of the administrative class generally.

12. These percentages are estimates; though broadly reliable they are only approximate.

13. L. W. Martin, *British Defence Policy, The Long Recessional* (London: Institute for Strategic Studies, 1969), Adelphi Paper No. 61.

14. See R. N. Rosecrance, *Defence of the Realm* (New York: Columbia University Press, 1968), chapter 6, for an account of the debate on and consequences of the 1952 Global Strategy paper.

15. See C. N. Parkinson, *Parkinson's Law, and other studies in administration* (Cambridge: Riverside Press, 1962).

16. L. W. Martin, 'The Market for Strategic Ideas in Britain: The Sandys Era', *American Political Science Review*, LVI (1962); also in R. Rose (ed.), *Policy-making in Britain* (London: Macmillan, 1969); Snyder, *Politics of British Defence Policy*.

11 Polemology: Promises and a Problem

ROGER A. BEAUMONT

Wayland Denton, a former army platoon leader: 'I went because I'm patriotic. But the more I think about all the guys getting messed up and blown away the more I wonder.... But the other night I went to see "Patton" and for a moment there I wanted to re-enlist.'[1]

Those 'over thirty' can be excused for impatience with traditional pacifism, with its moralizing and presumption of the triumph of good faith and reason, for many of them remember with personal pain the price paid for the democracies' acceptance of those doctrines in the 1920s and 1930s, and in the grim early years of the Second World War. Western adherence to naval limitation agreements and accompanying 'economies' cost the U.S. Navy dearly early in the Pacific War and left the Royal Navy critically short of convoy escorts. The 'too little-too late' days of 1942, the fall of China to communism and the Korean debacle after massive reduction in Western arms reinforced skepticism toward pacifism. It is not surprising, then, to reflect on the fact that the term 'polemology' – the study of war – was coined by Gaston Bouthoul in 1946 immediately after the Second World War.

In the intervening years, research and analysis has been under way in a variety of disciplines focussing on war and conflict. Social scientists active in the field include Anatol Rapaport, Morris Janowitz, Kenneth Boulding, Kurt Lang, Amitai Etzioni and Herman Kahn. Natural and 'hard' scientists have also contributed to the body of polemological knowledge, e.g. John Paul Scott, Nicholas Tinbergen and Konrad Lorenz. Popular accounts by Desmond Morris and Robert Ardrey have heightened general awareness of behavioral and genetic approaches to conflict. And various institutions and agencies have evolved which support various kinds of peace research – over fifty in the 1966 UNESCO list. Government-sponsored disarmament studies have been commissioned and the activities of the Institute for Strategic Studies reaches across official national and disciplinary boundaries.

In spite of this growing interest in empirical analyses of conflict phenomena, there is still resistance to the consideration of military affairs by academicians who 'ain't gonna study war no more', perhaps because of personal aversion to the subject itself, to ideological constraints or through the fear of its attraction to the young. Others may feel that military analysis may be militaristic power fantasy – or lead to fixation on trivial mechanical aspects rather than larger patterns and meaning. There is, unfortunately, enough evidence to bear out the latter. Often military studies are 'drum and trumpet' replays, and other frankly didactic, all of which constitutes a kind of academic ideological schism, throughout the West to some degree, but perhaps most markedly in the United States. In the slowly crystallizing 'discipline',[2] polemology, there are many problems to be examined. The lack of initial bias or assumption regarding cause may be the strongest element in polemology, and a detached position is vital to any diagnostic system of thought. The traditional moralist-polemic position does not, for example, allow clinical examination of the critical question of the aesthetic of war. Nor is the problem apparent when researchers on conflict and aggression are meticulous in defining terms to the point of scientific abstraction with a focus on game models and mathematical quarrels. Others have used a micro-organismic approach.[3] And some have tried to see violence as a result of social tensions and organized living as they apply to groups.[4] Psychiatrists, beginning with Freud in his later years,[5] have examined group conflict and aggressiveness. There have also been multi-disciplinary attempts to bring together 'micro' and 'macro' considerations.[6]

The literature of pacifism ranges from sermons to the Carnegie Foundation studies. The man who made the boldest attempt to shift pacifistic discussion from moralizing to scientific investigation was Lewis Richardson in his use of mathematical indices to determine the shape and flow of human conflict, bringing together data from history and geography and applying statistical instruments.[7] Yet such discussions (excluding perhaps Charles Francis Adams' 'moral equivalent of war') do not deal directly with the problem posed by the aesthetics of mass violence. Yet there are virtual 'subcults' outside the military which take pleasure in intensive and elaborate considerations of the historical experience of man-in-arms,* thousands of buffs who lovingly study the minutiae of military heraldry, totemry and decoration. These include insignia and uniform collectors, land, naval and air war gamers, weapons 'enthusiasts' and even skeletal military organizations which drill or, in the United States, fire antique weapons dressed in period uniforms.

When Bernard Shaw suggested early in the century that the khaki uniform would end war because of the loss of military pomp and pageantry, he did not allow for human ingenuity in embellishing pedestrian uniforms with symbols which would evoke the totemic, tribal aspects so important in military life. The proliferation of small elites, virtual replications of the classical warrior band[8] in the First and Second World Wars underlines the viability of the pattern.[9] One can then ask in the Shavian vein, why, in terms of utility, do soldiers need separate garrison and field uniforms? Would not a single functional design be adequate? (The French *paras* were eager to wear their mottled field dress in town.) What leads men to embellish the tools of war lovingly, elaborately and sometime with good

* A whole array of publications are supported by this loosely linked group, including many which have no direct utility for military professionals, but which emphasize the minutiae, color, ceremony and form of military life, e.g. *Air Classics, Sea Classics, Tradition, Military Historian and Collector, Alnavco Log, The General, Strategy and Tactics, Guns and Ammunition,* etc. There is little functional tactical or strategic analysis, overall technological-logistical mechanics, or value discussions – but rather attention to narrative details, anecdotes and visual spectacle.

taste and great sensitivity – with no relation to their overt function? Wilfred Owen saw the love of weapons, not unlike Spengler in *Man and Technics*, as the human equivalent of a claw.

Some would view as aberrant psychopathy Lee's comment on war's splendor and horror at Gettysburg, Moltke's view of war as the scourge of empty materialism and Patton's eulogies to the attraction of combat. Yet the issue intrudes itself at other levels continually. If controls are to be designed and imposed to further ritualize war, then the parameters of the condition have to be studied and understood. Yet the current fashion in America runs toward avoidance of such questions, leading, as Robin Higham noted recently,[10] to an 'unrealistic approach to the training of doctoral candidates in military history', the proposition that ignorance will lead to improved condition.

While the classic pacifist novels as *War and Peace*, and *The Red Badge of Courage* were written by those without personal experience of the scenes they described, first-hand accounts have been closer to the problem of the martial aesthetic. G. Frederick Manning, in *Her Privates We*,[11] noted that 'War is waged by men; not by beasts nor by gods ... to call it a crime against mankind is to miss at least half of its significance; it is also the punishment of a crime. That raises a moral question, the kind of problem with which the present age is disciplined to deal ... there is nothing in war which the present age is disinclined to deal ... there is nothing in war which is not in human nature.'[12] Teilhard de Chardin, a combat medical corpsman in the First World War, noted a transcending heightening of the senses and a communal spirit (not dissimilar from Lorenz's concept of 'the bond').[13] Guy Chapman[14] digressed in his memoirs on the aesthetics of shell-fire, comparing them to the engravings on French title pages of the eighteenth century,[15] and noted that toward the end of the war he felt a 'compelling fascination' in which, he noted, 'lies War's power. Once you have lain in her arms, you can admit no other mistress. You may loathe, you may execrate, but you cannot deny her ... even those who hate her most are prisoners to her spell.'[16] This tone appears in Graves' *Goodbye to All That* and perhaps in its most extreme form in Ernst Junger's *Storm of Steel*, evocative of the bellicose trumpetings of Homer,

Tyrtaeus, Homer Charles Lea, Moltke and Bernhardi. Even Sassoon went back to the trenches.

Another problem stems from the tendency of the academic to view violence – from body contact sport to warfare – in terms of his own values. Naturally, the verbally skilled prefer conflict restricted to the milieu in which they are most likely to win, even though the human damage which they cause may ultimately result in violence. It certainly touches on a contemporary article of faith to discuss the proposition that man has loved war long and ardently.[17] The uniform – consider, the *Iliad's* loving cataloguing of armor and arms acts as a powerful emotional catalyst. Service journals in Britain feature arguments from time to time for returning to the red coat. Old soldiers invoke its aphrodisiac powers, suggesting a fringe benefit which would not have to be paid out of the Ministry of Defense budget directly. American marines agitate for an issue of blues dress. The functionless embellishment of weapons systems, of course, is a main theme in the history of military innovation.[18] Whatever popular tributes may be paid to the ideal of peace, expensive periodicals and books on airplane heraldry and camouflage sell well in the United States and Europe.*

The question posed by such esthetics of violence hinges on the human sense of beauty and its evolutionary roots and functions. Did four million years of hunting and survival through glaciation and tectonic outbursts serve as a screen which produced a half-mad animal, only able to glimpse the essential randomness and meaningless of himself and the world? Can the sense of beauty, perhaps a guard against the despair of consciousness, operate at any level of horror? Does man have a reflex to invest the events of life with implicit or transcendental meaning to dull the pain of the knowledge of his own death, thus masking the sordid 'realities' of his even impulses to violence? How close is the hand that plays with form

---

* The shape of ritual violence, e.g. sports, are also reflective of these basic forms and sensitivities, from mock battles of pre-literate tribes through the Olympics and medieval tournaments to modern American football. The language of the sportswriter is a patois of military analogs; martial bands thunder through the contest. The increase in the sensory impact through color television has turned professional football into a near-cult, a kind of electronic *circe* furnishing violent fantasy for the adult male population of America which upstaged the Vietnam War.

and produces art to the hand that holds the dagger? Is the simile of Mussolini's son on the impact of a bomb on a crowd of Ethiopians resembling the opening of a rose aberrant – or normative? We do know, after all, that states of sexual excitation and aggressiveness are physiologically similar.[19] These are all unpleasant questions. Yet the visual spectacle of war peers out of the pages of broadly marketed four colour histories of the Revolution, Civil War and the World Wars, in dozens of military museums and has been a principle theme of epic films since *Birth of a Nation*.[20]

Academic arguments[21] against the study of war have come from Marxists protecting the image of *homo economicus*, Utopian pacifists, or behavioralists who reject the significance of genetics. The current attack in the United States is against an undefined 'militarism' – often blurring with 'defense'. R.O.T.C. is, for example, seen as a contaminant of youth. Yet the argument that a low level of militarization is a defense against bloody war was buried in the American Civil War, when tiny seedlings of military professionalism – a thousand men on both sides – gave birth to mass armies and mass slaughter. Sweden and Switzerland, on the other hand, have total conscription. These paradoxes are not singular. While technology has led to butchery, as in the Russo-Japanese and First World Wars, it has also had a ritualizing effect in other cases. Chemicals, rubber bullets and water have reduced casualties in riots, once quelled by swords and guns. The naval battles of the century have exacted far less from the ranks of seamen than from their comrades on land. More Englishmen died in automobile accidents than in the air during the Battle of Britain. Medical technology has dramatically reduced the gross losses that disease used to exact from armies in the field. The First World War was the first major conflict where as many men were killed in action as died from disease. But the excess of the 'perverted lights of science', real and projected, do not give optimists more than a fleeting glimpse of hope.

The analysis of man's affinity for mass violence is obscured by biasses and predispositions, theories and fears. But the search for answers will not come from ignoring the violent past, from pretending that man is afflicted by an impersonal, external thing called war, nor from ignoring that he has taken pleasure in it and shaped his values and institutions around it. In the evolution of polemology as a working instrument for understanding conflict, historians can pay a role in filling in many blank spaces – if they overcome their aversion to looking into the sockets of the leering skull and no longer scuttle past with an invocation. Neither apathy nor prayer conquered the great epidemics of the past. While it may still be a reflex, even among professionalized elites, to revert to withdrawal or dogma when faced with unpleasantness, more and more disciplines are converging on the phenomena of conflict and aggression. It may be that ultimately the gestalt psychologists and neurobiologists will be able to tell us more about the organismic roots of human admiration for the configurations and trappings of war. The record of its impact on society is one which historians, anthropologists, political scientists and sociologists can analyze and interpret if they choose to. But the change in the model of war implied by contemporary research in this field and the multi-disciplinary approach required may prove too great an inertia for the promising momentum of polemology. In the grimmest sense, time will tell.

NOTES TO CHAPTER 11

1. E. Drummond Ayres, Jr, 'Few Hurrahs When Johnny Comes Marching Home', *New York Times* News Service feature (8 Nov 1970).
2. One constructive development is the emergence of polemology, a view of war as clinically normative but pathological. The polemological approach avoids pacifistic sermon or militaristic eulogy (see 'The Scientific Basis of Peace' issue of *Impact of Science on Society*, Vol XVII, 2 Apr–June 1968, particularly pp. 103–10). The more general term of 'peace research' has also been applied to this area of interest, but distinctions can be drawn between the two approaches in terms of value assumptions.
3. See S. Grattini and E. B. Sigg (eds), *Aggression Behavior* (Excerpta Medica Foundation, 1969) for an example of this kind of symposium approach.
4. J. G. Starke, *An Introduction to the Science of Peace (Irenology)* (Leyden: A. W. Sitjhoff, 1968), pp. 53–68, and Amitai Etzioni, *The Hard Way to Peace* (New York: Crowell-Collier Press, 1962).
5. Sigmund Freud, *Civilization and Its Discontents* (London: Hogarth Press, 1957); Anthony Storr, *Human Aggression* (New York: Atheneum, 1968); Edward Glover, *War, Sadism and Pacificm: Further Essays on Group Psychology and War* (London: George Allen and Unwin, 1945).
6. See J. D. McCarthy and F. J. Ebling (eds), *The Natural History of Aggression: Proceedings of a Symposium held at the British Museum* (London: Academic Press, 1964).

7. Lewis Richardson, *Statistics of Deadly Quarrels* and *Arms and Insecurity* (Pittsburgh: The Boxwood Press, 1960).
8. For an unconscious, neo-Homeric lyricization see Peter Young, *Commando* (New York: Ballantine Books, 1969).
9. See R. A. Beaumont, 'Military Elites: Waste of Human Resources?', *Army* (May 1967); Morris Janowitz and Edward Shils, 'Cohesion and Disintegration in the Wehrmacht in World War II', *Public Opinion Quarterly*, XII (summer 1948); also Gilles Perrault, *Les Parachutistes* (Paris: 1961), in which he suggests elites are a response to growing conscript indifference.
10. *Military Affairs*, XXIV 3 (Oct 1970) pp. 98–9.
11. G. Frederick Manning, *Her Privates We* (New York: Berkley, 1964).
12. Ibid.
13. R. P. Teilhard de Chardin, *Lettres à Claude Arragones*, excerpted in André Ducasse, Jacques Meyer and Gabriel Perreux (eds), *Vie et Mort des Francais, 1914–1919* (Paris: Hachette, 1962), p. 102.
14. *A Passionate Prodigality* (New York: Holt, Rinehart and Winston, 1956).
15. Ibid., p. 77.
16. Ibid., p. 226.
17. Which led Ardrey to suggest that the history of man should be read out in terms of weapons development rather than tool-making, Robert Ardrey, *African Genesis* (New York: Dell 1967).
18. Elting Morison in 'A Case Study of Innovation', *Engineering and Science Magazine* (Apr 1950); B. H. Liddell Hart, *The Memoirs of Captain Liddell Hart* (London: Cassell, 1965 and 1968).
19. Storr, *Human Aggression*, p. 16. In his *Verdun* (New York: Knopf, 1939), Jules Romain's character Geoffrey reflects while watching a heavy artillery battery: '... Geoffrey was able to enjoy twice ... [the gun's] recoil ...'! There must be something sexual in our delight.... We poor little male creatures are thrown into ecstasy by this familiar movement carried out on a supernatural scale ... this miraculous organ ... appeased, but never exhausted, by its formidable release of energy.'.
20. e.g. *Intolerance*; *The Four Horsemen of the Apocalypse*; *All Quiet on the Western Front*; *Hell's Angels*; *Gone with the Wind*; *Henry V*; *Bridge on the River Kwai*; *Lawrence of Arabia*; *Patton*; *Tora, Tora, Tora*.
21. Louis Morton, 'The Writing of Official History', *Army*, II no. 10 (May 1961) noted: 'Military history is still regarded by the historical profession at large with some suspicion and skepticism....'.

12 Summing Up

ROGER A. BEAUMONT

The contributors to this volume have looked at a broad spectrum of factors which may shape the paths which lead to war, limited war or peace in this last quarter of an already bloody century. It is interesting to consider the interests of those who have dared to project. Some are organizational, some ideological, others mechanical. Much has, naturally enough, been omitted of vital concern. For instance, the shroud of classification hanging over A.S.W., the short renaissance of the battleship, the fate of the *Elath* and the tenuous future of the aircraft carrier are barely touched upon. The variety of projective vectors suggests that while a cross-disciplinary view of war in isomorphic terms is emerging, it is uneven.

This may be due to the values associated with prophecy in our society. One reason that prophets are without honor in their own land is that when they are making their projections they appear to be lunatics, and when their projections are fulfilled, they are not loved the more for being right. Who, for instance, would have been taken seriously in 1950 if he had predicted that the United States would, in the next decade, elect a Catholic president contrary to all cliches to the contrary? That it would get involved in a brush-fire war larger and less conclusive than Korea, and end up punch-drunk, internally divided and dazed, with its economy overheated? Who could have foreseen the dramatic growth and intrusion of the Russian high seas fleet in the Mediterranean and beyond, filling the power vacuums left by a Britain whose army shrank below the 1914 level, whose air force was forced to rely on foreign sources of supply for its fighter aircraft? Could even a psychedelic Ian Fleming have projected the 'Profumo Affair' and its impact on the seemingly implacable and imperturbable Conservative government? Who, in 1950, would have bet that France would leave Algeria, let alone NATO? How could repeated major clashes between India and Pakistan be anticipated without major confrontation?

Defense theoretics since the end of the Second World War have focussed more and more on hardware, theoretical model-building and on organizational design and gross resource allocation. There has been less and less deft, intuitive sense of the tribal and human dimensions of military life best manifested by Swinton in *The Defense of Duffer's Drift*. Depersonalizing effects of technology and growing bureaucracy have increased the size and the destructive power, but the tuning knob does not control energy expenditures effectively. More recently, the U.S. army chief of staff has outlined a plan for moving human beings from the battlefield completely, replacing the man-machine system with a system of receptors and responders which would achieve the much-to-be-sought-for time when war becomes an expensive game, but causes no direct human suffering or pain. It might seem dangerous to talk optimistically about hopes for further ritualizing war. Yet such ritualization has taken place, producing a relative stabilization of casualties in relation to the growth in world population. There is no data to support the idea that this is a holding pattern – which may mean that it is all the more likely.

Attempts to rationalize the control of human conflict have had very mixed results. It is heartwarming (except to Luddites) to see complex and expensive systems fail to respond to self-important, complacent, 'rational' systems analysis and planned program. At the same time, it may be that controls were really designed to insure civilian or military elitist control. If there is one lesson that warfare in the twentieth century with its growing mixture of man and machinery has underlined, it is that there is an irrational component in the mechanism of war. The emotions and trappings that go with it cannot yet be crammed into a box or a mold. If the irrationality

Summing Up   213

as well as the atrition of those who use war as an instrument of policy and waste can be driven home, then at least some conflicts may be eliminated. If, as Arthur C. Clarke suggests, evolution has to include carnivorous and militaristic phases to sharpen intelligence, perhaps evolution will move beyond these.

We are at a crucial point where romanticism and paranoia are allied in a desire to bring man into a kind of subdued, restful and unambitious posture as the denizen of a beautiful globe in space. Opposed, the adventurous and elitist see man's future lying in the conquest of space – an interesting choice of words – and the ultimate destiny of man as Chardinian 'omega'.

Perhaps the 1970s will see a resolution of this argument. If the control machinery gets out of hand and brings about the long foretold holocaust, then those left will face new existential terrors. Yet what is not even appreciated by the 'average man' is that he, wherever he may live, is a combatant and a potential participant in the next major war. Since Douhet and Trenchard envisioned the city dwellers as prime military targets, it has become less and less reasonable for people to ignore military problems or view war as a form of vicarious entertainment. We are all soldiers – or, at least, all targets.

The study of military affairs, then, is not an idle academic exercise, a referral of aggressive impulses or cathexis based on military totemry and decoration. The problem of war and human affairs cannot be treated or cured by ignoring symptomology, any more than plague was eradicated by people crowding into churches to pray it away. There is a lot of dirty, hard work to be done. In the end, a problem is best brought under control when viewed as an epidemiological analog requiring constant exercise of caution. Preventive expense may come to equal that of maintaining sanitation and health care systems. If effective prevention ever becomes real, those who face the problem as pathology will have contributed far more than those who have made *a priori* value judgments on the basis of moral or emotional considerations. The missionaries who went into the various corners of the world meant well and prayed hard. But in the end, those with medical skills, lay and clerical, had the most profound effect. It is not comforting to note that when they solved one set of problems, another emerged.

If the variety in this volume is not always clinical, it does reflect that military analyses are drifting away from searching for the lesson of battles or the loving recounting of heroic deeds as more concern is shown for implication, impact and values. Clinical observation itself also has a fragmented quality since pre-definition of problems has much to do with the shaping of research. The fragment may never be effectively synthesized except in hindsight. The development of medicine seems to be a more rational process when reading medical history than when surveying contemporary practice and research. Until something better comes along, the promise of polemology as an analogy to disease prevention and cure will be most effective for students of war and peace in an age when the convergence of crisis presents only alternatives of destruction.

Notes on the Contributors

ROGER A. BEAUMONT is Associate Director of the Center for Advanced Study in Organization Science, and Assistant Professor at the Department of Organization Science, University of Wisconsin. Professor Beaumont has served in both staff and line managerial roles in the private sector and in the army. He has published essays in *Horizon, The Royal United Service Institution Journal, Army, Military Affairs, Infantry, U.S. Naval Institute Proceedings, An Cosantoir* and *Truppendienst* as well as contributing a chapter to *Bayonets in the Streets* (edited by Robin Higham).

MARTIN EDMONDS is Senior Lecturer in Politics and Defence Lecturer in Civil-Military Relations in the Department of Politics, University of Lancaster. From 1972–3 he was Research Associate in the Institute of War and Peace Studies, Columbia University, doing research with a grant from the Carnegie Corporation of New York into public accountability and the defence-oriented corporation. His publications include contributions to *Military Technical Revolution, Civil Wars in the Twentieth Century, The New Political Economy, Dilemma of Accountability in Modern Government, A Source Guide to British Military History*, and several academic journals.

ROBERT SNOWDEN FICKS is a project assistant at the Center for Advanced Study in Organization Science at the University of Wisconsin. Mr Ficks served four years with the United States marine corps, including a tour of duty in Vietnam as an infantryman. He is currently studying the emerging Soviet naval infantry and strategic weapons evolution.

COLIN GRAY is currently a Ford Foundation scholar attached to King's College, London, researching into a forthcoming book, *Strategic Studies as a Policy Science*. He is a consultant to the RAND Corporation, and to the Hudson Institute, and was Executive Secretary of the Strategic and International Studies Commission, Canadian Institute of International Affairs. He is author of *Canadian Defence Priorities*, and has articles in *World Politics, Bulletin of Atomic Scientists, Foreign Policy, Orbis, International Journal, Military Review*, et. al.

MORRIS JANOWITZ, Department of Sociology, University of Chicago, is the author of *The Professional Soldier, A Social and Political Portrait* and numerous other works on the sociology of the military, war and peace. He is chairman of the Inter-University Seminar on Armed Forces and Society, an interdisciplinary group of social scientists concerned with research and teaching. Professor Janowitz has been actively associated with disarmament, arms control, and peace-keeping issues.

PHILIP S. KRONENBERG is Assistant Professor of Political Science at the University of Indiana. Dr Kronenberg has done research on interorganizational planning for mental health in the States, the political character of military reserve forces, and the responses of public organizations to civil disorder. He is co-editor and a contributor to two recent volumes: *National Security and American Society: Theory Process, and Policy* and *New Civil-Military Relations: The Agonies of Adjustment of Post-Vietnam Realities*.

Notes on the Contributors

PETER NAILOR is Professor of Politics and Head of Department in the Department of Politics, University of Lancaster. He was formerly an Assistant Secretary in the Ministry of Defence. He is currently engaged on a study of the *British Polaris Missile Programme*, and is a contributor to *International Security: Britain in the EEC*, *The Management of Britain's External Relations*, and several academic journals. He has been the universities' representative on the Council of the Royal United Services Institution, and visiting lecturer to the NATO Staff College, Rome, and the Imperial Defence College.

LAURENCE I. RADWAY is Chairman of the Government Department at Dartmouth College and is a member of the New Hampshire state legislature. He is co-author of the leading study of officer education in the United States: *Soldiers and Scholars: Military Education and National Policy*, and he has recently published *Foreign Policy and National Defense*. He has been a member of the civilian faculty of the National War College as well as a civilian aide to the Secretary of the Army.

ROGER WILLIAMS is Senior Lecturer in the Department of Government, University of Manchester, currently on leave of absence as Scientific Advisor to the Canadian Government, sponsored by the Science Research Council of Canada. He is author of *European Technology*, and *Politics and Technology*, and contributor to *The Dilemma of Accountability in Modern Government*. He is currently engaged on a study of the British nuclear reactor programme.

T. ALDEN WILLIAMS is Associate Professor of Political Science at Kansas State University. He is a member of the executive committee of the Inter-University Seminar on Armed Forces and Society, and the governing council and the Military Forces Section of the International Studies Association.